4

Best Hikes Near
Spokane

HELP US KEEP THIS GUIDE UP TO DATE

Every effort has been made by the author and editors to make this guide as accurate and useful as possible. However, many things can change after a guide is published—trails are rerouted, regulations change, techniques evolve, facilities come under new management, and so on.

We would appreciate hearing from you concerning your experiences with this guide and how you feel it could be improved and kept up to date. While we may not be able to respond to all comments and suggestions, we'll take them to heart, and we'll also make certain to share them with the author. Please send your comments and suggestions to the following address:

GPP
Reader Response/Editorial Department
PO Box 480
Guilford, CT 06437

Or you may e-mail us at: editorial@globepequot.com

Thanks for your input, and happy trails!

Best Hikes Near
Spokane

FRED BARSTAD

FALCONGUIDES ®

GUILFORD, CONNECTICUT
HELENA, MONTANA

AN IMPRINT OF GLOBE PEQUOT PRESS

FALCONGUIDES®

Copyright © 2014 Morris Book Publishing, LLC

FalconGuides is an imprint of Globe Pequot Press.
Falcon, FalconGuides, and Outfit Your Mind are registered trademarks of Morris Book Publishing, LLC.

Photos by Fred Barstad unless otherwise noted.

Text design: Sheryl P. Kober
Project editor: Ellen Urban
Layout: Maggie Peterson
Maps by Hartdale Maps © Morris Book Publishing, LLC.

Library of Congress Cataloging-in-Publication Data

Barstad, Fred.
  Best hikes near Spokane / Fred Barstad.
    pages cm.
  Includes index.
  ISBN 978-0-7627-8532-2
  1. Hiking—Washington (State)—Spokane Region—Guidebooks. 2. Spokane Region (Wash.)—Guidebooks. I. Title.
  GV199.42.W22S643 2014
  796.5109797'772—dc23
                                                              2014001092

Printed in the United States of America

10 9 8 7 6 5 4 3 2 1

Contents

Overview

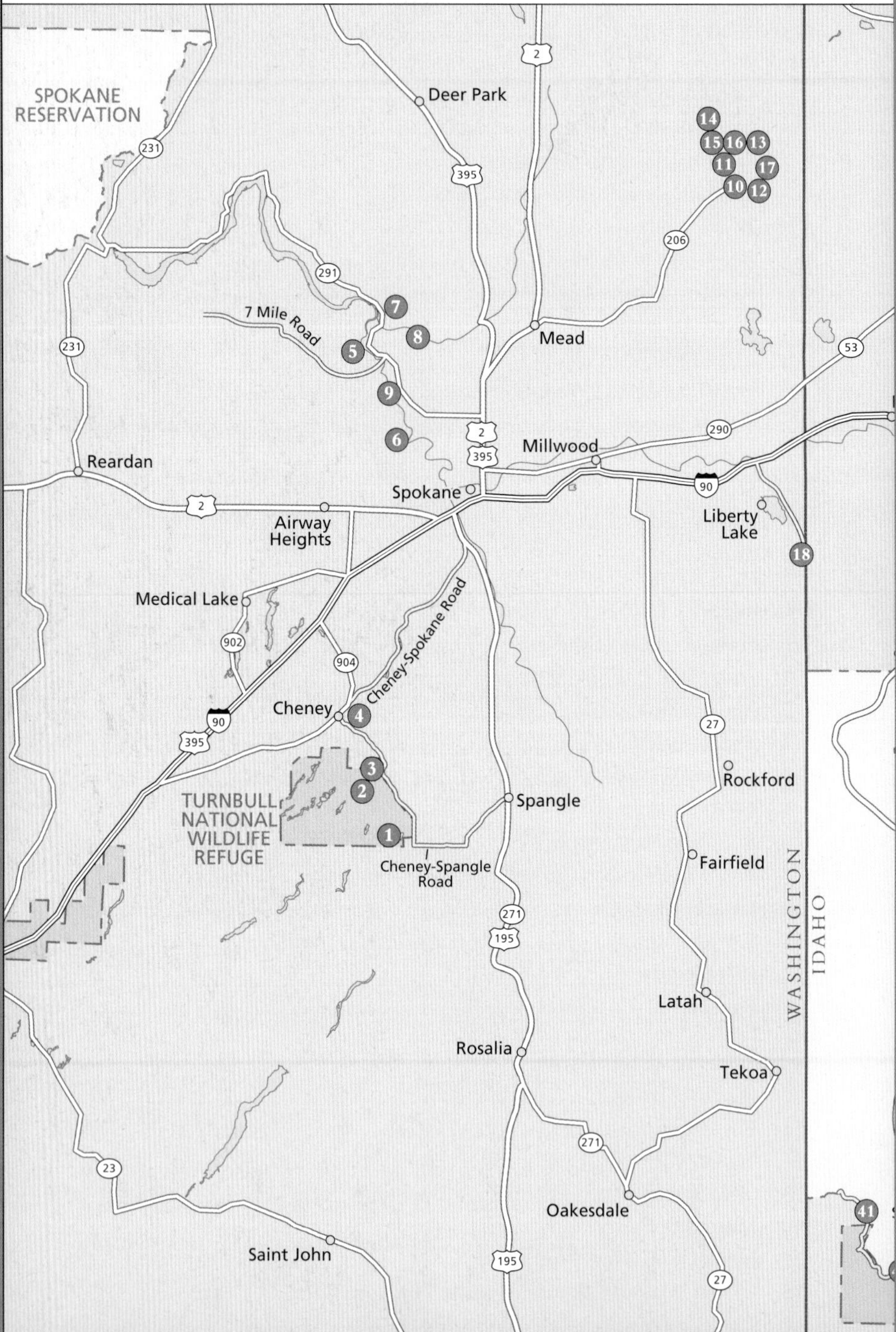

SPOKANE RESERVATION
Deer Park
Mead
Millwood
Spokane
Reardan
Airway Heights
Medical Lake
Cheney
Cheney-Spokane Road
7 Mile Road
Liberty Lake
Rockford
Spangle
Fairfield
TURNBULL NATIONAL WILDLIFE REFUGE
Cheney-Spangle Road
Latah
Rosalia
Tekoa
Oakesdale
Saint John
WASHINGTON
IDAHO

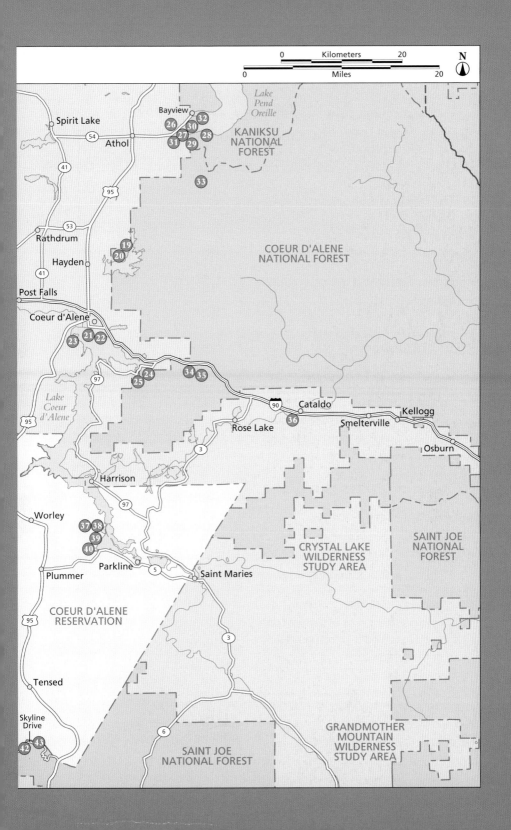

Acknowledgments

Thanks to the people from the land-management agencies that reviewed portions of my text: Steve Cristensen from Mount Spokane State Park, Sandy Rancourt from Turnbull National Wildlife Refuge, and Brian White from the Bureau of Land Management. Thanks also to Monte McCully of Coeur d'Alene Parks Department, Randall Butt from Farragut State Park, and to Ron Hise from Heyburn State Park for their reviews. Thanks to Andy Boggs of the Idaho Panhandle Forest and Geoff Harvey, Fourth of July Park and Ski Area Manager for the Panhandle Nordic Ski and Snowshoe Club, for reviews and information. Thanks to Megan Schmelzer of Riverside State Park for information and Lori Cobb, formerly of Riverside State Park, for information and reviewing portions of my text. Thanks to Jim and Lynn Frew, hosts at Bald Knob Campground in Mount Spokane State Park, Joan Kerptu from McCroskey State Park, and Stacy and Brenda Clinesmith for furnishing valuable information. Thanks also to Alex Hoppe for joining me while collecting information. Most of all, thanks to my wife, Sue Barstad, for all her computer help.

Scotch broom, Hike 8

Introduction

If you live in or plan to visit the Spokane–Coeur d'Alene area, a wide array of hiking opportunities await you. The hikes included here range from the subalpine summit of Mount Spokane to the semiarid Columbia Plateau and the timbered slopes of Chilco Mountain, Fourth of July Pass, and Mineral Ridge. At the lower elevations hiking possibilities are available nearly year-round.

Many of the hikes described in this book are within the five large state parks that are within a 45-minute drive of either Spokane or Coeur d'Alene.

Geography and Climate

Spokane is located at 1,900 feet elevation, near the poorly defined boundary between the grass and sagebrush of the semi-arid Palouse Prairie to the southwest and the timbered plateau and well watered mountains to the north and east. In general, rainfall (and snowfall) increases as you go farther east (toward Coeur d'Alene) and/or gain altitude in this part of the Northwest. The terrain also becomes more mountainous as you head east from Spokane. The average

Evening at Bald Knob Campground, Hike 13

January high temperature in Spokane is 33°F and the average low is 22°F. In July the average high temperature is 82°F and the low is 55°F. Twenty-five miles to the east, the city of Coeur d'Alene sits at 2,160 feet elevation in the pines next to beautiful Lake Coeur d'Alene. Coeur d'Alene is generally slightly cooler and wetter than Spokane.

Large Wildlife

White-tailed deer, mule deer, and Rocky Mountain elk are common along most of the hikes included in this guide. These are generally docile animals, although both the bucks and bulls can be somewhat aggressive during the fall rut (breeding season). Some cow elk seem to have a strong dislike for dogs and occasionally cause injuries. Bears and cougars are not often seen but are possible on all the hikes described here. Moose sightings are possible on many of the hikes. The Shiras moose (aka Wyoming moose) that roam this area are large animals, although not as large as their cousins in northern Canada and Alaska. They should never be closely approached or challenged in any way. Gray wolves (they are really almost any color from black to white), which were reintroduced into central Idaho in the mid-1990s, have established themselves very well. Many wolves inhabit Idaho and several packs have taken up residence in Washington. Wolves are very wide-ranging animals and could be found in almost any of the areas described in this book.

Hazards and Being Prepared

Weather conditions can change rapidly, even in the short time it may take to complete a 2- or 3-mile hike. The danger of adverse weather conditions generally increases with elevation and the length of the hike. Always take clothes that are adequate for all possible conditions. Water, food, and a map should be taken along on all but the shortest hikes. A guidebook and GPS receiver are also very handy. You must, however, know how to use the GPS receiver for it to be effective. Don't count on your GPS too heavily as a satellite may malfunction or, more likely, your batteries may go dead. Cell phone service can generally be had on at least part of most of the hikes described here, but don't count on it. Just when you need it, you may find yourself in a dead spot or your battery may be dead. There are a few simple things you can do that will improve your chances of staying safe and healthy while you are on your hike.

- First, check the weather report before heading out on the trail.
- Inform friends or relatives of your plans and when you plan to return.
- If you are planning a long or difficult hike, be sure to get into shape ahead of time. This will make your trip much more pleasant as well as safer.
- Know the basics of first aid, including how to treat bleeding, bites and stings, strains or sprains. Always pack a first-aid kit.
- Know the symptoms of both cold- and heat-related conditions, including

hypothermia, heatstroke, and heat exhaustion. The easiest way to avoid these afflictions is to wear proper clothing, dress in layers, and keep adequately fed and hydrated.

- One of the most important things to do is be mindful of your drinking-water supply. On most of these hikes, the best thing to do is to take along all the water you will need from a known safe source. All surface water should be filtered, chemically treated, or boiled before drinking.
- Afternoon and evening thunderstorms are common in the Spokane area from spring through early fall, and can include heavy rain and hail as well as lightning. Snow is possible at almost any time of the year at the highest elevations. If a storm is approaching, get off the ridgelines if possible and retreat to your car or other protected location. Protective clothing is always a good idea.
- On all but the shortest hikes, carry a backpack for your extra clothing and gear. This is much more comfortable than trying to carry this stuff in your hands.
- If you have children along, keep a close eye on them. A few of the hikes described here have cliffs or steep drop-offs close to the trail. In some places stinging and or poisonous plants are present, and there is always the chance, although slim, of meeting a rattlesnake. Children should carry a whistle to use if they are lost—and only if they are lost.
- Of all the safety tips, the most important is to take your brain with you when you venture into the wilds. Without it, these tips will not help, and with it, almost any obstacle can be avoided or overcome. Think about what you're doing, be safe, and have a great time in the outdoors.

Encounters with Bikers and Stock

Bikers use many of the trails covered in this book. It is the responsibility of bikers to yield to other users, but in some rare cases they may not see a hiker quickly enough to prevent a collision. Bikes are quiet, so the hiker should keep a careful watch for their approach.

Meeting stock traffic is not a common occurrence on most of the trails described here. It is possible, however, on a few of them, so it's a good idea to know how to pass stock with the least possible disturbance or danger. If you meet parties with stock, try to get as far off the trail as possible. Equestrians prefer that you stand on the downhill side of the trail, but there is some question as to whether this is the safest place for a hiker. If possible, I like to get well off the trail on the uphill side. It is often a good idea to talk quietly to the horses and their riders, as this seems to calm many horses. If you have the family dog with you, be sure to keep it restrained and quiet. Read the "Canine compatibility / other trail users" sections at the beginning of each hike description to get information about including your dog on that particular hike and what other users you are likely to encounter.

Zero Impact

Many of the trails in the Spokane–Coeur d'Alene region are heavily used. As trail users, we must be vigilant to make sure our passing leaves no lasting mark. Here are some basic guidelines for preserving the trails in our region.

- Pack out all your trash, including biodegradable items like orange peels. You might also pack out garbage left by other, less considerate hikers.
- Don't pick wildflowers or pick up rocks or antlers along the trail. Leave these things so that others may also enjoy them.
- Don't cut switchbacks, as this promotes erosion.
- Be courteous by not making loud noises while hiking.
- Many of these trails are multiuse, which means that you will share them with runners, bikers, and equestrians. Familiarize yourself with proper trail etiquette and yield the trail when appropriate.

White-tailed buck next to the trail, Hike 26

- If possible, use the restrooms at the trailhead. If not, dispose of the waste properly, well away from the trail and any water sources.

Roads to the Trailheads

All of the hikes in this guide are under an hour's drive from either Spokane or Coeur d'Alene. The I-90 freeway traverses the region from west to east. All of the driving directions begin at an exit off I-90 or from downtown Spokane at the junction of I-90 and Division Street. Nearly all the roads leading to the trailheads are paved or have good gravel surfaces. If this is not the case, the "Finding the trailhead" section at the beginning of the hike description will so state.

A Note about State Highway Designations

In Washington State highways are designated "SR" for state route. In Idaho state highways are designated "SH" for state highway. In this book the state highways are designated as they are on maps and road signs in each of the two states.

Land Management

The hikes in this book are nearly all located on public lands. These lands are managed by several different agencies. The few sections that are not on public land have easements to allow hiking.

Hikes 1 through 3 are on the Turnbull National Wildlife Refuge, which is managed by the US Fish and Wildlife Service. Hikes 5 through 9 are located in Riverside State Park, part of Washington's fantastic state park system. Washington State Parks and Recreation Commission manages the Columbia Plateau Trail (Hike 4). Hikes 10 through 17 are in Mount Spokane State Park, another of Washington's great state parks. Hike 18 is in the Liberty Lake Regional Park, which is managed by Spokane County Parks and Recreation, and Golf Department. The US Forest Service oversees the trails at English Point, including Hikes 19 and 20, Mount Coeur d'Alene (Hike 25), Chilco Mountain (Hike 33), and Hikes 34 and 35 at Fourth of July Pass. The US Bureau of Land Management (BLM) manages the ground beneath the Mineral Ridge Trail system (Hike 24). Hikes 26 through 32 are in or connected to Farragut State Park. Hikes 37 through 43 are within Heyburn State Park or Mary Minerva McCroskey State Park and are administered by Heyburn State Park. The Trail of the Coeur d'Alenes (Hike 36) is jointly administered by the Coeur d'Alene Tribe Project and Idaho Department of Parks and Recreation. Hikes 21 and 22 are on land administered by Coeur d'Alene's Park Department and Hike 23 is on Nature Conservancy land.

How to Use This Guide

This guide is designed to be as easy to use as possible. With each hike description, there is a map and summary information that includes the trail's length, difficulty, fees, and permits required. Also included is information on canine compatibility and trail contacts. Directions to the trailhead and what to expect along the trail are also covered. The "Miles and Directions" section at the end of each hike description provides mileage between significant points along the trail. A few of the hike routes are fairly complicated. Take your map and this book along to follow your progress.

How These Hikes Were Chosen

The hikes included here were picked to be compatible with the abilities of a wide variety of hikers. Many of the hikes are in the easy and moderate categories, which generally meet the needs of most hikers. There are, however, several strenuous hikes to keep the aerobic animals among us happy. There are also hikes that are wheelchair accessible.

Blue grouse, Hike 25

Trail Mileage

Trail mileage is mostly derived from the use of a GPS receiver. Hiking time at a known speed was also taken into consideration, as was the layout of the trail. In some cases, such as a series of short switchbacks, a GPS unit may record slightly less mileage than the true distance.

The mileages in the "Miles and Directions" section are rounded to the closest tenth of a mile. This may cause some discrepancy when reaching the total mileage for a hike. For instance, if the turnaround point on an out-and-back hike is 1.34 miles from the trailhead, it would be rounded to 1.3 miles. At the end of the hike, the one-way distance would be doubled to 2.68 miles, which would be rounded to 2.7 miles.

Asters beside Lake Pend Oreille, Hike 32

Difficulty Ratings

The hikes in this book are rated as to difficulty.

Easy hikes are generally fairly short and will have very little elevation gain or loss.

Moderate hikes can be several miles long and may have significant elevation gain and/or loss. The grades of moderate hikes are mostly gentle. Most hikers in relatively good condition will have no trouble with these hikes.

Hikes rated strenuous may have sections of steep, narrow, rough, and rocky trail. They are generally longer and may have an elevation gain of 2,000 feet or more. None of these hikes will be difficult for a person in good physical condition, but they may be grueling for people who are not.

The hiking times given are for hikers in fairly good physical condition. Hiking times do not include time spent sightseeing or picnicking. If there are children along, the hiking times should be increased to allow for the inspection of bugs, flowers, and other interesting things along the trail.

Maps

Up-to-date topo maps for many of the hikes in this guide are difficult to obtain. In most cases the maps provided in this guide are adequate for hiking the trails described here. Other maps are recommended at the beginning of each hike description. In some cases, the USGS quad maps and National Geographic topo maps on CD-ROM don't show the trails described here.

Montana Mapping & GPS LLC's Hunting and GPS maps for your GPS unit are also good topos and are in many cases easier to read. These maps also show land ownership, however, they too fail to show all the trails described here.

The *Riverside State Park Multi-use Trail Map,* produced by the Inland Empire Backcountry Horsemen, is an excellent map for hikes in Riverside State Park, as is the map in the *Turnbull National Wildlife Refuge* brochure for the hikes on the refuge. For Hikes in Mount Spokane State Park, Dharmamaps's *Mount Spokane State Park* is an up-to-date topo. The *Mount Spokane State Park* map produced by Washington State Parks, with donated proceeds made when renewing motor vehicle licenses, is free and adequate for the less complicated hikes. The *Farragut State Park Trail Guide* and the *Heyburn State Park Trail System* maps, available free at the visitor centers in these parks, are adequate for most of the hikes in these parks. For hikes in McCroskey State Park, a trail map is available as you enter the state park from the south. Although it covers the area and shows the trails, this map is small scale and not a topo. Often there will be a map on a reader board at the trailhead that will be helpful.

Map Legend

90	Interstate Highway	Bench	Bench

Interstate Highway

US Highway

State Road

County Road

Unpaved Road

Railroad

Selected Route

Trail or Fire Road

Paved Trail or Bike Path

Steps/boardwalk

Rapids

Waterfalls

Small River or Creek

Wetland

Pond or Lake

Bench

Boat Ramp/Launch

Bridge

Building/Point of Interest

Campground

Gate

Lodging

Mountain/Peak

Parking

Pass/Gap

Picnic Area

Ranger Station

Restaurant

Restroom

Scenic View/Viewpoint

Tower

Town

Trailhead

Visitor/Information Center

Trail Finder

Hike No.	Hike Name	Best Hikes Along Streams	Best Hikes for Peaks and Ridges	Best Hikes for Lakeshores and Lake Views	Best Hikes for Waterfowl and Wildlife Veiwing	Best Hikes for Historical Interest
1	Pine Lakes–Stubblefield Lake Loops			●	●	
2	30-Acre Lake			●	●	
3	Kepple Lake			●	●	
4	Columbia Plateau Trail				●	
5	Deep Creek Loop	●				
6	Bowl and Pitcher Loop	●				
7	Valley Trail–Indian Painted Rocks Trail Loop	●	●		●	
8	Little Spokane River	●			●	
9	Centennial Trail	●				●
10	Entrance Loop					
11	Burping Brook Loop	●				
12	Trail 120					
13	Bald Knob to Lower Loop Road Trailhead			●		

Trail Finder

Hike No.	Hike Name	Best Hikes Along Streams	Best Hikes for Peaks and Ridges	Best Hikes for Lakeshores and Lake Views	Best Hikes for Waterfowl and Wildlife Veiwing	Best Hikes for Historical Interest
14	Mount Kit Carson–Day Mountain Loop		●			
15	Mount Kit Carson Summit		●			
16	Mount Spokane Summit–Saddle Junction		●			
17	Quartz Mountain Lookout		●	●		
18	Camp Hughes Loop	●		●		
19	English Point East			●		
20	English Point West			●		
21	Tubbs Hill Loop			●	●	
22	Tubbs Hill Summit		●	●		
23	Tubbs Hill Summit		●	●	●	
24	Cougar Bay Nature Conservancy Preserve		●	●		●
25	Mineral Ridge Trail System		●	●		
26	Mount Coeur d'Alene					●
27	Lynx Trail			●		●
28	Bernard Peak / Scout Trail		●	●		

Trail Finder

Hike No.	Hike Name	Best Hikes Along Streams	Best Hikes for Peaks and Ridges	Best Hikes for Lakeshores and Lake Views	Best Hikes for Waterfowl and Wildlife Veiwing	Best Hikes for Historical Interest
29	Highpoint Trail		•	•		
30	Beaver Bay Shoreline Loop			•	•	
31	Buttonhook Bay Loop			•	•	•
32	Willow Lakeview Loop			•	•	•
33	Chilco Mountain National Recreation Trail		•	•		
34	Fourth of July Pass Inner Loop					
35	Fourth of July Pass Outer Loop					
36	Trail of the Coeur d'Alenes	•		•	•	
37	Whitetail–Shoeffler Butte Loops		•		•	
38	Indian Cliffs Trail		•	•		
39	CCC Nature Trail					•
40	Lakeshore Loop Trail			•	•	
41	James E. Dewey–Iron Mountain Loop		•			
42	Fireplace to Mission Mountain Summit		•			
43	Lone Pine Viewpoint		•			

Moose beside trail

South of Cheney, Washington, in part of what is called the Channeled Scablands, is the Turnbull National Wildlife Refuge. The Channeled Scablands were created when huge Ice Age floods washed away the prairie soils, leaving channels, basalt outcrops, and depressions. This was not just one flood but possibly as many as one hundred, which successively rushed across the landscape as the glacial ice dam that was holding back ancient Lake Missoula broke and reformed. Many of the depressions in the channels left by the floods are now lakes and ponds. These wetlands are the top-notch waterfowl habitat that you now see in the Turnbull National Wildlife Refuge. In addition to the abundant waterfowl, the wetlands are home to many other species of birds.

The upland areas in the northern part of the refuge are covered with open ponderosa pine forest and groves of aspen. Along the refuge's southern boundary, grasslands generally take over the uplands. White-tailed deer and elk are common on the refuge and are often seen in the morning and evening. A few moose are also present, and coyotes can often be heard howling.

Hike 1 takes you along lakeshores, through pine forest, and across grasslands. This hike also offers excellent waterfowl- and other wildlife-viewing opportunities. For shorter walks, Hikes 2 and 3 take you along lakeshores and through semi-open forest and also offer great waterfowl viewing.

Right on the western edge of the city of Spokane is Riverside State Park. At approximately 10,000 acres, it's the second-largest state park in Washington. Fifty-five miles of trails open to hiking and biking crisscross the park's river bottoms and rocky uplands. Hikes 5, 6, and 9 traverse the open pine forest, with good views of the churning Spokane River. Hike 9 offers easy walking on a wide paved trail that is accessible for visitors with physical challenges. Hike 7 climbs high above the Little Spokane River through the Little Spokane Natural Area, then drops back to river level to return to the trailhead. Hike 8 follows the lush valley of the Little Spokane River.

Water iris fields along Little Spokane River, Hike 7

Pine Lakes–Stubblefield Lake Loops

The Pine Lakes–Stubblefield Lake Loops provide a good overall cross section of the types of terrain and species of wildlife that can be found on the Turnbull Refuge. In the upland areas watch for coyotes, deer, and elk. On the lakes a wide variety waterfowl may be spotted. Moose are possible in all areas but most likely along the shorelines of the lakes.

Start: Pine Lakes Trailhead

Distance: 6.3-mile double lollipop-loop day hike

Hiking time: About 3 hours

Difficulty: Moderate, mostly because of the distance; the grades are gentle

Best season: Year-round, weather permitting

Canine compatibility/other trail users: Open to hikers only. Dogs are discouraged on the refuge, however, they are permitted as long as they are on a leash less than 5 feet long.

Fees and permits: A daily or annual Refuge Pass is required Mar–Oct. No fee is charged Nov–Feb. A Federal Duck Stamp as well as several other federal passes allow you to get onto the refuge free. Daily Refuge Passes are self-purchased at the entrance to the refuge. Annual passes must be obtained at the refuge headquarters.

Maps: The *Turnbull National Wildlife Refuge* brochure has a map that is adequate for the hikes in the Turnbull Refuge, or just use the one in this book. Montana Mapping & GPS LLC's Hunting and GPS maps are good topos of the area. The National Geographic map on CD-ROM covers the area and shows the Stubblefield Lake Loop portion of this hike (as a roadbed) but doesn't show the Pine Lakes Loop.

Trail contact: Turnbull National Wildlife Refuge, 26010 S. Smith Rd., Cheney, WA 99004; (509) 235-4723; www.fws.gov/turnbull

Special considerations: Much of this route is without shade and may be very hot during the summer. If you happen to see a moose on this hike or any other hike, give it plenty of space, at least 100 yards. Even that may not be enough in some cases. Moose are unpredictable and potentially very dangerous.

THE HIKE

Leaving the parking area, walk across the road and pass a viewing area complete with binoculars on a post at the trailhead. The paved track winds its way down for a short distance to near lake level, then turns right (southwest). Winslow Pool is the marshy lake on your left. In 0.2 mile there is a trail junction where you bear right (nearly straight ahead). A few yards farther there is another junction. This junction is the beginning of the Pine Lakes Loop. You will hike part of this loop now and the rest of it upon your return from Stubblefield Lake.

Bear right (nearly straight ahead again) at the second junction and hike south-southwest along the lakeshore. On the right side of the trail, away from the lake, are cattails (*Typha latifolia*), rosebushes, and an occasional orange-barked ponderosa pine (*Pinus ponderosa*). To the left watch the lake for the many varieties of ducks that inhabit this refuge. There is also a chance you might see a trumpeter swan (*Cygnus buccinator*). Shortly you will come to a reader board that discusses these colorful waterfowl. The route crosses the outlet of the lake a little less than 0.2 mile past the reader board. Once across the outlet the track makes a turn to the left and quickly arrives at another trail junction. Turn right at this junction and follow the connector trail to the Stubblefield Lake Trail, which is another lollipop loop.

Turn right on the Stubblefield Lake Trail (roadbed) and hike south for 0.2 mile to another junction and the beginning point of the Stubblefield Lake Loop portion of this hike. There is a good view to the right of Pine Lakes before reaching the junction, as you hike across the grassland surrounded by pine trees. Hike straight ahead (south) from this junction.

For the next 0.7 mile, the route descends very gently. Then, close to the southern end of Cheever Lake, you reenter the timber. At the southern end of the lake, there is another junction. When I hiked this route, the willows to the right, near the junction, were heavily browsed to moose height. If you see a moose (*Alces alces*), don't approach or challenge it in any way. All moose are unpredictable and potentially dangerous, and some of them have poor attitudes. As with all wildlife, watch moose from a distance.

Turn left at the junction. Then climb gently to the southeast through the open ponderosa pine woods. There is another roadbed to your right shortly after leaving the junction. Bear left to stay on the loop. The course is now dirt surfaced rather than gravel.

The route leaves the timber 0.8 mile past the junction at the south end of Cheever Lake. Hike southeast across the grassland for 0.4 mile, then turn east along a fence line. This fence line is along the southern boundary of the Turnbull National Wildlife Refuge.

The track (roadbed) follows the fence for almost 0.3 mile, then turns northeast, leaving the fence line. A very poor road roadbed follows the fence to the east. You will reach the junction near Stubblefield Lake in another 0.6 mile. The course reaches its highest elevation, about 2,360 feet, between the fence line

Bull moose battle

and the junction near Stubblefield Lake. Stubblefield Lake and the meadow around it, which are to the right, are important habitat for shorebirds and migrating waterfowl. The lake itself is small or almost nonexistent at times.

At the junction next to Stubblefield Lake, the route turns left. Hike to the northwest, across the grass-covered prairie. Small groves of aspens (*Populus tremuloides*) stud the rolling terrain. Watch for elk (*Cervus canadensis*) in this semi-open country, especially if you're here in the morning or evening. After leaving the junction near Stubblefield Lake, the route passes between a marsh and a small pond in about 0.7 mile. In another 0.1 mile the track turns to the west. Then you climb over a small rise to the junction that ends the loop. This junction is 1.5 miles from the junction close to Stubblefield Lake.

Turn right at this junction and retrace your steps for 0.2 mile to the junction with the connector trail to the Pine Lakes Loop. Turn left on the connector trail, retracing your steps for slightly less than 0.2 mile west, to the junction with the Pine Lakes Loop. The west end of this connector trail forms a triangle. Bear right at the first junction and hike the last few yards to meet the Pine Lakes Loop.

At the junction turn right, on the paved trail. Hike north slightly back from the lakeshore, through the aspens and ponderosa pines. The route reaches Ice Pond Viewpoint in 0.2 mile. Just before reaching the viewpoint, there is a bench next to the trail. California quail (*Callipepla californica*) are often present in the brush close to the Ice Pond Viewpoint. Soon you will pass another reader board about the waterfowl. The tread crosses the earthen dam that divides Winslow Pool, which is on the right, and Pine Lake, which is on the left, 0.1 mile farther along. There are two trail junctions just across the dam. Bear left at the first one, then turn right at the second. This junction is the end of the Pine Lakes Loop, so retrace your incoming steps for the 0.3 mile back to the Pine Lakes Trailhead.

MILES AND DIRECTIONS

0.0   Begin your hike from Pine Lakes Trailhead.

0.3   Bear right (nearly straight ahead) at the second trail junction.

0.5   Turn right on the path that connects the Pine Lakes Loop with the Stubblefield Lake Trail.

0.7   Turn right on the Stubblefield Lake Trail.

0.9   Hike straight ahead at the junction starting the Stubblefield Lake Loop.

1.6   Turn left at the junction at the south end of Cheever Lake.

3.1   Bear left at the trail (road) junction, leaving the fence line.

3.6   Turn left and hike northwest from the junction next to Stubblefield Lake.

Pine Lakes–Stubblefield Lake Loops

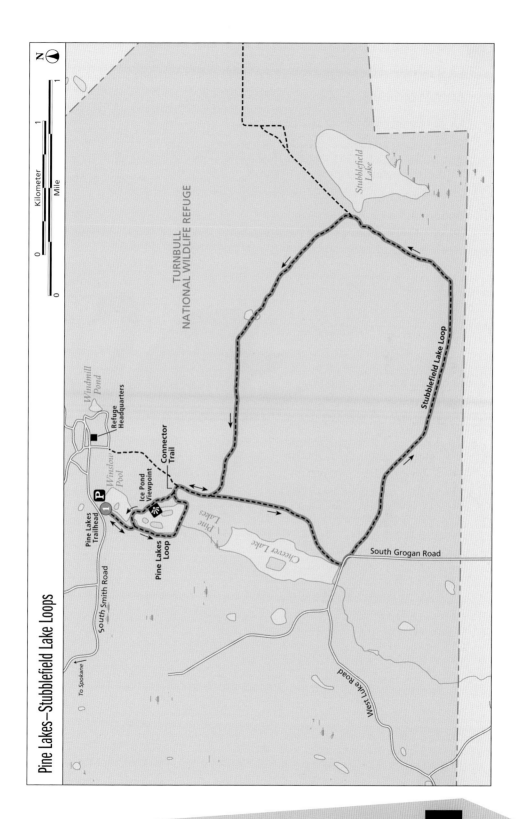

5.2 Turn right at the junction ending the Stubblefield Lake Loop.

5.4 Turn left on the connector trail to Pine Lakes Loop.

5.6 Turn right on the Pine Lakes Loop.

6.0 Turn right at the junction, ending the Pine Lakes Loop.

6.3 Arrive back at the Pine Lakes Trailhead.

Option
Hike the 30-Acre Lake Trail (Hike 2) on the same trip because it's short and close by.

30-Acre Lake

The hike past 30-Acre Lake is a fairly short, easy, and somewhat remote hike that follows a dirt service road on the Turnbull National Wildlife Refuge. Hiking this route offers excellent wildlife-viewing possibilities, especially in the early morning.

Start: South 30-Acre Lake Trailhead
Distance: 1.6 miles out and back or 0.8-mile shuttle day hike
Hiking time: About 1 hour out and back, 0.5-hour shuttle
Difficulty: Easy
Best season: Year-round, weather and snow conditions permitting
Canine compatibility / other trail users: This route is for hikers only. Dogs are discouraged on the refuge, however they are permitted as long as they are on a leash less than 5 feet long.
Fees and permits: A daily or annual Refuge Pass is required Mar–Oct. No fee is charged Nov–Feb. A Federal Duck Stamp as well as several other federal passes allow you to get onto the refuge free. Daily Refuge Passes are self-purchased at the entrance to the refuge. Annual passes must be obtained at the refuge headquarters.
Maps: The *Turnbull National Wildlife Refuge* brochure has a map that is adequate for the hikes on the Turnbull Refuge, or just use the one in this book.
Trail contact: Turnbull National Wildlife Refuge, 26010 S. Smith Rd., Cheney, WA 99004; (509) 235-4723; www.fws.gov/turnbull

Finding the trailhead: Take I-90 west from downtown Spokane. Drive 11 miles to exit 270. Take the exit and drive south for 6 miles on SR 904 to Cheney. Near the west end of Cheney, turn left (south) on the Cheney-Plaza Road. Head south for 4 miles to the entrance road for the Turnbull National Wildlife Refuge (South Smith Road). Turn left and follow the signs toward the refuge headquarters. Just after leaving the Cheney-Plaza Road, there is a reader board and pay station on the right where you can obtain a daily Refuge Pass. Drive 3.5 miles to the entrance for the Pine Creek Auto Tour Route, which is a one-way road. You will pass the tour route exit before you reach the entrance. Turn left on the tour route and go 1.1 miles north, to the southern 30-Acre Lake Trailhead and parking area. Only limited parking and no other facilities are available at the south trailhead. GPS: N47 25.681' /W117 32.279'

If you are making this a shuttle hike, the north trailhead is 2.1 miles farther along the tour route. The north trailhead also has only limited parking and no other facilities. GPS: N47 26.226' /W117 32.494'

An early morning in September is the best time to make this hike. Bull elk may be bugling, their high-pitched, almost birdlike calls challenging each other for dominance. Coyotes may also be making themselves heard, and other wildlife is often seen. Even moose can occasionally be seen here. If you should spot a moose, watch from a distance and don't challenge it in any way.

Head north-northwest from the parking area on the dirt service road, which is closed to unauthorized vehicles. There is a sign marking 30-Acre Lake a little less than 0.2 mile into the hike. The lake is to the right of the trail (roadbed). Take a few minutes here to observe the waterfowl that may be sitting on the lake.

Continuing on to the north-northwest, you will cross a marsh and a small creek, which may be dry, before reaching a grove of aspen trees (*Populus tremuloides*). Soon the tread passes the north end of another marsh. Past the marsh you climb a few feet, then continue northwest. Open ponderosa pine (*Pinus ponderosa*) forest is on both sides of the course, for the short distance remaining to the junction with the Pine Creek Auto Tour Route at the north trailhead. The north trailhead is 0.8 mile from the south trailhead. Unless you have somehow arranged for a vehicle at this trailhead, this is your turnaround point, so retrace your steps back to the south trailhead.

Elk

Of all North American antlered animals, elk (*Cervus canadensis*) are second in size only to moose. A full-grown bull (male) stands about 5 feet high at the shoulders and may weigh 700 to 1,000 pounds. The crowning glory of a bull elk is its large set of antlers. On a mature bull the antlers normally have six points on a side and may reach a length of over 5 feet. Most are much shorter than that, however. Elk are quite vocal during the late summer and early fall breeding season, called the rut. Their high-pitched bugles can be heard for long distances, challenging other bulls to combat. The size and age of a bull can be told by his bugle. Young bulls, which are most often heard, have a much higher-pitched voice than do mature bulls.

Elk are also noisy when they run, especially through woods with down logs. They seem to gauge their steps a little low and hit most of the logs with their hooves. They also do this when jumping fences, often knocking off the top wire or rail. This habit makes them unpopular with some ranchers.

Spotted elk calves weigh 30 or so pounds and are born in May and June. The spots only last a couple of months, fading into the normal tawny elk coat by late summer. Elk are social animals and are normally seen in herds.

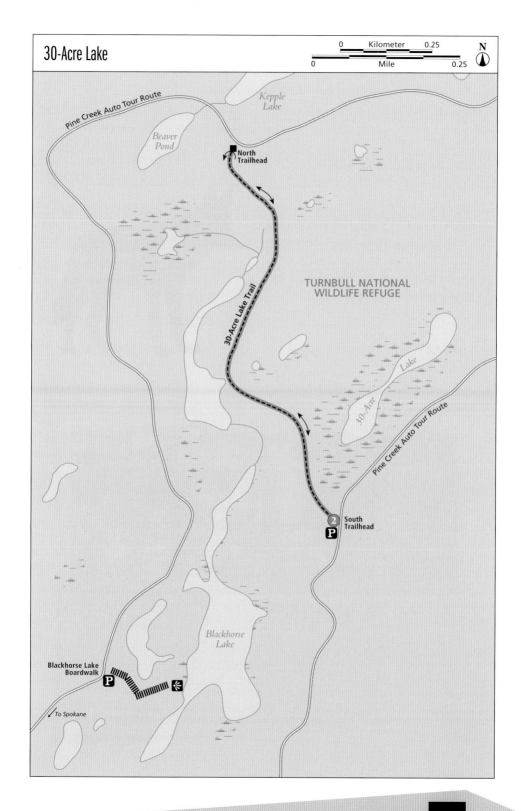

30-Acre Lake

0 Kilometer 0.25

0 Mile 0.25

N

Pine Creek Auto Tour Route

Kepple Lake

Beaver Pond

North Trailhead

TURNBULL NATIONAL WILDLIFE REFUGE

30-Acre Lake Trail

30-Acre Lake

Pine Creek Auto Tour Route

South Trailhead

Blackhorse Lake

Blackhorse Lake Boardwalk

To Spokane

MILES AND DIRECTIONS

0.0 Hike north-northwest from the south trailhead.

0.2 Pass the 30-ACRE LAKE sign.

0.8 Turn around at the north trailhead.

1.6 Arrive back at the south trailhead.

Option

You may want to stop and walk the very short Blackhorse Lake Boardwalk on the same trip. It's only 1.4 miles past the north 30-Acre Lake Trailhead on the Pine Creek Auto Tour Route.

Young bull elk

Kepple Lake

The trails at Kepple Lake consist of two short lollipop loops with a couple of very short side trips. The trailheads for the two loops are only 0.3 mile apart, close enough together that it's easy to walk between them and take in both hikes without moving your car. Waterfowl watching is one of the main attractions of this hike.

Start: Kepple Lake Peninsula Trailhead

Distance: 1.9 miles, 2 loops

Hiking time: About 1 to 1.5 hours

Difficulty: Easy

Best season: Year-round, weather permitting

Canine compatibility / other trail users: This route is for hikers only. Dogs are discouraged on the refuge, however they are permitted as long as they are on a leash less than 5 feet long.

Fees and permits: A daily or annual Refuge Pass is required Mar–Oct. No fee is charged Nov–Feb. A Federal Duck Stamp as well as several other federal passes allow you to get onto the refuge free. Daily Refuge Passes are self-purchased at the entrance to the refuge. Annual passes must be obtained at the refuge headquarters.

Maps: The *Turnbull National Wildlife Refuge* brochure has a map that is adequate for the hikes in the Turnbull Refuge, or just use the one in this book.

Trail contact: Turnbull National Wildlife Refuge, 26010 S. Smith Rd., Cheney, WA 99004; (509) 235-4723; www.fws.gov/turnbull

Special considerations: If you happen to see a moose on this hike or any other hike, give it plenty of space, at least 100 yards. Even that may not be enough in some cases. Moose are unpredictable and potentially very dangerous.

3

Finding the trailhead: Take I-90 west from downtown Spokane. Drive 11 miles to exit 270. Take the exit and drive south for 6 miles on SR 904 to Cheney. Near the west end of Cheney, turn left (south) on the Cheney-Plaza Road. Head south for 4 miles to the entrance road for the Turnbull National Wildlife Refuge (South Smith Road). Turn left and follow the signs toward the refuge headquarters. Just after leaving the Cheney-Plaza Road, there is a reader board and pay station on the right where you can obtain your Refuge Pass. Drive 3.5 miles to the entrance for the Pine Creek Auto Tour Route. You will pass the tour route exit before you reach the entrance. Turn left on the tour route and go 2.6 miles north, northeast, then west to the Kepple Lake Peninsula Trailhead. Parking and restrooms are available at the trailhead. GPS: N47 26.321' /W117 32.052'

THE HIKE

Hike north from the trailhead, soon passing the Kepple Peninsula Environmental Education Shelter, which is on the left. Buttercups (*Ranunculus glaberrimus*), grass widows (*Sisyrinchium inflatum*), and yellow bells (*Fritillaria*

Kepple Lake

pudica) line this section of the trail in April. A little farther along you will reach a trail junction and an informational sign about waterfowl. Bear left here and walk out to the wildlife observation blind, which is next to Kepple Lake. Take a few minutes at the blind and see if you can observe any wildlife, then walk back to the junction and bear left. This section of the route is along the lakeshore through the ponderosa pine (*Pinus ponderosa*) woods. The track, which is surfaced with bark and wood chips, passes a bench and returns to the paved trail, which was your inbound route, in slightly over 0.3 mile. Another 0.1 mile of walking brings you back to the Kepple Lake Peninsula Trailhead. You could end your hike here at your car, but checking out the rest of Kepple Lake is well worth the effort.

To continue your hike, turn left on the Pine Creek Auto Tour Route (road) and walk 0.3 mile east to the Kepple Lake Overlook parking area. From the parking area, hike northeast on a roadbed that is only open to foot traffic. Bluedicks (*Brodiaea douglasii*) line the route beneath the tall ponderosa pines in early summer, while squirrels and chipmunks scurry about their business. In 0.1 mile turn left, leaving the roadbed on another trail surface of bark and wood chips. Soon you will reach a sign describing several species of waterfowl, followed immediately by a trail junction. Bear left here and soon reach a bench atop a rocky outcrop overlooking Kepple Lake. This is Kepple Lake Overlook so sit down and enjoy watching the waterfowl and possibly other wildlife that may be on or around the lake. Coots (*Fulica americana*) can often be seen from here and ring-necked ducks (*Aythya collaris*) are sometimes present. When you are ready, return to the last junction and turn left.

In a short distance the trail reaches a roadbed (same road that you followed leaving the Kepple Lake Overlook parking area). Turn left on the roadbed and hike 0.1 mile northeast to a gate, which is only about 50 yards from the South Cheney-Spangle Road. This is your turnaround point, so turn around and follow the roadbed back to the Kepple Lake Overlook parking area. Turn right at the parking area and retrace your steps along the Pine Creek Auto Tour Route to the Kepple Lake Peninsula Trailhead.

MILES AND DIRECTIONS

0.0 Hike north from the Kepple Lake Peninsula Trailhead.

0.1 Kepple Peninsula Environmental Education Shelter is on the left.

0.2 Turn around at the wildlife-viewing blind.

0.6 Return to Kepple Lake Peninsula Trailhead and walk east on the Pine Creek Auto Tour Route.

0.9 Hike northeast from the Kepple Lake Overlook parking area.

1.0 Turn left, leaving the roadbed.

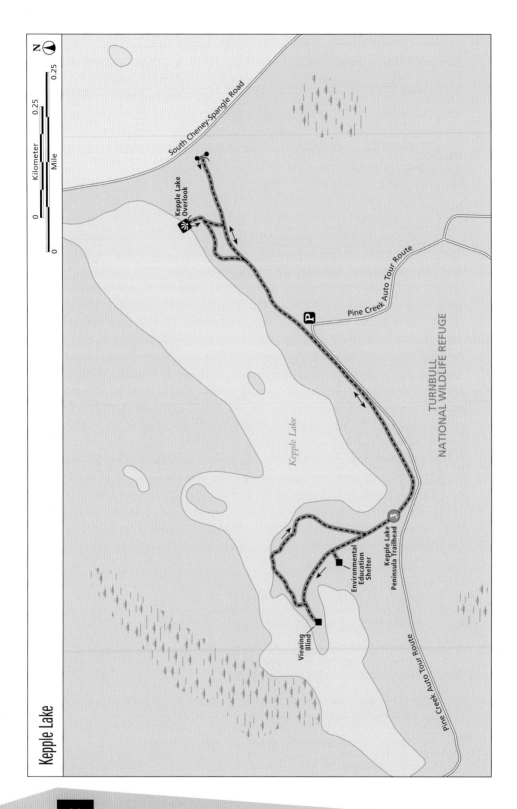

1.1 Arrive at Kepple Lake Overlook.

1.3 Turn around next to South Cheney-Spangle Road.

1.9 Arrive back at the Kepple Lake Peninsula Trailhead.

Options
Hike the 30-Acre Lake Trail (Hike 2) on the same trip. It is on the opposite side of the Pine Creek Auto Tour Route. You passed the 30-Acre Lake south trailhead before reaching the Kepple Lake Peninsula Trailhead and the 30-Acre Lake north trailhead is a short distance west of (past) the Kepple Lake Peninsula Trailhead.

The Blackhorse Lake Boardwalk, which reaches into Blackhorse Lake for a better view of the waterfowl and occasionally a moose (*Alces alces*), is but a short drive ahead along the Pine Creek Auto Tour Route.

> 🌿 Green Tip:
> *Pass it down—the best way to instill good green habits in your children is to set a good example.*

Kepple Lake observation blind

Columbia Plateau Trail

The section of the Columbia Plateau Trail described here is the only part of that trail that is presently paved. For kids that like trains, this is a great hike. You may get a close look at a train on a parallel track or crossing overhead on a bridge. This hike can be made one-way, cutting the total distance in half, if a car shuttle to the Fish Lake Trailhead can be arranged. The Columbia Plateau Trail is a Rails-to-Trails project.

Start: Cheney Trailhead

Distance: 7.7 miles out and back or 3.8-mile shuttle day hike

Hiking time: About 3 hours out and back, 1.5-hour shuttle

Difficulty: Easy

Best season: Year-round, snow conditions permitting

Canine compatibility / other trail users: The most common users of this section of the Columbia Plateau Trail are bicyclists. Horses and motorized vehicles are prohibited. This portion of the Columbia Plateau Trail is accessible for people with physical challenges. Dogs must be kept on a leash, which is very important for safety here because of the numbers of bicyclists.

Fees and permits: Discover Pass is required for parking at the trailheads. The pass is available online at www.discoverpass.wa.gov and wherever fishing and hunting licenses are sold.

Maps: The map in this book is more than adequate for this hike. Many maps show this route as a railroad track, which it once was.

Trail contact: At present the Columbia Plateau Trail is managed by Riverside State Park, 9711 W. Charles Rd., Nine Mile Falls, WA 99026; (509) 465-5064; riverside statepark.org

Special considerations: Even though pedestrians have the right-of-way over bicyclists, it is always a good idea to be courteous and move to the side to allow them to pass safely.

Finding the trailhead: From downtown Spokane, take I-90 west for 11 miles to exit 270. Take the exit and drive south for 6 miles on SR 904 to Cheney, Washington. Drive south from Cheney on the Cheney-Spangle Road for 1 mile. The parking area and trailhead are on the left side of the road. Shaded picnic tables and restrooms are available at the trailhead, but there's no water. The trailhead is at 2,300 feet elevation. GPS: N47 28.767' / W117 33.652'

THE HIKE

At the northwest corner of the parking area, descend the paved path for a few yards to the Columbia Plateau Trail and turn right. A sign informs you here that it is 0.25 mile to the Water Station and 3.75 miles to the Fish Lake Trailhead. The actual distances are slightly farther in both cases. Other signs let you know that the maximum speed is 15 mph for bicycles and that you are entering the city of Cheney. The route leads northwest following the old railroad grade through a cut rimmed with aspen (*Populus tremuloides*) and ponderosa pine (*Pinus ponderosa*) trees.

Three-tenths of a mile from the trailhead, you pass Mile Mark 361. The mile markers are the distances from Portland, Oregon, along the old railroad. On the left 0.1 mile past the mile marker, you will reach the Water Station, which has a shaded bench and a fountain. As you pass the Water Station, the course enters a more open area. For about 0.2 mile the broad, paved trail traverses open country. Then, as the route passes through a cut in the layered basalt, trees show up again. A sluggish stream follows the grade through the cut. Muskrats (*Ondatra zibethicus*) are occasionally seen in this stream.

The track leaves the city of Cheney 1.1 miles from the trailhead. Soon the tread passes Mile Mark 362, then goes beneath a railroad overpass. The trail goes under a wooden bridge 0.2 mile farther along. The trail leaves the cut about 2 miles from the trailhead. Past the cut there is a field and a house to the left of the trail. To your right is a railroad track. The route passes Mile Mark 363 before long, then enters another cut. The Anderson Road Bridge crosses overhead, 2.7 miles after leaving the Cheney Trailhead.

Four-tenths of a mile farther along, the trail passes beneath another railroad bridge and reaches Mile Mark 364 in another 0.2 mile. Fish Lake comes into view to the left just past the mile marker. The Fish Lake Trailhead is reached slightly over 3.8 miles from the Cheney Trailhead. If you haven't arranged a car shuttle, turn around here and retrace your steps back to the Cheney Trailhead.

MILES AND DIRECTIONS

0.0 Descend the path from the Cheney Trailhead, then turn right.

0.4 Pass the Water Station.

3.8 Reach the Fish Lake Trailhead, turn around (if you haven't arranged for a car shuttle), and retrace your steps to the Cheney Trailhead.

7.7 Arrive back at the Cheney Trailhead.

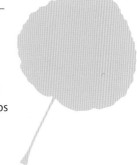

Columbia Plateau Trail

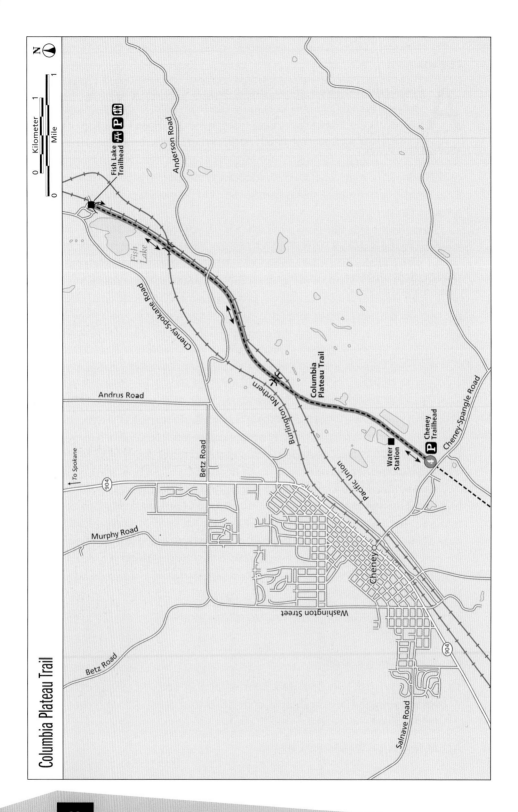

Options

Hike one of the routes in the Turnbull National Wildlife Refuge (Hike 1, 2, or 3) on the same trip, as they are close by. Walking the gravel part of the Columbia Plateau Trail west from the Cheney Trailhead is also a good, nearly flat, hike. Hike out and back as far as you like, watching for waterfowl along the way. Horses are allowed on the trail west of the Cheney Trailhead.

Muskrat

The muskrat (*Ondatra zibethicus*) is not a close relative of the beaver, despite their many similar habits. Muskrats are 16 to 25 inches in length (including the nearly hairless tail) and may weight up to three pounds. They are covered with thick, glossy, brown fur that has been and is still to some extent valuable. Being excellent swimmers, muskrats never stray far from water. Like beavers, they can stay underwater for 15 minutes or slightly longer.

Columbia Plateau Trail

Deep Creek Loop

Hike through mostly ponderosa pine forest above Deep Creek Canyon and take in the view of the rugged canyon and lava flows from Deep Creek Overlook. Then descend to the Centennial Trail next to Nine Mile Reservoir. Soon leave the broad, paved Centennial Trail and climb through the lava and jagged rock pinnacles to the forested bench above the west side of Deep Creek Canyon, and follow it back to the trailhead.

Start: Pine Bluff Trailhead

Distance: 4.0-mile loop day hike with a very short side trip

Hiking time: About 2.5 hours

Difficulty: Moderate, with a couple of strenuous spots

Best seasons: Spring, summer, and fall. Also winter if there isn't snow cover.

Canine compatibility / other trail users: Dogs are permitted on a leash. Bicycles are allowed on this route and are the most common traffic on the Centennial Trail portion of this loop.

Fees and permits: Discover Pass available wherever hunting and fishing licenses are sold or online

at www.discoverpass.wa.gov

Maps: *Riverside State Park Multi-use Trail Map,* produced by the Inland Empire Backcountry Horsemen, PO Box 30891, Spokane, WA 99223; iebch.com. This map may be purchased at the state park.

Trail contact: Riverside State Park, 9711 W. Charles Rd., Nine Mile Falls, WA 99026; (509) 465-5064; riversidestatepark.org

Special considerations: The hike description below may seem complicated because of the many trail junctions on this route. Watch the map closely as you hike and the directions will become much simpler.

Finding the trailhead: There are many ways to reach this trailhead; this is the route from the center of Spokane. Take Division Street north from I-90 to Francis, which is also SR 291. Turn left on Francis and follow it to 9-Mile Road (SR 291). Bear right on 9-Mile Road and drive northwest for 2 miles to 7-Mile Road. Turn left on 7-Mile Road and head west for 2.5 miles to the Pine Bluff Trailhead at the junction with Pine Bluff Road. The trailhead and parking area are on the right side of 7-Mile Road. There is adequate parking but no restrooms at the Pine Bluff Trailhead. The elevation at the trailhead is 1,840 feet. GPS: N47 44.864' /W117 33.152'

THE HIKE

From the Pine Bluff Trailhead, hike northeast on the dirt roadbed (closed to motor vehicles). The route reaches a junction after a few yards of hiking through the open ponderosa pine (*Pinus ponderosa*) woods. There are no signs at the junction so bear right and continue to traverse the open woods to the northeast. The roadbeds rejoin each other in 0.3 mile.

At the point where the roadbeds come back together, you leave the road-bed and head north on the singletrack. The course descends for about 100 yards into the small canyon. The trail reaches the bottom of the canyon very close to the point where Coulee Creek joins Deep Creek. Both of these creeks may be dry. Cross the creekbed, then climb north for slightly under 0.2 mile to State Park Drive and the Deep Creek Trailhead. The trailhead, at 1,820 elevation, is little more than a wide spot in the road.

North of the trailhead the road is closed to motorized traffic and blocked by a metal gate. Walk around the gate and follow State Park Drive north. In 0.2 mile the 25-Mile Trail crosses the road. A quarter mile after passing the 25-Mile Trail junction, you reach the junction with a short side trail that goes to the Deep Creek Overlook. Turn left at the junction and walk the short distance to the overlook. The GPS coordinates at the overlook are N47 45.671' / W117 32.928'.

Deep Creek Overlook

After taking in the view, return to State Park Drive and turn left (northeast). Continue another 0.3 mile on the now-paved State Park Drive. The route traverses through the ponderosa pines and Douglas firs (*Pseudotsuga menziesii*), with balsamroot (*Balsamorhiza sagittata*) and lupine (*Lupinus*) on the forest floor. Then you descend a hill and pass a gate before reaching the junction with the broad, paved Centennial Trail. At the junction a sign states that you have come "¼ mile" from Deep Creek Overlook and "1 mile" from the Deep Creek Trailhead (a slight overestimation). The elevation at this junction is 1,710 feet.

Turn left at the junction and follow the Centennial Trail. Nine Mile Reservoir (a reservoir in the Spokane River) is to your right as you hike west-northwest. The route descends gently to a bridge over the mouth of Deep Creek. Cross the bridge and soon reach the junction with Trail 411. At this junction you are 1.7 miles into this hike and at 1,620 feet elevation. The unsigned junction with Trail 411 is just past a metal bench, after passing the junction on a path that follows Deep Creek upstream (see map for clarification).

Turn left on Trail 411 and immediately begin to climb to the southwest. Soon the route makes a couple of steep rocky switchbacks. The track then crosses an area covered with lava. Large rock outcrops loom overhead as you traverse the rough talus slopes. Six-tenths of a mile after leaving the Centennial Trail and climbing 160 feet, Trail 411 reaches a junction with the 25-Mile Trail.

Turn right at the junction and hike west along the 25-Mile Trail. The track climbs for 0.25 mile to another junction. Here you turn left, leaving the 25-Mile Trail. Then the tread climbs, making six switchbacks in the 0.1 mile to the junction with Trail 410. Bear left (nearly straight ahead) on Trail 410 and hike south. The track climbs slightly, following the bench for 0.25 mile, then flattens out at about 1,950 feet elevation. Continue south on the bench to another junction with the 25-Mile Trail. This Y junction is 2.9 miles into this hike.

At the Y junction, bear left and hike south on the 25-Mile Trail. The track descends a little before flattening out again on the bench. The course gets close to the rim of Coulee Creek Canyon 0.4 mile from the junction. Above the trail to your right are rugged rock cliffs. After you have followed the top of the bench for 0.6 mile, you descend for a short distance to the junction with Pine Bluff Road. At the junction with the road, the elevation is 1,910 feet. Turn left on Pine Bluff Road and hike mostly downhill for 0.4 mile, back to the Pine Bluff Trailhead.

Deep Creek Loop

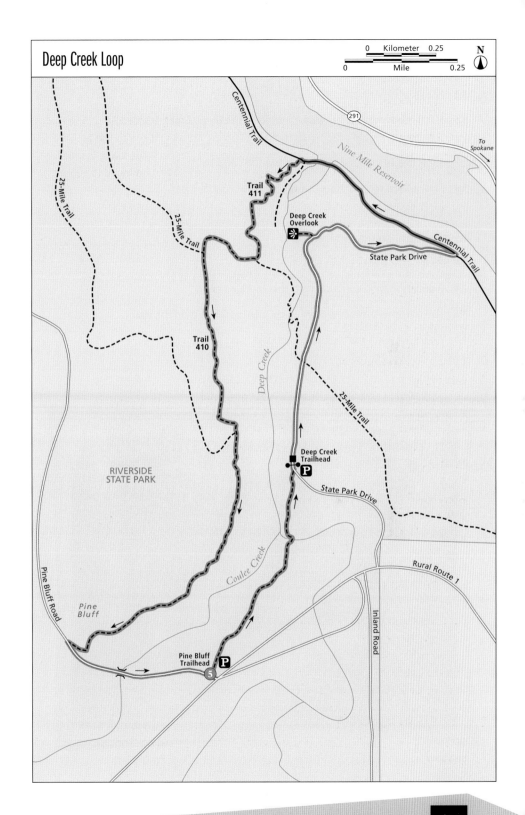

0 — Kilometer — 0.25
0 — Mile — 0.25

N

Centennial Trail

291

Nine Mile Reservoir

To Spokane

Trail 411

Deep Creek Overlook

Centennial Trail

State Park Drive

25-Mile Trail

25-Mile Trail

Trail 410

Deep Creek

25-Mile Trail

Deep Creek Trailhead

P

State Park Drive

RIVERSIDE STATE PARK

Rural Route 1

Coulee Creek

Pine Bluff Road

Pine Bluff

Inland Road

Pine Bluff Trailhead

P

5

MILES AND DIRECTIONS

0.0 Hike northeast from the Pine Bluff Trailhead.

0.5 Head north along State Park Drive from the Deep Creek Trailhead.

0.9 Reach the junction with the side trail to the Deep Creek Overlook. Walk the short distance to the left to the overlook and back.

1.3 Turn left on the Centennial Trail.

1.7 Turn left on Trail 411.

2.3 Turn right on the 25-Mile Trail.

2.5 Bear left at the junction with Trail 410.

2.9 Bear left at the Y junction with the 25-Mile Trail.

3.6 The trail intersects Pine Bluff Road. Hike southeast on the road.

4.0 Arrive back at the Pine Bluff Trailhead.

Lava fields

Bowl and Pitcher Loop

Hike through rock gardens, draws, and uplands of Riverside State Park, Washington's second largest. The park covers 10,000 acres of forests, rocky canyons, and riverfront, as well as several miles of the splashing and frothing Spokane River. A large section of this hike follows the 25-Mile Trail, which is a 25-mile-long loop through Riverside State Park. Signposts mark much of the 25-Mile Trail.

Start: Swinging Bridge Trailhead

Distance: 5.5-mile double-loop day hike

Hiking time: About 3 hours

Difficulty: Easy to moderate

Best seasons: Spring, summer, and fall. Also winter if there isn't snow cover.

Canine compatibility / other trail users: Bicyclists and equestrians also use this trail. Dogs are permitted on a leash.

Fees and permits: Discover Pass available wherever hunting and fishing licenses are sold or online at www.discoverpass.wa.gov

Maps: *Riverside State Park Multi-use Trail Map,* produced by the Inland Empire Backcountry Horse-men, PO Box 30891, Spokane, WA 99223; iebch.com. This map may be purchased at the state park. The National Geographic *Washington* topo on CD-ROM, disk 4, and Montana Mapping & GPS LLC's Hunting and GPS maps are good topos of the area.

Trail contact: Riverside State Park, 9711 Charles Rd., Nine Mile Falls, WA 99026; (509) 465-5064; riversidestatepark.org

Special considerations: This is a fairly complicated route to follow, so be sure to keep your map handy and follow your progress. On the last 3.4 miles of this hike (and some sections before that), follow the 25-Mile Trail markers.

Finding the trailhead: From exit 281 on I-90, take Division Street north to Francis, which is SR 291. Turn west (left) on SR 291 and go 3.8 miles to the junction with Rifle Club Road. A sign here points to the Bowl and Pitcher area. Turn left on Rifle Club Road and drive 0.4 mile southwest to Aubrey L. White Parkway. Turn left on Aubrey L. White Parkway and drive 2 miles south to the Bowl and Pitcher area, which includes a campground and day-use area. The trailhead is on the west side of the area, at the east end of the Swinging Bridge. Signs point out the way. There is plenty of parking, restrooms, and a campground close to the trailhead. The *Riverside State Park Multi-use Trail Map* may be helpful here. GPS: N47 41.801' /W117 29.818'

THE HIKE

Before you cross the Swinging Bridge and begin your hike, read the reader board at the east end of the bridge. The Bowl and Pitcher rock formation is to your right as you cross the Swinging Bridge. Once across the bridge the course climbs a short distance to the junction with the 25-Mile Trail. Turn right (north) at the junction onto the 25-Mile Trail.

As you hike north the route works its way through the dark rock outcroppings. You will reach the junction with Trails 210 and 211 in 0.3 mile. Turn right at the junction, staying on the 25-Mile Trail, and start the first loop. You soon reach another junction, where you'll hike straight ahead, staying on the main trail. To the right below the trail, the Spokane River froths and sloshes through a set of rapids. The track follows the top of the riverbank as you hike northeast, well above the clear, rushing waters.

Six tenths of a mile from the trailhead, the course goes under some power lines. There is an unsigned trail junction 0.25 mile farther along. The trail to the left is a shortcut, but it misses some of the best river views on this hike. Bear right here, staying on the main trail, which follows the riverbank. A column of rock called the Devils Toe Nail rises from the center of the frothing river, 0.3 mile

Bowl and Pitcher

farther along. Soon the track passes Mile Marker 20. There is another trail junction just past the mile marker. Turn left here, temporarily leaving the 25-Mile Trail. The route climbs a short distance west to a junction with Trail 211, which is an abandoned roadbed. The trail that turned left off the 25-Mile Trail 0.5 mile back also rejoins the route (coming in from the southeast; see map for clarification) here.

Turn left on Trail 211 and hike south. Three-tenths of a mile after leaving the junction, rock outcroppings rise above the trail on your right. The course returns to the junction with Trail 210 and the 25-Mile Trail in another 0.2 mile. This junction, 1.6 miles into this hike, is the end of the first loop and the beginning of the second. If you would like to make this a shorter outing, you can retrace your steps from here back to the Swinging Bridge Trailhead.

To continue on to the second loop, turn right at the junction and head west on Trail 210. The track makes a couple of switchbacks then continues to climb to the northwest, passing a viewpoint. In 0.4 mile Trail 210 crosses the wide, paved Centennial Trail. In a little more than 0.1 mile more, you reach the junction with Trail 200, which is marked on a trail sign. Turn left here and quickly reach the junction with the 25-Mile Trail, which you will be following all the way from here back to the Swinging Bridge Trailhead. By the time you reach this junction, you have climbed a little over 200 feet of elevation from the junction with Trail 211 where you started this loop.

Turn to the left on the 25-Mile Trail and head south. In the open areas, lupine (*Lupinus*) and death camas (*Zigadenus venenosus*) sprout beside the trail. After climbing another 150 feet in 0.3 mile, the track levels out. The course follows an abandoned grade for 0.3 mile then turns left, leaving the grade and making a couple of descending switchbacks. The route then flattens out on a meadow-covered bench beneath some power lines. This section of the route parallels the Centennial Trail, which is to your left (east). After following the power lines for about 0.6 mile, the tread turns left and descends to another junction with the Centennial Trail. At this point you have hiked 3.6 miles since leaving the Swinging Bridge Trailhead.

Turn left at the junction, onto the Centennial Trail. Walk a few yards to the north, passing the junction with the road that leads to the equestrian trailhead. Then turn right, staying on the 25-Mile Trail and leaving the paved Centennial Trail. The route now heads east-northeast and shortly reaches a trail junction where you bear right and quickly cross an abandoned roadbed. In 0.3 mile the trail turns right on another abandoned roadbed and descends a short distance to the junction with Trail 101. Bear right here, then turn quickly left on another abandoned roadbed. There are "pipeline" signposts at these turns. Shortly, you turn right, leaving the pipeline. A little farther along is another junction. The trail (roadbed) to the right leads 100 yards to an equestrian trailhead. Hike left (east) here, staying on the 25-Mile Trail.

In 0.1 mile the route turns right, leaving the roadbed, and soon crosses two abandoned roadbeds. Then you enter the parking area for another equestrian trailhead. Turn left (northeast) at the parking area on a road and soon bear left, staying on the main road (25-Mile Trail). You quickly pass two more junctions—bear left at both. Then the route crosses the pipeline road and Trail 101. You will reach the junction with Trail 100 0.2 mile past the second equestrian trailhead.

At the junction with Trail 100, the 25-Mile Trail turns to the left (west), with the Spokane River below to your right. The track follows the river west for about 0.6 mile. In places other trails parallel the main trail. There are several junctions

Squirrel above the trail

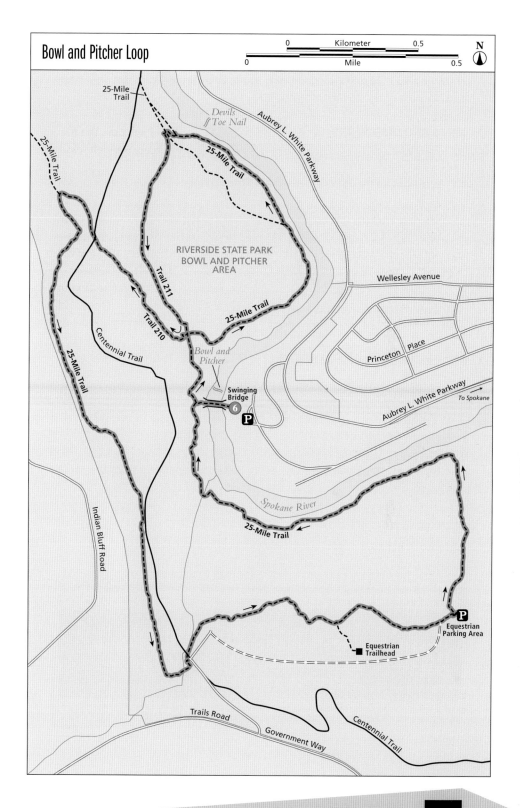

Bowl and Pitcher Loop

with these side trails. After 0.6 mile the course turns right to head north for the remaining 0.3 mile to the junction next to the Swinging Bridge. Turn right here and cross the bridge to the trailhead.

MILES AND DIRECTIONS

0.0 Leave the Swinging Bridge Trailhead and cross the Swinging Bridge.

0.4 Turn right on the 25-Mile Trail, starting the first loop.

1.1 Turn left on Trail 211 (roadbed).

1.6 Turn right at the junction with Trail 210 and the 25-Mile Trail.

2.0 Cross the Centennial Trail.

2.1 Turn left on the 25-Mile Trail.

3.6 Cross the Centennial Trail again.

4.0 Pass a roadbed to an equestrian trailhead.

4.3 Pass another equestrian trailhead.

4.5 At the junction with Trail 100, stay on the 25-Mile-Trail.

5.5 Arrive back at the Swinging Bridge Trailhead.

Options
The two loops described here can easily be hiked separately from the same trailhead.

Valley Trail–Indian Painted Rocks Trail Loop

Starting close to the Little Spokane River, hike up a lush valley. Then climb over the top of a ridge with great views and descend back down to the Little Spokane River. Head upstream along the meandering waterway back to the trailhead.

Start: Indian Painted Rocks Trailhead

Distance: 6.3-mile loop day hike

Hiking time: About 4 hours

Difficulty: Moderate

Best seasons: Summer and fall

Canine compatibility / other trail users: Most of this trail is hikers only, no dogs, bikes, or camping.

Fees and permits: A Discover Pass is needed for parking at the trailhead. Discover Passes are available wherever hunting and fishing licenses are sold or online at www .discoverpass.wa.gov.

Maps: *Riverside State Park Multiuse Trail Map,* produced by the Inland Empire Backcountry Horsemen, PO Box 30891, Spokane, WA 99223; iebch.com. This map may be purchased at the state park. Montana Mapping & GPS LLC's Hunting and GPS maps are good topos of the area as are National Geographic maps on CD-ROM.

Trail contact: Riverside State Park, 9711 W. Charles Rd., Nine Mile Falls, WA 99026; (509) 465-5064; riversidestatepark.org

Special considerations: Watch for moose along this route. For safety, watch moose from a distance

and don't challenge them in any way. When I hiked this trail, there was a large bull about 1.5 miles from the trailhead. Most of this route is within the Little Spokane River Natural Area, which is part of Riverside State Park. However, in a couple of places, the route crosses private property (with an easement), so be sure to stay on the route to avoid conflicts here. At times of high water, the Indian Painted Rocks Trail section of this loop may be temporarily flooded and closed. If this is the case, there is usually a sign so stating at the Indian Painted Rocks Trailhead.

Finding the trailhead: There are many ways to reach this trailhead; this is a route from the center of Spokane. Take Division Street north from I-90 to Francis, which is SR 291. Turn left on Francis and follow it to 9-Mile Road (SR 291). Bear right on 9-Mile Road and drive northwest for 6 miles to Rutter Parkway, which is just as you enter Nine Mile Falls. Turn right on Rutter Parkway. In 2.4 miles you will reach the junction with Indian Trail Road. Turn left at the junction, staying on Rutter Parkway. In 0.9 mile Indian Painted Rocks Trailhead, where this hike begins and ends, is on your left. There is ample parking and restrooms at the trailhead. The elevation at the trailhead is 1,575 feet. GPS: N47 46.961'/W117 29.808'

THE HIKE

Hike northeast from the north side of the Indian Painted Rocks Trailhead parking area, paralleling the Rutter Parkway. In a little less than 0.2 mile, you will reach a junction with a dirt roadbed, which is closed to unauthorized vehicles. Turn left and hike northeast on the roadbed. Larkspur (*Delphinium*), lupine (*Lupinus*), and arrowleaf balsamroot (*Balsamorhiza sagittata*) cover the ground beneath the Rocky Mountain maples (*Acer glabrum*) and Douglas firs (*Pseudotsuga menziesii*). The track climbs gently and soon enters a draw. You climb along the bottom of the fairly narrow draw for a mile. Then the draw broadens and flattens out. This flatter area appears to have been select-logged some time ago. Mule deer (*Odocoileus hemionus*) are often seen in this area and moose (*Alces alces*) are possible.

The route temporarily leaves state park property 1.6 miles from the trailhead. A fence post and rod marks this boundary, but they could be easily missed. Be sure to stay on the route, especially in this area. In another 0.3 mile the route (still a roadbed) makes a turn to the left to head southwest. At this turn you have climbed to slightly over 2,100 feet elevation. The track then climbs out of the now-broad draw. After leaving the draw the route climbs moderately, reaching a ridgeline in 0.5 mile. Along the ridge is a viewpoint with a bench. The view is to the west overlooking the Spokane River Valley. Shortly after passing the viewpoint, you reach the highest point on this loop, at 2,450 feet elevation.

Past the high point the tread descends to the south. The course passes a small pond 0.3 mile into the descent. Another 0.3 mile and you pass a structure that appears to be some kind of reservoir. The course then descends steeply, soon passing signs that say No Trespassing and Keep Out on both sides of the trail. Stay on the route here. The tread makes a left turn at a signpost 0.4 mile farther along. The signpost points to the Highway 291 Trailhead. At the turn you are close to a paved private road and a house. In a short distance the track crosses the paved road. Angle slightly to the left at the crossing.

The trail makes a right turn at another signpost 0.2 mile farther along. Then you cross a flat bench before descending again. The route descends for another 300 yards to a junction with the paved road and the Indian Painted Rocks Trail, which is the return route to the Indian Painted Rocks Trailhead. This junction, at 1,550 feet elevation, is 4.6 miles into the loop. To the right along the paved road, it's only a short distance to the Highway 291 Trailhead. Bear left, crossing the road, and pick up the Indian Painted Rocks Trail on its south side.

Spokane River

The trail, which is an abandoned roadbed here, passes a signboard, then heads east. Ponderosa pines (*Pinus ponderosa*) and cottonwoods (*Populus tricho-carpa*) tower above the route. To the right the wet flats along the Little Spokane River are covered with yellow water iris, a nonnative species brought here by early settlers. In 0.5 mile the route turns left at a short wooden fence. On the fence is a sign that states STAY ON THE TRAIL. The track climbs moderately for 0.1 mile, then descends some steps and crosses a draw. You climb slightly after crossing the draw. Brown-eyed Susans (*Gaillardia aristata*) often bloom beside the trail here during the summer. The track then descends back nearly to river level.

Soon the course reaches a short fence that blocks an alternate section of trail. Stay on the main trail and in a short distance you will be close to the river. A few yards farther along there is a trail junction. The trail to the left goes to a bench and soon rejoins the main trail. The route climbs over a tilted granite slab 0.25 after passing the bench. There are two paths to the right that lead to the riverbank 0.1 mile past the granite slab. Granite cliffs loom above the trail on the left in another 0.25 mile. Here another path turns to the right, but don't take it. Continue to the east along the main trail, and reach the Indian Painted Rocks Trailhead in 0.2 mile. The Indian Painted Rocks Trailhead is 1.7 miles from the point where you last crossed the paved road.

MILES AND DIRECTIONS

0.0 Hike northeast from the Indian Painted Rocks Trailhead.

0.2 Turn left on a roadbed.

1.9 The trail makes left turn, leaving the draw.

4.6 Cross the paved road to Indian Painted Rocks Trail.

6.3 Arrive back at the Indian Painted Rocks Trailhead.

Options

You may want to hike the Little Spokane River Trail (Hike 8) on the same outing. The Little Spokane River hike ends at the Indian Painted Rocks Trailhead, and it's only a short drive to the trailhead where it starts.

> ## 🌿 Green Tip:
> *Enjoy and respect this beautiful landscape.*
> *As you take advantage of the spectacular scenery offered by the Spokane Coeur d'Alene area, remember that our planet is very dear, very special, and very fragile.*
> *All of us should do everything we can to keep it clean, beautiful, and healthy, including following the Green Tips you'll find throughout this book.*

8

Little Spokane River

This trail is mostly within the Little Spokane River Natural Area of Riverside State Park. Watch for wild turkeys all along this route. When I last hiked this trail, I spent at least 15 minutes watching a hen turkey with her brood. Moose are also possible anywhere along this trail.

Start: Lower St. George's Trailhead

Distance: 4.0-mile shuttle or 7.7-mile out-and-back day hike

Hiking time: About 2-hour shuttle, 4 hours out and back

Difficulty: Easy to moderate

Best season: Spring through fall

Canine compatibility / other trail users: Hikers and cross-country skiers only; no dogs, bikes, or camping

Fees and permits: A Discover Pass is needed if you are going to park at the Indian Painted Rocks Trailhead. Discover Passes are available wherever hunting and fishing licenses are sold or online at www.discoverpass.wa.gov.

Maps: *Riverside State Park Multi-use Trail Map*, produced by the Inland Empire Backcountry Horsemen, PO Box 30891, Spokane, WA 99223; iebch.com. This map may be purchased at the state park. Montana Mapping & GPS LLC's Hunting and GPS maps are good topos of the area, as is the National Geographic map on CD-ROM, *Washington*, disk 4.

Trail contact: Riverside State Park, 9711 W. Charles Rd., Nine Mile Falls, WA 99026; (509) 465-5064; riversidestatepark.org

Finding the trailhead: There are many ways to reach this trailhead; this is a route from the center of Spokane. Take Division Street north from I-90 to Francis, which is also SR 291. Turn left on Francis and follow it to 9-Mile Road, also SR 291. Bear right on 9-Mile Road and drive northwest for 6 miles to Rutter Parkway, just as you enter Nine Mile Falls. Turn right on Rutter Parkway. In 2.4 miles you will reach the junction with Indian Trail Road. Turn left at the junction, staying on Rutter Parkway. In 0.9 mile Indian Painted Rocks Trailhead, where this hike may end if you have a shuttle available, is on the left. To reach your starting point, follow Rutter Parkway another 3 miles, then turn right and go 0.1 mile to Lower St. George's Trailhead. The elevation at the trailhead is 1,630 feet. The *Riverside State Park Multi-use Trail Map* can be a big help when trying to find this trailhead. GPS: N47 45.852' / W117 27.338'

L eaving the trailhead, the trail quickly passes through a hiker-only gate. A few yards farther is a signboard, where you bear right. Then you turn left where a short fence blocks the abandoned trail that goes straight ahead. Now the route climbs fairly steeply, making nine switchbacks and climbing a bit over 300 feet of elevation before reaching a trail junction. This junction is 0.5 mile into the hike.

Turn right at the junction and descend—a trail marker post points the way. The track, which is an abandoned roadbed, loses only a few feet before climbing again through brush that is more than head high on both sides of the trail. In 0.5 mile more of gentle climbing through the lupine (*Lupinus*) and ninebark bushes (*Physocarpus malvaceus*), you will reach another trail junction. This junction is also marked with a trail marker on a fiberglass post. Bear right (nearly straight ahead) at the junction. This junction is 1.1 miles from the trailhead at approximately 2,100 feet elevation.

The trail leaves state park property, entering land owned by St. George's School, in slightly over 0.1 mile. Then you descend gently mostly through the Douglas fir (*Pseudotsuga menziesii*) forest. Soon the course turns to the right and drops a little more steeply, passing several large, healthy-looking rosebushes.

Water iris

A little farther along, the tread crosses a draw, where the forest changes from Douglas fir to ponderosa pine (*Pinus ponderosa*). Soon the trail flattens and makes a turn to the left as you pass a group of nonnative Scotch broom (*Cytisus scoparius*) bushes. Soon after turning left the tread passes a gate and reenters state park land. A short distance farther there is another trail junction. Bear right onto a bench covered with young to medium-age ponderosa pines.

Slightly over 0.3 mile more of hiking brings you to yet another trail junction with a rock outcrop to the right. Bear left here. There is a trail marker post at this junction. Soon the tread passes a small marsh and a bench and you begin descending a draw. The route soon turns left, leaving the draw and climbing slightly, passing a signpost. The course soon flattens and then descends to near river level. The marshy area to the right is nearly covered with yellow water iris.

The trail follows the river bottom downstream in and out of the flower-covered meadows. You will pass a path to the right that leads to a bench in a meadow.

A few more minutes of hiking brings you to the junction with Rutter Parkway. There is no roadside parking where the trail meets Rutter Parkway. If you have a shuttle waiting, turn right. Walk along the roadway and cross the bridge over the Little Spokane River to the Indian Painted Rocks Trailhead. The trailhead is on the left side of the road at 1,575 feet elevation, and it is 4 miles from the Lower St. George's Trailhead, where this hike started.

If you don't have a car waiting, turn around at the junction with Rutter Parkway and retrace your steps to the Lower St. George's Trailhead.

Yellow water iris is a nonnative species that was brought to the area by European settlers for use as an ornamental plant. These invasive but beautiful plants have become very well established in the marshy areas along the Little Spokane River bottom.

Scotch Broom

Scotch broom (*Cytisus scoparius*) was introduced on Vancouver Island, British Columbia, in 1850. It has become very widespread in the Northwest, mostly west of the Cascade Mountains. Scotch broom seems to grow best in areas that have been disturbed, where it often outcompetes native plants to become dominant. The scrub may stand up to 10 feet tall and has green branches that are covered with small deciduous leaves. The bright-yellow flowers of the Scotch broom strongly resemble those of the sweet pea. When dry, the resinous Scotch broom scrub is highly flammable.

Little Spokane River

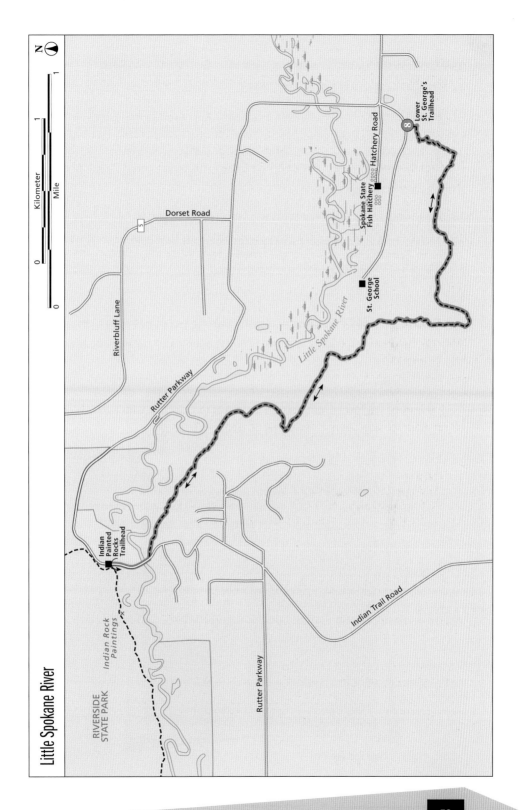

MILES AND DIRECTIONS

0.0   Start at the Lower St. George's Trailhead.

0.5   At the trail junction, turn right.

1.1   Bear right at the trail junction.

2.1   Pass a gate and reenter Riverside State Park.

2.5   Bear left at the trail junction.

3.6   Pass a path to the right that leads to a bench in the meadow.

3.8   At the junction with Rutter Parkway, turn around or turn right.

4.0   Reach the Indian Painted Rocks Trailhead.

Options

Hike the Indian Painted Rocks Trail on the same trip. The Indian Painted Rocks Trail continues down the Little Spokane River for another 1.7 miles to the Highway 291 Trailhead.

Little Spokane River

Centennial Trail

Hike the paved Centennial Trail from Sontag Park Trailhead near Nine Mile Falls through Riverside State Park to Military Cemetery Trailhead. This is the most scenic part of the 37-mile-long Centennial Trail and the section that is best adapted to hikers. Allow plenty of time to enjoy the viewpoints overlooking the sometimes calm, sometimes frothing Spokane River.

Start: Sontag Park Trailhead

Distance: 9.4-mile shuttle day hike

Hiking time: About 5 hours

Difficulty: Easy

Best seasons: Spring, summer, and fall. Winter can also be good depending on snow conditions.

Canine compatibility / other trail users: Dogs are permitted on a leash. Bicycles are the most common users of the Centennial Trail. This entire trail is accessible for people with physical challenges.

Fees and permits: Discover Pass, available wherever hunting and fishing licenses are sold or online at www.discoverpass.wa.gov

Maps: *Washington State Parks Riverside State Park* brochure and map available free at state park headquarters and Bowl and Pitches campground entrance. *Riverside State Park Multi-use Trail Map,* produced by the Inland Empire Backcountry Horsemen, PO Box 30891, Spokane, WA 99223; iebch.com. This map may be purchased at the state park. The National Geographic *Washington* topo map on CD-ROM, disk 4. Montana Mapping & GPS LLC's Hunting and GPS maps are available at huntinggpsmaps.com.

Trail contact: Riverside State Park, 9711 Charles Rd., Nine Mile Falls, WA 99026; (509) 465-5064; riversidestatepark.org

Special considerations: Watch for fast bicycle traffic, especially on hills and blind corners.

Finding the trailhead: There are many ways to reach this trailhead; this is a route from the center of Spokane. Take Division Street north from I-90 to Francis, which is SR 291. Turn left on Francis and follow it to 9-Mile Road, also SR 291. Bear right on 9-Mile Road and drive northwest for 6.3 miles to Charles Road. Turn left and cross the bridge over the Spokane River below Nine Mile Falls Dam. Follow Charles Road for 0.3 mile to Sontag Park Trailhead. The park and trailhead are on the right side of Charles Road. GPS: N47 46.686' /W117 32.966'

To reach the Military Cemetery Trailhead where this hike ends, return to 9-Mile Road, turn right and drive south to 7-Mile Road. Turn right and follow 7-Mile Road to Inland Road. Turn left on Inland Road and follow it and Old Trails Road south to Government Way. Turn left on Government Way and drive to the trailhead, which is a short distance off Government Way, on your left. *The Washington State Parks Riverside State Park* brochure and map is helpful when trying to find the Military Cemetery Trailhead.

THE HIKE

The Centennial Trail leads south from the Sontag Park Trailhead, quickly crossing Charles Road. After crossing Charles Road the route follows Carlson Road. This section of the Centennial Trail is shared with motorized traffic so watch for cars. After climbing gently for 0.7 mile, the route makes a left turn, leaving Carlson Road. The track here becomes, for now, a nonmotorized route. You will reach the junction with Trail 400, which is to the right, 0.5 mile after leaving Carlson Road. Another 0.3 mile brings you to the junction with Trail 411. If you would like to make a side trip, Trail 411 climbs to your right, reaching some interesting lava formations in a short distance.

After passing the junction with Trail 411, the Centennial Trail crosses the Deep Creek Bridge and begins to climb toward the junction with State Park Drive. The junction is reached in a little less than 0.7 mile after climbing about 90 feet in elevation, through mostly Douglas fir (*Pseudotsuga menziesii*) woods. State Park Drive is closed to unauthorized motor vehicles and is a popular biking and hiking route. To your right on State Park Drive, its only a short side hike of about 0.4 mile to Deep Creek Overlook. The view from the overlook includes the rugged Deep Creek Canyon and the chaotic lava lands across it.

Leaving the junction with State Park Drive, the route continues southeast, passing beneath some power lines and reaching the McLellan Trailhead in 0.6 mile. Past the trailhead the route is again a road that is shared with motorized traffic. You pass some houses next to the road and in about 0.5 mile cross 7-Mile Road. For the next 0.7 mile, the route is still shared with cars, and then you reach the Wilber Road Trailhead. A short distance after passing the Wilber Road Trailhead, the 25-Mile Trail crosses the Centennial Trail. Shortly thereafter there is a fireplace and a kiosk with information about it to the right of the trail.

You reach the first junction with Trail 211 1.3 miles after passing the Wilber Road Trailhead. Continue southeast on the paved trail for 0.5 mile more to another junction with Trail 211. To the left Trail 211 leads to the Bowl and Pitcher area in about a mile. Stay on the Centennial Trail, heading south. In 0.7 mile Trail 210 crosses the route. The Centennial Trail then climbs a little before flattening out. Eight-tenths of a mile after passing the junction with Trail 210, you will pass a gate. Here the route becomes shared with cars again. Shortly after passing the gate, you reach the Bowl and Pitcher Overlook Trailhead. There is an excellent view from here looking down on the Bowl and Pitcher formation in the Spokane River.

Green Tip:
Never let your dog chase wildlife.

Spokane River

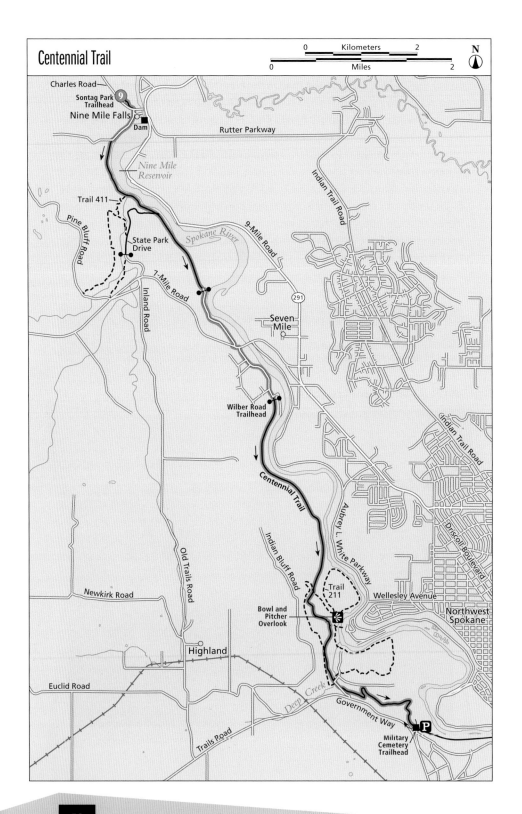

Kilometers
0   2

Miles
0   2

N

Charles Road
Sontag Park Trailhead
Nine Mile Falls
Dam
Rutter Parkway
Nine Mile Reservoir
Trail 411
Pine Bluff Road
State Park Drive
Spokane River
9-Mile Road
Indian Trail Road
291
Seven Mile
7-Mile Road
Inland Road
Wilber Road Trailhead
Centennial Trail
Old Trails Road
Indian Bluff Road
Aubrey L. White Parkway
Indian Trail Road
Driscoll Boulevard
Newkirk Road
Trail 211
Wellesley Avenue
Northwest Spokane
Bowl and Pitcher Overlook
Highland
Euclid Road
Deep Creek
Government Way
Trails Road
Military Cemetery Trailhead
P

The broad, paved track continues south after passing the overlook. In 0.4 mile there is a junction with the road to the Equestrian Area. In another 100 yards turn left, leaving the shared road. Now the Centennial Trail heads southeast. The course makes a descending S turn 0.3 mile ahead. Stay to the edge of the trail here and watch for bicycle traffic on these nearly blind corners. Past the S turn the route heads east, then south, reaching the Military Cemetery Trailhead in another 1.2 miles.

This is by no means the end of the Centennial Trail, but it is a good place to end your hike. Much of the rest of the trail is through the city.

MILES AND DIRECTIONS

0.0 Hike south from Sontag Park Trailhead.

1.5 Pass the junction with Trail 411.

2.2 Pass the junction with State Park Drive.

3.3 The route crosses 7-Mile Road.

4.0 Pass the Wilber Road Trailhead.

5.8 Pass Trail 211 for the second time.

7.4 Pass the Bowl and Pitcher Overlook Trailhead.

9.4 Reach the Military Cemetery Trailhead.

Options

A short side trip on Trail 411 to the lava formations is well worth the time and effort, as is the 0.8-mile round-trip side trip to Deep Creek Overlook on State Park Drive. It is not necessary to cover this entire route in one trip. If you want a shorter hike, you can easily begin and/or end your hike at any one of the trailheads mentioned above. The *Washington State Parks Riverside State Park* brochure and map is helpful when trying to find these trailheads.

A. *Honorable Mention*

Beacon Hill

Beacon Hill, east of downtown Spokane, has an extensive trail system. There are plenty of hiking possibilities here, but at present the signing is almost nonexistent. Beacon Hill Recreation Area maps of the trails are available at outdoors stores. The Beacon Hill area is easily accessed from East Upriver Drive. The hiker can expect a good workout on these up and down trails, as well as views of the Spokane River and the city.

Wild turkey along Quartz Mountain Lookout hike

At nearly 14,000 acres, Mount Spokane State Park is Washington's largest state park. Most of the hikes described here traverse mountain forest, the exception being the uppermost portion of Mount Spokane, which is clothed in subalpine timber and high-elevation grassland. The open grassland and especially the strips that are used as ski runs in winter bloom with a profusion of flowers in the early summer. White-tailed and mule deer, black bear, cougar, elk, and moose inhabit every corner of the huge park.

Hikes 10 and 11 are short loops mostly through the dense forest. Hikes 12 and 13 are descending hikes that can be ended at the bottom with a shuttle pickup, or you can get a better workout and return by hiking back up. Much of Hike 14 follows a roadbed around Mount Kit Carson and Day Mountain that is closed to all but authorized traffic. Hike 15 climbs to the rocky summit of Mount

Kit Carson and a 360-degree view of the surrounding terrain. Hike 16 takes you on a strenuous descent and then ascent of Mount Spokane, and Hike 17 leads to a lookout that can be rented for an overnight stay on the top of a mountain. Nearly all the hikes in Mount Spokane State Park interconnect, adding to the hiking route possibilities.

Beargrass, Hike 12

Entrance Loop

Hike along abandoned dirt roadbeds, which make up the Entrance Loop, through widely diverse second-growth forest. The route is never very steep, wide all the way, and has no cliffs close to it, making it an excellent hike on which to include children.

Start: Entrance Loop Trailhead

Distance: 1.4-mile loop day hike

Hiking time: About 1 hour

Difficulty: Moderate

Best seasons: Late spring, summer, and fall for hiking. This is a great snowshoeing trail during the winter.

Canine compatibility / other trail users: Pets must be on a leash and under physical control at all times. These trails are open to bicyclists and equestrians during the summer season. In the winter Entrance Loop is used as a snowshoe route. Snowmobiles may only use the 0.3-mile-long Trail 120 section of this loop.

Fees and permits: Discover Pass available wherever hunting and fishing licenses are sold or online at www.discoverpass.wa.gov. A snopark permit is required during the winter season.

Maps: The *Mount Spokane State Park* map produced by Washington State Parks, with donated proceeds made when renewing motor vehicle licenses, is free and adequate for the less complicated hikes, like this one. Dharmamaps's *Mount Spokane State Park* is a good topo of the state park that shows all the trails. Montana Mapping & GPS LLC's Hunting and GPS maps are good topos of the area as are National Geographic maps on CD-ROM, however, neither of these show all the trails.

Trail contact: Mount Spokane State Park, 26107 N. Mount Spokane Park Dr., Mead, WA 99021; (509) 238-4258; mount.spokane@ parks.wa.gov

Special considerations: Keep an eye out for snowmobiles on the Trail 120 portion of this hike (snowshoe) during the winter season.

Finding the trailhead: From downtown Spokane, head north on Division Street to the junction with US 2 (Newport Highway). Follow US 2 to the junction with SR 206 (Mount Spokane Park Drive). Turn right on SR 206 and drive 15.3 miles to the Mount Spokane State Park entrance. Pass the entrance and go another 0.3 mile to the Entrance Loop Trailhead. Parking and restrooms are on the left side of the road. This hike begins across the road from the parking area, at 3,230 feet elevation. GPS: N47 53.292' / W117 07.510'

After crossing the highway begin your hike up Trail 122. Of the two trails that leave this trailhead, Trail 122 is the one on the right. Your return trail (121) is the trail to left. The route climbs moderately to the south-southwest as you leave the trailhead.

Douglas fir (*Pseudotsuga menziesii*), western larch (*Larix occidentalis*), western red cedar (*Thuja plicata*), and western hemlock (*Tsuga heterophylla*) as well as grand fir (*Abies grandis*) shadow the course, with Rocky Mountain maple, aka Douglas maple (*Acer glabrum*), providing an understory in the more open spots.

Soon the route makes a turn to the left (southeast). About 0.5 mile from the trailhead, you reach the junction with Trail 120. At the junction you have climbed to 3,580 feet elevation. Turn left at the junction and head easterly on Trail 120. For the 0.3 mile to the junction with Trail 121, the course remains at about that elevation. Trail 120 continues to the trailhead and parking area next to the junction of Mount Spokane Park Drive and Mount Spokane Summit Road. See "Options" below.

Entrance Loop Trail

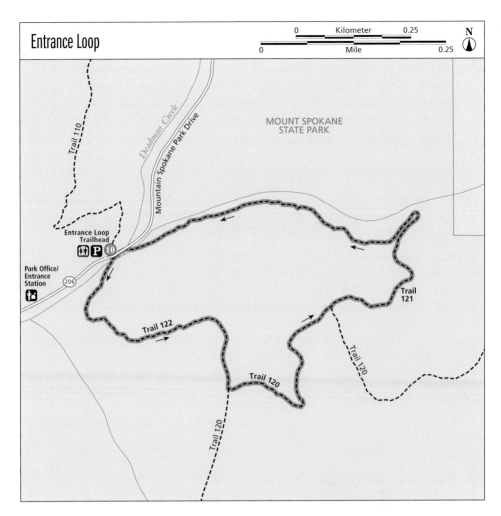

Entrance Loop

MOUNT SPOKANE STATE PARK

Trail 110

Deadman Creek

Mountain Spokane Park Drive

Entrance Loop Trailhead

Park Office/ Entrance Station

206

Trail 122

Trail 120

Trail 120

Trail 121

Trail 120

0 Kilometer 0.25
0 Mile 0.25
N

Turn left on Trail 121 and descend to the north. Soon the trail makes a wide switchback to the left and crosses a tiny stream. There is a larger stream on the right side of the trail after you pass the switchback. The route soon crosses another small stream, which passes beneath the abandoned roadbed in a culvert. As you hike the last part of the route back to the Entrance Loop Trailhead, bracken fern (*Pteridium aquilinum*) lines much the course.

Grand Fir

Generally found at low to middle elevations, the grand fir (*Abies grandis*) is a large conifer, reaching 140 feet or more in height. One of the keys to identifying the grand fir is the needles, which are arranged in two rows opposite each other on the branch. The dark-green needles also have a notch in the tip. The grand fir is also called white fir in most of the Northwest. This is a reference to its light-colored wood, as compared to the red heartwood of the Douglas fir, which is often referred to as red fir in the inland Northwest. The light-green cones on the grand fir's upper branches are 3 or 4 inches long. Like other true firs (*Abies*) the cones stand erect from the twigs.

The wood of the grand fir is not highly valued as lumber, but it is often used for plywood and chipboard. Its value as firewood cannot be underrated, as it provides limited heat and lots of ash.

MILES AND DIRECTIONS

0.0   Cross the highway and hike south-southwest on Trail 122.

0.5   Turn left at the junction onto Trail 120.

0.8   Turn left again at the junction onto Trail 121.

1.4   Arrive back at the Entrance Loop Trailhead.

Options
This hike can be combined with Trail 120 (Hike 12) to make an 8.2-mile lollipop loop from the snowmobile snopark parking area next to the junction of Mount Spokane Park Drive and Mount Spokane Summit Road.

Burping Brook Loop

Hike on several trails through conifer forests and along bubbling streams. This route is not very physically demanding but has enough turns and junctions to be challenging. The Burping Brook Loop hike is an exercise in following directions and reading a map.

Start: Lower Loop Road Trailhead
Distance: 1.8-mile loop day hike, including an out-and-back side trip
Hiking time: About 1 to 1.5 hours
Difficulty: Moderate
Best seasons: Summer and early fall
Canine compatibility / other trail users: Pets must be on a leash and under physical control at all times. Mountain bikes and horses are also allowed on these trails. Most of this route is marked with blue diamond cross-country-ski markers and is a designated ski trail during the winter season.
Fees and permits: A Discover Pass, available wherever hunting and fishing licenses are sold or online at www.discoverpass.wa.gov, is required for parking.
Maps: *Washington State Parks*

Mount Spokane State Park or the map in this book are adequate for this hike. Dharmamaps's *Mount Spokane State Park* is a good topo of the state park that shows all the trails. Montana Mapping & GPS LLC's Hunting and GPS maps are good topos of the area as is the National Geographic map on CD-ROM, *Washington,* disk 4, however, neither of these show all the trails.
Trail contact: Mount Spokane State Park, 26107 N. Mount Spokane Park Dr., Mead, WA 99021; (509) 238-4258; mount.spokane@parks.wa.gov
Special considerations: The hiking directions included here are fairly complicated (more so than the route really is). Keep a close eye on the map as you hike so that you don't miss a turn.

Finding the trailhead: From downtown Spokane at exit 281 on I-90, head north on Division Street to the junction with US 2 (Newport Highway). Follow US 2 to the junction with SR 206 (Mount Spokane Park Drive). Turn right on SR 206 and drive 17.2 miles to the first junction with Mount Kit Carson Loop Road and the Lower Loop Road Trailhead. There is a large paved parking area along the road 50 yards southeast of the trailhead but no other facilities. The elevation at the trailhead is 3,880 feet. GPS: N47 54.281' /W117 07.486'

THE HIKE

eaving the parking area, hike north for about 50 yards along Mount Spokane Park Drive to the trailhead at the junction with the Mount Kit Carson Loop Road. Head northeast on the loop road and pass the gate, which blocks it from motor vehicle traffic. Turn right in about 50 yards, leaving the roadbed and heading toward Trail 100. There is another trail junction a short distance after leaving the roadbed. To the right is Trail 100 heading east, and to the left Trail 100 heads west. Bear right and hike northeast for a few yards to another trail junction, where Trail 100 turns to the right.

Hike straight ahead here, leaving Trail 100 and starting on the out-and-back side trail. The trail climbs northeast on the right side of the creek. Soon the track, which is a poorly maintained and long-abandoned roadbed, crosses a five-log bridge over a tiny stream. Then you climb, sometimes steeply, through the western hemlock (*Tsuga heterophylla*), western red cedar (*Thuja plicata*), and fir forest. Below the forest canopy, bracken fern (*Pteridium aquilinum*), two species of huckleberry (*Vaccinium* spp.) bushes, and Rocky Mountain maple (*Acer glabrum*) make up much of the understory.

This side trail comes to an end before long—at 4,130 feet elevation—0.4 mile from the trailhead. Retrace your steps for 0.3 mile back to the lower junction with Trail 100.

Turn right at the junction and head west on Trail 100. You will cross the creek and quickly reach the junction with Trail 110. Bear right (northwest) at the

Gate at the Lower Loop Road trailhead

junction. Trails 110 and 100 follow the same route here. You will come to another trail junction in about 0.3 mile. This junction is at 4,040 feet elevation. Bear left here, leaving Trail 110 and staying on Trail 100.

The tread soon crosses Burping Brook, then starts to head downhill. The course reaches yet another trail junction in 0.3 mile. Turn left here, leaving Trail 100, and descend five switchbacks in the short distance to the junction with the Mount Kit Carson Loop Road. At this junction you are 1.5 miles into this hike, at 3,800 feet elevation.

Turn left here and head east on the roadbed. The route soon crosses Burping Brook again, as the stream flows beneath some large western red cedar trees. There is a picnic table to the left just across the creek. Next to the table the roadbed crosses Trail 110. To the right along Trail 110, there is a restroom a short distance away. Keep hiking east on the Mount Kit Carson Loop Road. Then cross another creek and head south to the junction with Mount Spokane Park Drive and the Lower Loop Road Trailhead.

Western Hemlock

The stately western hemlock (*Tsuga heterophylla*), the state tree of Washington, grows best in cool, wet areas at lower to middle elevations. Mature trees here can attain a height of 170 to 200 feet and live for more than 500 years. The western hemlock is a very shade-tolerant species and prefers sites where the soil is high in humus content.

The drooping central leader (at the very top of the tree) is the easiest way to identify a hemlock from a distance. Western hemlock needles are short and uneven in length, varying from 0.3 to 0.7 inch long and yellow-green in color. The needles are irregularly spaced along the twigs. The cones are very small, 0.7 to 1.3 inches long, and brown in color. After maturing and spreading their seeds, the cones drop to the ground intact. These cones may be thick on the forest floor beneath a mature tree. Western hemlock bark is rough, scaly, and brown. On old trees it becomes thick and furrowed. The bark is high in tannin and can be used for tanning purposes. Bark slivers from the western hemlock can be inflammatory and should be quickly removed. When cut, mature western hemlock trees are often hollow and in some cases may be nearly filled with water. When wet, hemlock wood is very heavy and may not even float on water.

MILES AND DIRECTIONS

0.0 Hike north from the Lower Loop Road Trailhead.

0.4 The trail ends. Turn around.

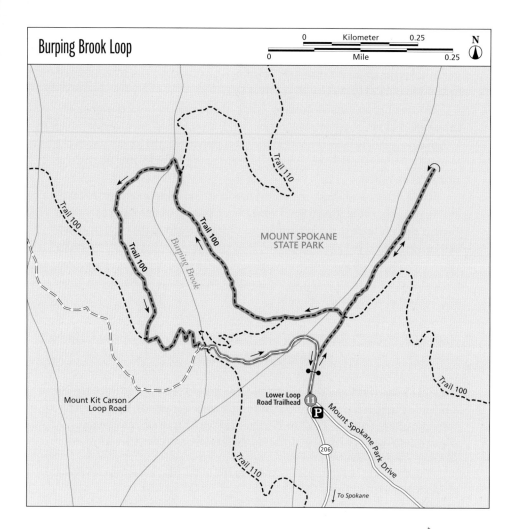

Burping Brook Loop

0 Kilometer 0.25
0 Mile 0.25

N

Trail 110

Trail 100

Trail 100

Trail 100

Burping Brook

MOUNT SPOKANE
STATE PARK

Trail 100

Mount Kit Carson
Loop Road

Lower Loop
Road Trailhead

Mount Spokane Park Drive

206

Trail 110

To Spokane

0.7 Return to the lower junction with Trail 100 and turn right.

0.8 Bear right at the junction with Trail 110.

1.1 Turn left on Trail 100, leaving Trail 110.

1.4 Bear left, leaving Trail 100.

1.5 Turn left on Mount Kit Carson Loop Road.

1.8 Arrive back at the junction with Mount Spokane Park Drive and the Lower Loop Road Trailhead.

Options

This hike could be combined with Hike 13 to make a complicated 8.4-mile lollipop loop from the Bald Knob Picnic Area and Trailhead.

Trail 120

Hike downhill through dense midmountain forest. Then, if you have not arranged for a car shuttle, get a good workout climbing back up.

Start: Snowmobile snopark parking area next to the junction of Mount Spokane Park Drive and Mount Spokane Summit Road
Distance: 3.3-mile shuttle or 6.6-mile out-and-back day hike
Hiking time: About 1.5-hour shuttle or 3.5 hours out and back
Difficulty: Easy shuttle, moderate out and back
Best seasons: Summer and early fall
Canine compatibility / other trail users: Pets must be on a leash and under physical control at all times. Mountain bikers often use this route.
Fees and permits: Discover Pass available wherever hunting and fishing licenses are sold or online at www.discoverpass.wa.gov
Maps: Dharmamaps's *Mount*

Spokane State Park is a good topo that shows all the trails. The *Mount Spokane State Park* map produced by Washington State Parks, with donated proceeds made when renewing motor vehicle licenses, is free and adequate for the less complicated hikes like this one. Montana Mapping & GPS LLC's Hunting and GPS maps are good topos of the area as is the National Geographic map on CD-ROM, *Washington,* disk 4.
Trail contact: Mount Spokane State Park, 26107 N. Mount Spokane Park Dr., Mead, WA 99021; (509) 238-4258; mount.spokane@parks.wa.gov
Special considerations: Trail 120 is a snowmobile route during the winter.

Finding the trailhead: From downtown Spokane, head north on Division Street to the junction with US 2 (Newport Highway). Follow US 2 to the junction with SR 206 (Mount Spokane Park Drive). Turn right on SR 206 and drive 18.5 miles to the junction with Mount Spokane Summit Road. At the junction turn right into the large snowmobile snopark parking area. The trailhead is to the right of the restroom, close to the southwest corner of the parking area. The elevation at the trailhead is 4,550 feet. GPS: N47 54.266' / W117 06.114'

Trail 120, which is an abandoned roadbed and cleared wide enough for winter snowmobile traffic, leads south as you leave the trailhead. As is the case with many snowmobile trails, the route is marked with orange diamonds. The track descends very gently, through the mixed conifer forest of western hemlock (*Tsuga heterophylla*), Douglas fir (*Pseudotsuga menziesii*), grand fir (*Abies grandis*), western white pine (*Pinus monticola*), lodgepole pine (*Pinus contorta*), and western larch (*Larix occidentalis*). Beargrass (*Xerophyllum tenax*) and huckleberry (*Vaccinium* spp.) bushes cover the ground between the trees.

You will reach a junction with another roadbed 1 mile from the trailhead. The roadbed, which is to the right, is closed to entry. Hike straight ahead at the junction, heading southeast. Past the junction the course climbs gently for 150 yards then flattens and begins to descend gently again. Quickly you cross a

Tamarack in fall color

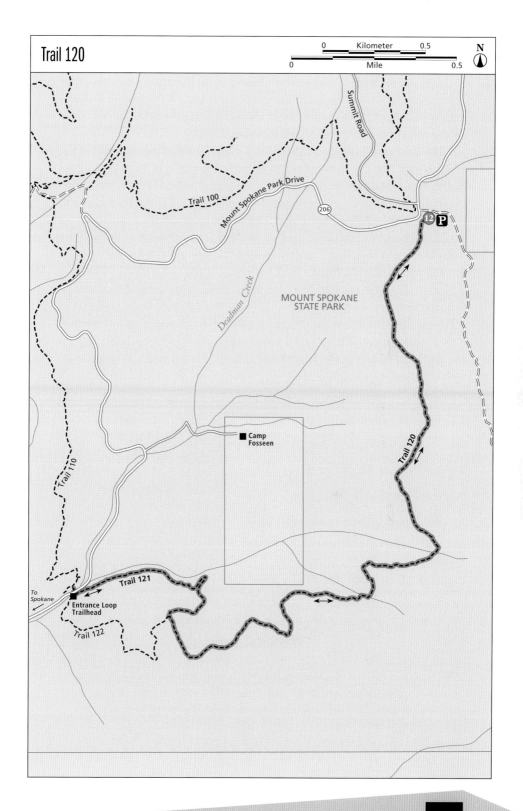

small stream at about 4,250 feet elevation. In another 150 yards the downgrade becomes steeper as you head west-southwest down a rounded ridgeline. After descending along the ridgeline for 0.25 mile and losing 200 feet of elevation, the track makes a sweeping switchback to the left, leaving the ridgeline. You cross another small stream 0.2 mile after leaving the ridgeline.

The tread crosses another tiny stream 0.4 mile farther along and reaches the junction with Trail 121 in another 300 yards. This junction is 2.6 miles into the hike at 3,590 feet elevation. Turn right at the junction on Trail 121 and descend to the northeast. The route crosses a couple more tiny streams, the second one as you make a hard left turn. For the next 0.4 mile, the route follows a creek heading west-southwest. The creek is to the right of the trail as you descend through the dark canyon bottom forest of western hemlock, western red cedar, and Douglas fir. In spots ferns line the route.

The trail reaches the Entrance Loop Trailhead 3.3 miles from the snowmobile snopark parking area where this hike started. The Entrance Loop Trailhead, at 3,230 feet elevation, is the end of your hike if you have arranged for a car shuttle. If this is to be an out-and-back hike, turn around and retrace your steps back up the 1,300 vertical feet to the snowmobile snopark parking area and trailhead.

MILES AND DIRECTIONS

0.0 Hike south from the snopark trailhead.

1.0 At the junction with a closed road, hike straight ahead.

2.6 Turn right at the junction with Trail 121.

3.3 Turn around at Entrance Loop Trailhead.

6.6 Arrive back at the snopark trailhead.

Options

Combine this hike with Hike 10 to make a 6.7-mile lollipop loop.

Western Larch

Western larch (*Larix occidentalis*) is a different kind of conifer as it is deciduous (sheds its leaves). The larch (often called tamarack) turns bright yellow in the fall, then it sheds its needles, making it look like a dead tree. Tamarack is the wood that many locals prefer to burn in their woodstoves.

Bald Knob to Lower Loop Road Trailhead

Descend through the high mountain forest from the Bald Knob Picnic Area and Trailhead into the Mount Spokane Ski Area. Enjoy the great views from the open runs and the fields of flowers and huckleberries. Then cross the Mount Spokane Summit Road and continue your descent to the junction with Mount Spokane Park Drive at the Lower Loop Road Trailhead. Nearly this entire hike is through beautiful widely diverse old-growth or medium-age second-growth forest. White-tailed deer are common and may be seen anywhere along this route.

Start: Bald Knob Picnic Area and Trailhead

Distance: 6.6-mile out-and-back day hike, with 1 short side trip and 2 shuttle options

Hiking time: About 4 hours for the entire hike

Difficulty: Moderate

Best seasons: Summer and early fall

Canine compatibility / other trail users: Pets must be on a leash and under physical control at all times. Mountain bikes allowed on this route.

Fees and permits: A Discover Pass, available wherever hunting and fishing licenses are sold or online at www.discoverpass.wa .gov, is required for parking.

Maps: Dharmamaps's *Mount Spokane State Park*. The *Mount Spokane State Park* map produced by Washington State Parks, with donated proceeds made when renewing motor vehicle licenses, is free and can be obtained at the park entrance. Montana Mapping & GPS LLC's Hunting and GPS maps are good topos of the area as are National Geographic maps on CD-ROM, however, they don't show all the trails.

Trail contact: Mount Spokane State Park, 26107 N. Mount Spokane Park Dr., Mead, WA 99021; (509) 238-4258; mount.spokane@ parks.wa.gov

Special considerations: This hike is somewhat complicated, so try to watch your map as you hike and follow the hike description below. This is a great hike on which to teach children to follow a map. Keep an eye out for mountain-bike traffic.

THE HIKE

There is no sign marking Trail 130 at the trailhead. From the large Bald Knob Picnic Area and Trailhead parking area, follow the trail southeast toward the picnic shelter. Turn left (east) approximately 20 yards before reaching the shelter and look for a sign ahead next to the timber. Another trail, this one coming from the picnic shelter, intersects the one you are on next to the sign at the edge of the woods. The course, which is a long-abandoned roadbed, descends into the timber and crosses a tiny stream 0.2 mile from the trailhead, Pearly everlasting (*Anaphalis margaritacea*), goldenrod (*Solidago canadensis*), beargrass (*Xerophyllum tenax*), and huckleberry bushes (*Vaccinium* spp.) grow beside the descending track. About 150 yards after crossing the stream, the junction with Trail 130a is reached. Hike straight ahead (east) at the junction, staying on Trail 130. Soon the track turns north.

You will reach the junction with Trail 130b, at 4,800 feet elevation, 0.5 mile into the hike. Trail 130b is also a long-abandoned roadbed. Hike straight ahead (north-northeast) at the junction, staying on Trail 130, to make a short side trip to some great views. Soon the track crosses an alpine ski run. The flower-covered run offers a great view to the east that includes Spirit Lake. Slightly less than 0.25 mile from the junction with Trail 130b, you will reach Chairlift 1. Enjoy the view for a little while, then turn around and head back to the junction with Trail 130b.

Turn left at the junction on Trail 130b and hike southeast. The abandoned roadbed is somewhat overgrown in spots, but the logs across it have been cut, making for easy travel. The route reaches a junction with Trail 130a in just over 0.5 mile. Both signs at this junction point out Trail 130 (which is not really the correct number for either trail). Hike straight ahead at the junction, heading south-southwest. Shortly the route makes a turn to the left, very close to the Mount Spokane Summit Road. There is a signpost here that points the way. The track passes some buildings and reaches a junction with the Mount Spokane Summit Road and Mount Spokane Park Drive, 0.3 mile from the junction with Trail 130a.

Across Mount Spokane Park Drive is a large parking area. This junction is 1.8 miles from the Bald Knob Trailhead at 4,540 feet elevation. See the options below to end your hike here.

To continue your hike, cross Mount Spokane Summit Road and pick up Trail 100 on the far side. Trail 100 (also a closed road here) heads west, paralleling the Mount Spokane Summit Road. The route, which is marked with blue diamond cross-country-ski markers, climbs slightly. You will reach an unmarked junction

Ski run on Mount Spokane

in 0.2 mile. The path to the right connects with the Mount Spokane Summit Road in a short distance. Hike straight ahead (northwest) here. In another 0.2 mile of hiking through the western hemlock (*Tsuga heterophylla*), grand fir (*Abies grandis*), and lodgepole pine (*Pinus contorta*) forest, you make a sweeping turn to the left and the route crosses a small stream. A few more steps and you reach the top of a ridge, at 4,660 feet elevation. Then the tread starts to descend moderately steeply.

The trail soon crosses another small stream next to mile marker 0.5. Goldenrod, bracken fern (*Pteridium aquilinum*), and thimbleberry bushes (*Rubus parviflorus*) cover the ground next to the stream beneath the canopy of Douglas fir (*Pseudotsuga menziesii*), western larch (*Larix occidentalis*), and alder (*Alnus*). About 0.9 mile after crossing the Mount Spokane Summit Road, you will reach the junction with Trail 101, which is to the right. Trail 101 climbs to the north and intersects the Mount Spokane Summit Road in about 0.5 mile. This route becomes quite steep and rocky before reaching the summit road.

Hike straight ahead (southwest) at the junction, staying on Trail 100. At 120 yards past the junction with Trail 101, Trail 100 leaves the roadbed you have been following. The route ungulates some but generally descends, crossing another long-abandoned roadbed in a little less than 0.4 mile. A bit farther along, the track makes a couple of switchbacks close to mile marker 1.0. Western red cedar (*Thuja plicata*) now joins the mix of trees. The trail soon crosses another tiny stream, then makes a switchback to the left very close to and slightly above Trail 103. Soon you cross a small bridge over a tiny stream, then make a switchback to the right. A few yards past the switchback, the track reaches the junction with Trail 103. This junction is 3.6 miles from the Bald Knob Trailhead, at 3,940 feet elevation.

Make a hard left at the junction and walk a few steps south to another junction. Bear left (nearly straight ahead) at this junction, leaving Trail 100. Shortly you will reach the junction with the Mount Kit Carson Loop Road. The loop road is closed to all unauthorized motor vehicles. Bear right on the Mount Kit Carson Loop Road and continue south for a few yards to the junction with the Mount Spokane Park Drive, at the Lower Loop Road Trailhead. At the trailhead your elevation is 3,880 feet and you are 3.7 miles from the Bald Knob Picnic Area and Trailhead.

If you have arranged for a car shuttle, you can end your hike here. If not, turn around and retrace your steps for 2.2 miles back to the junction with Trail 130a. Turn left on Trail 130a and climb fairly steeply through the mountain forest. Huckleberry bushes are thick beside the trail. The route climbs 230 feet in slightly over 0.4 mile to the junction with Trail 130. At the junction with Trail 130, turn left and retrace your steps for a little less than 0.3 mile to the Bald Knob Trailhead.

Bald Knob to Lower Loop Road Trailhead

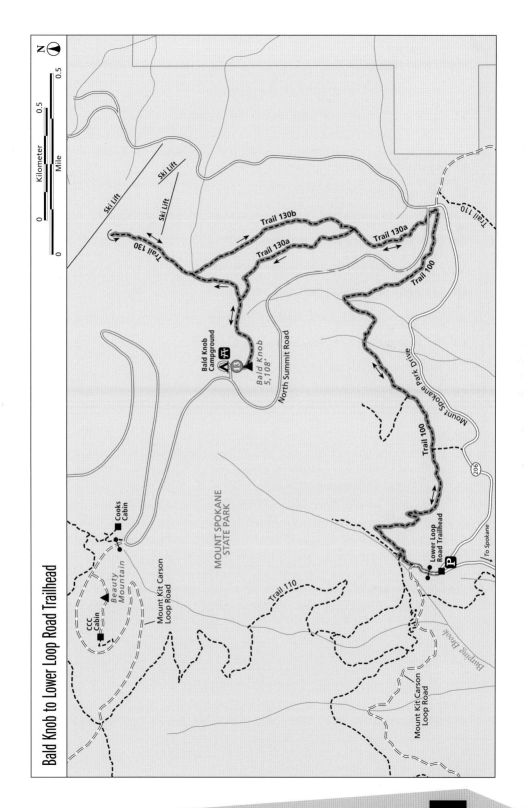

13

MILES AND DIRECTIONS

0.0 Begin at the Bald Knob Picnic Area and Trailhead.

0.3 At the junction with Trail 130a, hike straight ahead.

0.5 At the junction with Trail 130b, hike straight ahead.

0.7 Reach the turnaround point next to Chair #1.

1.0 Return to the junction with Trail 130b and turn left.

1.5 At the junction with Trail 130a, hike straight ahead to the southwest.

1.8 Cross Mount Spokane Summit Road.

2.7 At the junction with Trail 101, hike straight ahead.

3.6 At the junction with Trail 103, turn left.

3.7 Turn around at the Lower Loop Road Trailhead.

5.0 Return to the junction with Trail 130a and turn left.

6.3 Turn left at the junction with Trail 130.

6.6 Arrive back at the Bald Knob Picnic Area and Trailhead.

Options

For a shorter trek, you can end your hike at the junction with Mount Spokane Summit Road and Mount Spokane Park Drive and shuttle back the 1.2 miles to the Bald Knob Picnic Area and Trailhead.

If you don't want to climb back up to the Bald Knob Picnic Area and Trailhead from the Lower Loop Road Trailhead, you can arrange a shuttle. To make this shuttle, drive the 1.2 miles back down the Mount Spokane Summit Road to the junction with Mount Spokane Park Drive. Turn right and go 1.3 miles to the Lower Loop Road Trailhead. Fifty yards past the trailhead, there is a large parking area on the left side of the road.

Combine this hike with Hike 11 (Burping Brook Loop) to make an 8.4-mile lollipop loop.

Mount Kit Carson–Day Mountain Loop

First climb the moderately steep Trail 110, gaining over 1,600 feet of elevation. Then follow the Mount Kit Carson Loop Road (which is closed to unauthorized motorized traffic) as it descends very gradually through the diverse mountain forest, before retracing your steps for the last 1.8 miles to the Entrance Loop Trailhead. Watch for the fairly common white-tailed deer all along this hike.

Start: Entrance Loop Trailhead

Distance: 12-mile lollipop-loop day hike

Hiking time: About 4.5 to 7 hours

Difficulty: Moderate to strenuous

Best seasons: Summer and early fall

Canine compatibility / other trail users: Pets must be on a leash and under physical control at all times. These trails are open to bicyclists and equestrians during the summer season. Mountain bikers are the most common users of the Mount Kit Carson Loop Road portion of this hike. In the winter snowshoers and cross-country skiers use the route.

Fees and permits: Discover Pass available wherever hunting and fishing licenses are sold or online at www.discoverpass.wa.gov. A snopark permit is required during the winter season.

Maps: Dharmamaps's *Mount Spokane State Park* is an up-to-date topo of the state park. The *Mount Spokane State Park* map produced by Washington State Parks, with donated proceeds made when renewing motor vehicle licenses, is free and available at the state park entrance. Montana Mapping & GPS LLC's Hunting and GPS maps are good topos of the area as is the National Geographic map on CD-ROM, *Washington,* disk 4.

Trail contact: Mount Spokane State Park, 26107 N. Mount Spokane Park Dr., Mead, WA 99021; (509) 238-4258; mount.spokane@parks.wa.gov

Special considerations: A small portion of this route crosses private timberland. Please stay on the route (roadbed) in that area (it is clear-cut).

14

THE HIKE

Trail 110 heads north, climbing rather steeply, from the Entrance Loop Trailhead. Grand fir (*Abies grandis*), western red cedar (*Thuja plicata*), aspen (*Alnus*), and Rocky Mountain maple (*Acer glabrum*) line the track as you ascend. One-eighth of a mile from the trailhead, the course makes four switchbacks as you pass some fairly large Douglas firs (*Pseudotsuga menziesii*). Above the switchbacks the tread passes beneath power lines. Soon the grade moderates and some western white pines (*Pinus monticola*) and hemlocks show up next to the trail. Grouse can often be seen along this part of the route.

Soon the trail descends slightly and passes mile marker 0.5, at 3,570 feet elevation. You will reach a trail junction 0.1 mile after passing the marker post. Bear slightly right at the junction on what is now a dirt roadbed, lined in places with goldenrod (*Solidago canadensis*). The area to the left (west) here is closed to entry. The course crosses through a saddle at 3,540 feet elevation a little over 0.1 mile past the junction. Then you climb gently through the forest, which now includes western larch (*Larix occidentalis*) and lodgepole pine (*Pinus contorta*) trees, to another trail junction. Bear left here—the trail to the right also enters an area that is closed to entry. These side trails are not shown on Dharmamaps's *Mount Spokane State Park* map.

The route crosses a tiny stream, which flows beneath it in a culvert, and reaches mile marker 1.0, 0.2 mile after passing the junction. Soon after passing mile marker 1.0, Mount Spokane Park Drive comes into view to the right. The trail parallels the highway for about 0.25 mile, then bears left, leaving it. Before long the trace reaches mile marker 1.5 as you hike through a forest that is now nearly devoid of undergrowth. You will cross fern-lined Burping Brook 0.1 mile past mile marker 1.5. A little more hiking brings you to the first junction with the Mount Kit Carson Loop Road. The track passes a restroom and a table just before reaching the junction. The Mount Kit Carson Loop Road is closed to unauthorized motor vehicle access. This junction, at 3,800 feet elevation, is 1.8 miles from Entrance Loop Trailhead.

This is the beginning of the loop portion of this hike. Cross the Mount Kit Carson Loop Road, and climb through the cedar and hemlock forest, staying on Trail 110. This section of Trail 110 is marked with blue diamond cross-country-ski and snowshoe markers. The track makes three switchbacks before reaching the junction with Trail 100. Turn left at the junction. Trails 110 and 100 follow the same route for the next 0.3 mile. You reach the trail junction where trails 100 and 110 separate again, at about 4,100 feet elevation, after passing mile marker 2.0. Turn right at this junction and continue to climb on Trail 110, quickly crossing a tiny stream. Bracken fern (*Pteridium aquilinum*) lines the route through the open woods as you pass mile marker 2.5.

The course makes a wide switchback to the left 0.1 mile after passing mile marker 2.5. A couple tenths of a mile farther along, the track crosses a tiny stream. Soon thimbleberry (*Rubus parviflorus*) bushes crowd the trail. As you cross another small stream a little farther along, monkshood (*Aconitum columbianum*) joins the mix of flowers. Soon the trail bears left, leaving the long-abandoned roadbed that it has been following for some time. You pass mile marker 3 at about 4,450 feet elevation. Here huckleberry bushes and beargrass (*Xerophyllum tenax*) grow between the very old stumps that dot the forest floor beneath the medium-age trees.

Pearly everlasting

The trail makes three more switchbacks before reaching mile marker 3.5 at 4,720 feet elevation. Soon you make yet another switchback, then climb the last third of a mile to another junction with the Mount Kit Carson Loop Road at Saddle Junction. Besides the loop road, trails 140, 130, and 170 meet at Saddle Junction. There is also a restroom here. The forest at the junction has become more subalpine in character, with a mix of subalpine fir (*Abies lasiocarpa*), western larch, lodgepole pine, and western white pine. Beneath the trees a few mountain ash (*Sorbus scopulina*) and lots of huckleberry (*Vaccinium* spp.) bushes cover the ground. This junction, at 4,870 feet elevation, is 4.3 miles from the Entrance Loop Trailhead.

Turn left at Saddle Junction, and hike northwest on the wide, dirt and gravel Mount Kit Carson Loop Road. The track descends very gently, and in slightly less than 0.5 mile you will pass mile marker 5.0. These markers are for the Mount Kit Carson Loop Road and not a continuation of the markers on Trail 110, although the distance seems to almost match. Look to your right between here and mile marker 4.5 for a view of the summit area of Mount Spokane and the towers atop it. You will reach the junction with Trail 130 0.1 mile after passing the 4.5 mile marker. Trail 130, which is to the right at this junction, is also known as Chair Road. Trail 130 follows the Mount Kit Carson Loop Road for a short distance to the northwest, then leaves the loop by climbing steeply to the left.

Hike straight ahead at the junction, staying on the Mount Kit Carson Loop Road. In a short distance the route leaves Mount Spokane State Park and enters land owned by the Inland Empire Paper Company. This area was nearly clear cut several years ago so the view is good. Stay on the roadbed while on the private land. In 0.7 mile the course reenters Mount Spokane State Park and you are back in the timber again. There is a trail (road) junction 0.3 mile after reentering the state park. Hike straight ahead, staying on the Mount Kit Carson Loop Road, and soon pass mile marker 3.5. When I hiked this route, there were bear tracks and scat on the roadbed in this area.

The route crosses Little Deer Creek 0.4 mile after passing mile marker 3.5. Next to the creek is a table, which makes this a good spot to stop for a snack or lunch. Soon after crossing Little Deer Creek, you pass mile marker 3.0. Continue southwest, then south along the Mount Kit Carson Loop Road, passing mile markers 2.5 and 2.0. Shortly after passing mile marker 2.0, there is another table next to the tread as you cross a small stream. You will reach the junction with Day Road 0.25 mile farther along. This junction, at 3,950 feet elevation, is 8.6 miles into this hike. Hike straight ahead at the junction, staying on the Mount Kit Carson Loop Road.

Soon the track passes mile marker 1.5 and reaches another junction. The trail (roadbed) to the right is Trail 155. The junction with Trail 155 is 0.3 mile from the junction with Day Road. Hike straight ahead (east southeast), staying on the Mount Kit Carson Loop Road. A few yards after passing the junction with Trail

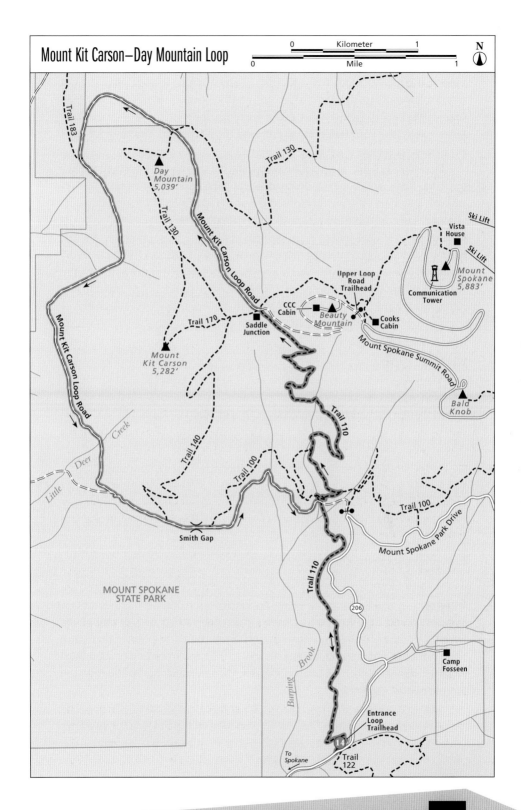

Mount Kit Carson–Day Mountain Loop

155, Trail 140 leaves the loop road to the right. Hike straight ahead. Shortly after passing the junction with Trail 140, Trail 100 turns off to the left. Hike straight ahead a few more yards to Smith Gap and another junction with Trail 140. Smith Gap, where you will find a table and a restroom, is at 4,170 feet elevation, 9.1 miles from where you started at the Entrance Loop Trailhead. You have 2.9 miles left to go to complete the hike.

Bear slightly left at the junction with Trail 140, staying on the Mount Kit Carson Loop Road, and begin to descend as you hike east-northeast. In 0.25 mile you will pass mile marker 1.0. Mount Spokane is now almost directly ahead. In about 0.2 mile the route passes another table next to a tiny stream. You will cross another small stream before reaching mile marker 0.5. In another 0.3 mile the junction with a short connector trail that goes to Trail 100 is reached. Stay on the Mount Kit Carson Loop Road, heading east, and quickly reach the junction with Trail 110, where the loop portion of this hike started. Turn right on Trail 110 and retrace your steps, descending for 1.8 miles to the Entrance Loop Trailhead.

MILES AND DIRECTIONS

0.0   Climb north from the Entrance Loop Trailhead.

1.8   Cross Mount Kit Carson Loop Road.

4.3   At Saddle Junction turn left on the Mount Kit Carson Loop Road.

5.4   At the junction with Trail 130 (Chair Road), hike straight ahead.

8.6   At the junction with Day Road, hike straight ahead to the southeast.

9.1   Cross Smith Gap. Hike slightly left, heading east-northeast.

10.2 Return to the junction of Mount Kit Carson Loop Road and Trail 110 and turn right.

12.0 Arrive back at the Entrance Loop Trailhead.

Options

This hike could be shortened by over 3 miles by starting and ending at the Lower Loop Road Trailhead, approximately 0.2 mile east along Mount Kit Carson Loop Road from its lower junction with Trail 110. To reach the Lower Loop Road Trailhead, drive another 1.6 miles northeast, then north along SR 206 from the Entrance Loop Trailhead.

Mount Kit Carson Summit

TRAIL 170

Mount Spokane State Park covers 13,643 acres, more than any other state park in the Evergreen State. In the heart of Washington's largest state park is 5,282-foot-high Mount Kit Carson. The hike to the summit of Mount Kit Carson is not particularly difficult, but the view from the top is one of the best in the park. Wildlife abounds here but is often difficult to spot because of the dense vegetation. You will, however, almost undoubtedly see the tracks of deer and elk and possibly those of a moose or a bear.

Start: Upper Loop Road Trailhead

Distance: 3.6-mile out-and-back day hike

Hiking time: About 2 to 2.5 hours

Difficulty: Moderate, with 0.6 mile that is fairly strenuous

Best seasons: Summer and early fall

Canine compatibility / other trail users: Pets must be on a leash and under physical control at all times. Mountain bikes and horses are also allowed on most of this route, as are cross-country skiers during the winter.

Fees and permits: Discover Pass, available wherever hunting and fishing licenses are sold or online at www.discoverpass.wa.gov. A snopark permit is required during the winter season.

Maps: Dharmamaps's *Mount Spokane State Park* or *Mount Spokane State Park* produced by Washington State Parks, with donated proceeds made when renewing motor vehicle licenses. Older maps may show Trail 140 as Trail 115 and or Trail 135.

Trail contact: Mount Spokane State Park, 26107 N. Mount Spokane Park Dr., Mead, WA 99021; (509) 238-4258; mount.spokane@parks.wa.gov

Finding the trailhead: From downtown Spokane, head north on Division Street to the junction with US 2 (Newport Highway). Follow US 2 northwest to the junction with SR 206 (Mount Spokane Park Drive). Turn right on SR 206 and drive 18.5 miles to the junction with Mount Spokane Summit Road. Turn left on Mount Spokane Summit Road and go 1.8 miles to the junction with Mount Kit Carson Loop Road, which is the Upper Loop Road Trailhead. There is adequate parking in the lot on the right side of the road, approximately 50 yards southeast of the trailhead, but no other facilities. The elevation at the trailhead is 5,200 feet. GPS: N47 55.067' /W117 07.377'

From the parking area, walk to the northwest, up the Mount Spokane Summit Road. In about 50 yards you will reach the junction with the Mount Kit Carson Loop Road, the starting point of your hike. Go around the white metal gate and head northwest through the forest of mountain ash (*Sorbus scopulina*), alder (*Alnus*), and fir trees along the Loop Road.

You will reach a junction in a little over 0.1 mile. A sign here directs bikes to stay on the Loop Road. At the junction turn left on the abandoned roadbed and follow it west. Hike over the top of Beauty Mountain to the Civilian Conservation Corps (CCC) Cabin. The route is open to hikers only from the Loop Road to the CCC Cabin.

Just before reaching the cabin, there is a road to the right—ignore it. Walk around the cabin to its west side, where you will find its front door. The cabin is usually unlocked and is open to the public. At the CCC Cabin you are 0.25 mile from the trailhead.

Heading on toward the summit of Mount Kit Carson, descend the cobblestone steps west of the cabin. Then follow the route to the west. These cobblestones may be slippery when wet. There is an unmarked trail junction a short distance ahead. Turn left (south) at the junction. A little farther along there is another trail junction. Turn right here and descend the last few feet to rejoin the

Mount Kit Carson summit

Mount Kit Carson Loop Road. Turn left on the road. The route makes a switch-back to the right in 0.2 mile after rejoining the roadbed. Then you continue west-northwest, descending gently to Saddle Junction at 4,890 feet elevation. There are restrooms available at Saddle Junction. Hikes 14 and 16 also reach Saddle Junction.

The Mount Kit Carson Summit Trail 170 is one of several trails that meet at Saddle Junction. Trail signs point the way here. Climb west-southwest on Trail 170, leaving Saddle Junction. You will reach the junction with Trail 140 in slightly less than 0.2 mile. Bear slightly right here and continue to climb the now steeper track. This part of the trail is lined with huckleberry (*Vaccinium* spp.) bushes. There is another path to the right about 20 yards past the junction with Trail 140 (Trail 115 on older maps). Keep on climbing to the southwest, staying on the main trail. As you climb, the trail becomes narrower.

On the summit ridge 0.3 mile from the junction with Trail 140, the route flattens out. You will reach another trail junction after following the ridge southwest for 0.1 mile. Hike straight ahead here, leaving Trail 170. Continue for the last 0.1 mile to the summit, which is on the unnumbered trail (that appears to be the main trail here). Then scramble up the last few feet to the summit of Mount Kit Carson.

The views from the rocky, 5,282-foot-high summit are great in all directions. Nearby to the east-northeast is Mount Spokane, and to the southwest the city of Spokane can be seen, often through haze. When you have finished taking in the view from the summit, turn around and retrace your steps back to the Upper Loop Road Trailhead.

MILES AND DIRECTIONS

0.0 Hike northwest from the Upper Loop Road Trailhead.

0.1 Turn left, leaving the Mount Kit Carson Loop Road.

0.3 Pass the Civilian Conservation Corps (CCC) Cabin.

1.1 Turn left onto Trail 170 at Saddle Junction.

1.3 Bear slightly right and continue climbing steeply past Trail 140.

1.7 Head southwest at a trail junction, leaving Trail 170.

1.8 Reach the summit of Mount Kit Carson and turn around.

3.6 Arrive back at the Upper Loop Road Trailhead.

Options
Combine this hike with Hike 16 to make a challenging, 6-mile-long double lollipop loop from the trailhead at the summit of Mount Spokane.

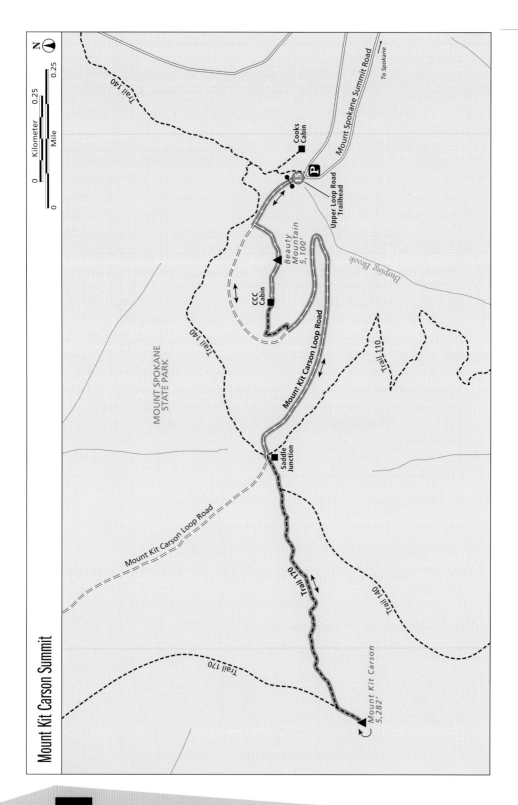

Mount Kit Carson Summit

Western Mountain Ash

Generally growing at middle to upper elevations, the western mountain ash (*Sorbus scopulina*), prefers open areas where it can get direct sunlight. It's a deciduous shrub or small tree. Blooming in early summer, the tiny, numerous white flowers form clusters up to 6 inches wide at the ends of the branches. These flowers mature into red berries that are eaten by birds of many species.

Mountain ash

Mount Spokane Summit–Saddle Junction

TRAILS 140, MOUNT KIT CARSON LOOP ROAD, AND 135A

Starting from the highest summit in Mount Spokane State Park, this lollipop loop descends to Saddle Junction. The return hike back to the summit of Mount Spokane is an excellent workout. White-tailed deer are often seen along this route. There is also a slight possibility of spotting a moose or at least seeing moose tracks.

Start: Mount Spokane Summit Trailhead

Distance: 3.5-mile lollipop-loop day hike

Hiking time: About 2.5 hours

Difficulty: Strenuous

Best seasons: Summer and early fall

Canine compatibility / other trail users: This route is open to mountain bikers and equestrians as well as hikers. Dogs must be on a leash and under physical control at all times.

Fees and permits: A Discover Pass is required. Discover Passes may be obtained wherever hunting and fishing licenses are sold and online at www.discoverpass.wa .gov.

Maps: Dharmamaps's *Mount Spokane State Park* is an up-to-date topo of the state park. The *Mount Spokane State Park* map produced by Washington State Parks, with donated proceeds made when renewing motor vehicle licenses, is free and available at the park entrance booth. Montana Mapping & GPS LLC's Hunting and GPS maps are good topos of the area as is the National Geographic map on CD-ROM, *Washington,* disk 4. Older maps may show Trail 140 as Trail 135.

Trail contact: Mount Spokane State Park, 26107 N. Mount Spokane Park Dr., Mead, WA 99021; (509) 238-4258; mount.spokane@ parks.wa.gov

Special considerations: When I last hiked this route, there was one very short section (the 100 yards or so of Trail 135a) that was difficult to see on the ground. There were also no signs there to direct you, so watch your map.

Finding the trailhead: From downtown Spokane, head north on Division Street to the junction with US 2 (Newport Highway). Drive northeast on US 2 to the junction with SR 206 (Mount Spokane Park Drive). Turn right on SR 206 and drive 18.5 miles to the junction with Mount Spokane Summit Road. Turn left on Mount Spokane Summit Road and go 4 miles to the summit of Mount Spokane and the trailhead. The trailhead is on the right just past the trail to Vista House. There is parking for several vehicles at the trailhead but no other facilities. GPS: N47 55.360' / W117 06.812'

THE HIKE

Trail 140 heads northwest, leaving the 5,870-foot-high trailhead near the summit of Mount Spokane. You descend steeply on the rough and rocky route through the short subalpine timber. Beargrass (*Xerophyllum tenax*) covers the ground in places between the stubby trees. The route makes a couple of switchbacks after you have descended about 200 vertical feet. About 0.4 mile into the hike you will cross a sloping meadow.

Pearly everlasting (*Anaphalis margaritacea*), bracken fern (*Pteridium aquilinum*), and fireweed (*Epilobium angustifolium*) cover the ground in the semi-open woods. Growing above the flowers are huckleberry (*Vaccinium* spp.) and elderberry (*Sambucus racemosa*) bushes.

A very vague path leads to the left 0.9 mile from the trailhead. Don't take it now; this path is Trail 135a, part of your return route. This is where the loop portion of this hike starts. One-tenth of a mile farther along is a more obvious path to the left that leads to the Mount Kit Carson Loop Road. Bear right here and stay on Trail 140, heading west. After descending a little more, the track traverses the wooded slope to Saddle Junction. You will pass mile mark 4 shortly before reaching the junction. Saddle Junction, 1.6 miles from the trailhead at 4,880 feet elevation, is the junction of Trails 140, 110, 170, and the Mount Kit Carson Loop Road. The loop road, like the trails it connects with here, is open to hikers, horses, and bikes but is closed to unauthorized motor vehicles. A restroom is available at Saddle Junction.

Turn left on the Mount Kit Carson Loop Road and continue your hike by heading southeast. The route makes a switchback to head northwest in 0.4 mile. You reach the junction with Trail 130a a little over 0.1 mile farther along. Trail 130a is to the right; stay on the loop road. The course reaches a junction with a spur road, next to a wooden gate, in another 0.1 mile. The spur road, which is to the right, leads to the Civilian Conservation Corps (CCC) Cabin. The CCC Cabin is a short distance up this spur road if you would like to visit it. Hike straight ahead on the main road to continue on the loop.

In the next 0.25 mile, before you reach the junction with the Mount Spokane Summit Road and Trail 135a, you pass two more trail junctions. The trail to the right leads back to the CCC Cabin and the one to the left goes a short distance to Trail 140 (the trail on which you descended to Saddle Junction). Hike a little farther along the Loop Road to the junction with the Mount Spokane Summit Road.

To your the left (north) at the junction there is another dirt road. Turn left on this road, which is Trail 135a. Hike north for slightly under 0.1 mile to a radio tower. This is where this route becomes hard to spot. Walk between the tower and the building next to it, then continue generally north, crossing a tiny stream. You will intersect Trail 140 in about 100 yards. The tower is in view through the trees all the way to Trail 140. There is little evidence of the trail on the ground between the tower and Trail 140, and there is no sign at this junction. This is the end the loop portion of this hike. Turn right on Trail 140 and climb fairly steeply, retracing your steps back to the summit of Mount Spokane and the trailhead where you started.

Civilian Conservation Corps cabin

Mount Spokane Summit–Saddle Junction

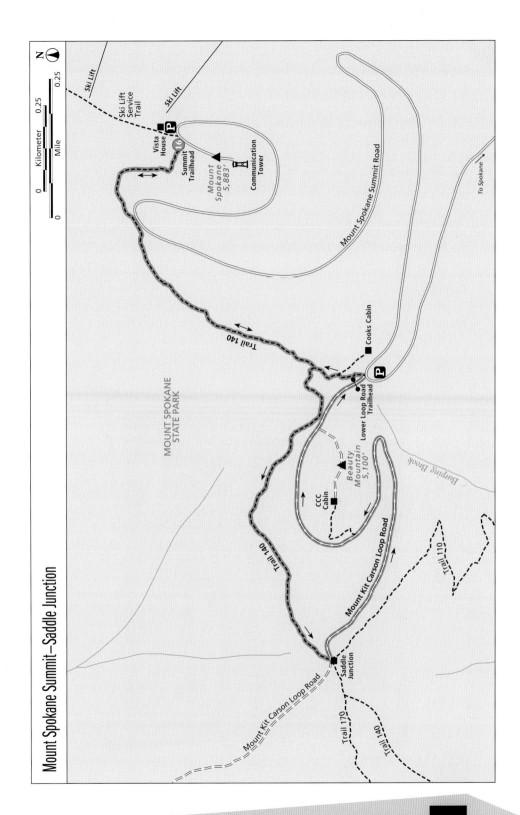

MILES AND DIRECTIONS

0.0   Hike northwest from the trailhead.

0.9   Pass the vague junction with Trail 135a.

1.6   Turn left at Saddle Junction on the Mount Kit Carson Loop Road.

2.2   Hike straight ahead at the junction with the roadbed to the CCC Cabin.

2.5   Turn left on Trail 135a.

2.6   Turn right on Trail 140.

3.5   Arrive back at the the trailhead near the summit of Mount Spokane.

Options

To lengthen this hike, continue west from Saddle Junction to the summit of Mount Kit Carson and return, before climbing back to the trailhead near the summit of Mount Spokane. See Hike 15 for a description of the route to the top of Mount Kit Carson. This side trip will add 1.4 miles round-trip to your hike.

Fireweed

Quartz Mountain Lookout

Hike the mostly gentle trails and roadbeds through diverse, mostly old-growth mountain forest to the lookout high atop Quartz Mountain. At the lookout take the time to admire the fantastic view in all directions. If you have the time, it is possible to rent the lookout for an overnight stay. The roadbeds that much of this hike follow are closed to motor vehicle access by the general public.

Start: Selkirk Lodge parking area

Distance: 4.6-mile out-and-back day hike or overnighter if you have rented the lookout

Hiking time: About 2.5 hours

Difficulty: Easy

Best seasons: Summer and early autumn

Canine compatibility / other trail users: Pets must be on a leash and under physical control at all times. These trails are open to hikers and bicyclists during snow-free times and cross-country skiers during the winter season. Hiking, snowshoeing, and dogs are prohibited during the winter season.

Fees and permits: A Discover Pass is required for parking. Discover Passes may be obtained wherever hunting and fishing licenses are sold and online at www.discover pass.wa.gov.

Maps: Dharmamaps's *Mount Spokane State Park* is an up-to-date topo of the state park. The map on the signboard next to the parking area shows this route well. The *Mount Spokane State Park* map produced by Washington State Parks, with donated proceeds made when renewing motor vehicle licenses, is free and adequate but not very detailed. Montana Mapping & GPS LLC's Hunting and GPS maps are good topos of the area as are National Geographic maps on CD-ROM, however, neither of these show all of the ski trails (which are what you will be following).

Trail contact: Mount Spokane State Park, 26107 N. Mount Spokane Park Dr., Mead, WA 99021; (509) 238-4258; mount.spokane@ parks.wa.gov

Special considerations: The Quartz Mountain Lookout can be rented from the state park for overnight use. It's a spectacular place to watch the sun set and rise.

Finding the trailhead: From downtown Spokane, head north on Division Street to the junction with US 2 (Newport Highway). Follow US 2 northeast to the junction with SR 206 (Mount Spokane Park Drive). Turn right on SR 206 and drive 18.5 miles to the junction with Mount Spokane Summit Road. At the junction turn right into a large parking area. Drive east through the parking area, then continue heading first south then west into another large parking area next to the Selkirk Lodge. This parking area is approximately 0.2 mile from SR 206. The route starts at a large signboard at the southeast corner of the parking area next to the Selkirk Lodge. The elevation at the trailhead is 4,630 feet. GPS: N47 54.187' / W117 05.992'

THE HIKE

Climb the few feet out of the parking lot and take a couple of minutes to look at the map on the large signboard at the trailhead. You will notice that you can take any of several trails to reach Junction #1. Probably the easiest and most direct one is the Mountain View Trail, which is the farthest one to the left (east) and the one described here. Follow the dirt roadbed that is the Mountain View Trail south through the mature hemlock (*Tsuga heterophylla*) and fir forest. Mountain ash (*Sorbus scopulina*), alders (*Alnus* spp.) and huckleberry (*Vaccinium* spp.) bushes form the understory beneath the large trees. Watch for wild turkeys as you hike, as they are fairly common here.

In slightly more than 0.3 mile, Junction #1 is reached. Go straight ahead at the junction on the Blue Jay Trail 220. The tread climbs gently and soon angles (straight ahead) across a gravel road. Another 0.6 mile of hiking brings you to Junction #2. This junction, at 4,690 feet elevation, is just over 1 mile into the hike.

At Junction #2 turn left on the dirt and gravel road that is Trail 220. Trail 220 is now called the Lodgepole Trail. The track climbs very gently. If you look behind you, you get a good view of Mount Spokane. Grouse are often seen along this section of the route. The Lodgepole Trail reaches Junction #3, at 4,770 feet elevation, 0.4 mile from Junction #2.

Leaving Junction #3, bear very slightly right, heading south-southeast and staying on the main roadbed. In a few yards there is another junction. Hike straight ahead, staying on the main roadbed. There is a restroom to the right at this junction. Soon you will pass another junction. Stay right (straight ahead on the main roadbed). The track soon passes two more junctions. There is no sign on the one to the left, but Abner's Way is to the right. Stay on the main roadbed, still heading south-southwest and climbing.

The course crosses another roadbed just after making a left turn a little more than 0.5 mile from Junction #3. Cross the other roadbed and hike straight ahead up the hill to the northeast. Soon, as the roadbed you are hiking on makes a hard right turn, you pass an unmarked junction with two trails, both of them to the left.

Quickly you come to yet another junction. Bear right here (really straight ahead). The roadbed to the left leads into a quartz quarry. Now the route climbs a little more steeply and winds to the left around the top of Quartz Mountain.

There is a restroom to the left of the roadbed 0.3 mile after passing the road into the quartz quarry. The lookout stands at the top of the mountain, above and a few yards south of the restroom. A short trail leads from the restroom to the lookout or you can continue a short distance on the roadbed to reach it.

Quartz Mountain Lookout, at 5,130 feet elevation, provides a commanding 360-degree view of east-central Washington and northern Idaho. Mountains in Montana can also be seen far to the east. Hauser Lake and Newman Lake are fairly close by to the south, and Mount Spokane is to the northwest. The Lookout is furnished with beds, a stove, lights and a table. It is, however, locked when not rented. It's easy to tell why this is called Quartz Mountain as quartz rocks and boulders are everywhere. When you are ready, return as you came to the Selkirk Lodge parking area.

Quartz Mountain lookout

Wild Turkey

Wild turkeys (*Meleagris gallopavo*) have become common in much of the Northwest since their introduction in the 1970s. Wild turkeys are the largest game bird in North America, attaining a length of 45 inches and a wingspan of up to 5 feet. They are slimmer than domestic turkeys, making them appear taller and longer-legged. Most of a wild turkey's plumage is dark brown to black with golden iridescent highlights. On the wings the flight feathers are barred white.

Gobblers (mature male turkeys) are easily distinguished from hens by the large red waddles that hang from below the beak and a fairly long beard (a tuft of feathers that hangs from the breast). Jakes (immature male turkeys) and hens lack the long beard and large red waddles.

With the turkey's stout beak and powerful grinding gizzard, even the toughest seed or nut can be eaten and ground up. Besides seeds and nuts, these fowl eat berries, roots, and some bulbs. Being omnivores, turkeys also eat insects, lizards, frogs, and some small mammals, like mice and voles.

Gobblers are polygamous, gathering a flock of hens with their strutting displays. Normally, a clutch of ten to twelve eggs is laid. The hen incubates the clutch for twenty-seven or twenty-eight days. Turkey chicks leave the nest soon after hatching and may make their first flight in as little as fourteen days.

These large fowl seem to prefer open woodland but have adapted to a wide variety of habitats, including the huge canyons of Snake River country, mountain forests, and much of the region's agricultural land. They do, however, need at least some trees for roosting. In some cases they have taken up residence in small towns and in the suburbs of larger cities. In urban or suburban settings, the big birds may quickly become a nuisance.

Green Tip:
Stay on the trail. Cutting through from one part of a switchback to another can destroy fragile plant life.

MILES AND DIRECTIONS

0.0 Hike south on the Mountain View Trail.

0.3 Hike straight ahead on the Blue Jay Trail 220 at Junction #1.

1.0 Turn left on the Lodgepole Trail 220 at Junction #2.

1.4 Hike straight ahead at Junction #3, staying on the main roadbed.

1.5 Hike straight ahead at the junction, staying on the main roadbed.

1.9 Cross another roadbed.

2.3 Reach Quartz Mountain Lookout and turn around.

4.6 Arrive back at the Selkirk Lodge parking area.

Mount Spokane from the south

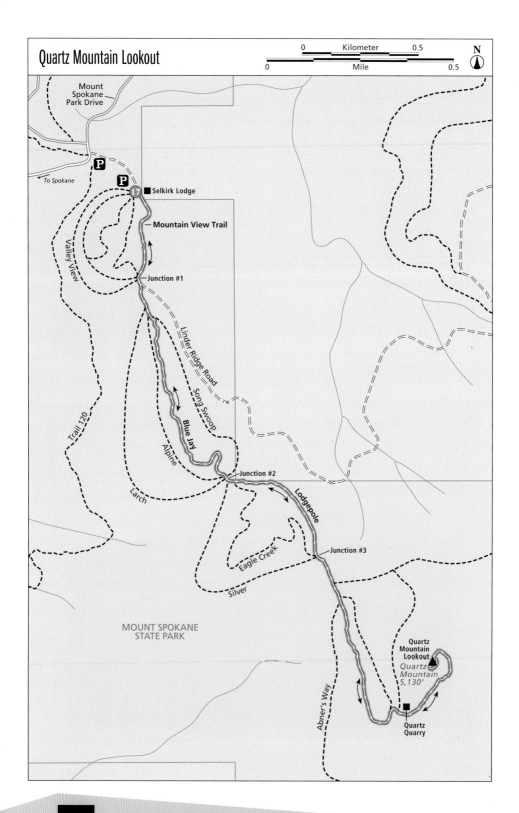

0   Kilometer   0.5

0   Mile   0.5

N

Mount Spokane Park Drive

← To Spokane

P

P

17   ■ Selkirk Lodge

— Mountain View Trail

Junction #1

Valley View

Trail 120

Linder Ridge Road

Song Swoop

Blue Jay

Alpine

Larch

Junction #2

Lodgepole

Eagle Creek

Silver

Junction #3

MOUNT SPOKANE STATE PARK

Abner's Way

Quartz Mountain Lookout

Quartz Mountain 5,130'

■ Quartz Quarry

B. Honorable Mention
Bald Knob–CCC Cabin

From Bald Knob Campground (the same trailhead as Hike 13), cross the Mount Spokane Summit road and hike west to the Civilian Conservation Corps Cabin. This route traverses semi open forests with lots of wild flowers in season. There are also good views to the south and southwest toward Spokane.

Lake Coeur d'Alene from Mineral Ridge

There are a wide variety of hikes available in or within 20 minutes driving time of downtown Coeur d'Alene. Many of these hikes are within the urban area, however, at least a couple are almost wilderness in character. Hike 18 takes you deep into the Liberty Lake Regional Park, through dense woods, past a waterfall, and on to great viewpoints. Hikes 19 and 20 are a bit of an oddity as they are on national forest land but are within a suburban area. Easy trails and beautiful diverse forest make these trails excellent family hikes. Within the city of Coeur d'Alene, Hikes 21 and 22 are close to the shoreline of spectacular Lake Coeur d'Alene. A short distance south of the city is the Nature Conservancy's Cougar Bay Preserve and Hike 23. Waterfowl viewing is the highpoint of this hike. Historically interpretive Hike 24 climbs a ridge in the mining area at the northeast end of Lake Coeur d'Alene. Besides its historical significance, this hike also has wonderful views. A mile or so south of Hike 24 is Hike 25, which takes you on a 2,200-foot-plus climb through forests and past viewpoints to the summit of Mount Coeur d'Alene.

Camp Hughes Loop

Starting along the marshland at the south end of Liberty Lake, this hike takes you through mixed forests, which consist of grand and Douglas fir, western hemlock, western red cedar, and several deciduous species, as well as three species of pines. Then you climb more than 1,200 feet to reach the Camp Hughes Cabin. Past the cabin the route descends, following abandoned roadbeds back to lake level. This route is open yearlong and camping along it is permitted in places. However, the trailhead, campground, and the road leading to them is closed during the winter months.

Start: Liberty Lake County Park
Distance: 7.4-mile lollipop-loop day hike or overnighter
Hiking time: About 3.5 to 5 hours
Difficulty: Moderate, except for a 1.6-mile strenuous section
Best seasons: Summer and fall
Canine compatibility / other trail users: Leashed dogs are permitted. Bikes are often ridden along this route. Stock is permitted on most of the return portion (west side) of this loop.
Fees and permits: None, although a fee is charged for camping at Liberty Lake County Park
Maps: *Liberty Lake and Mica Peak* USGS 7½ min. quads cover the area. The National Geographic *Washington* topo on CD-ROM disk 4 covers the area and shows parts of the route. Check out the map on the reader board at the trailhead before you start hiking, and use the one in this book.
Trail contact: Spokane County Parks and Recreation, 404 N.

Havana St., Spokane, WA 99202; (509) 477-4730
Special considerations: The route follows abandoned roadbeds, except for the 1.6-mile section from the Liberty Creek Cedar Forest to Camp Hughes, which is a steep, narrow, rough, and eroded dirt singletrack. Be sure to take along a map, as there are several unsigned junctions along this route.

Finding the trailhead: From I-90 at exit 296, drive south 0.2 mile to Apple-way Avenue. Turn left (east) on Appleway and go 0.9 mile to Molter Road. Turn right (south) on Molter Road, following the small signs toward Liberty Lake County Park, and drive 1.1 miles to Valley Way. Turn left on Valley Way and head east for 0.8 mile. Then the road turns right (south) and becomes Lakeside Road. Follow Lakeside Road for 1.6 miles to Zepher Road. Turn right on Zepher Road and soon enter Liberty Lake County Park. You will reach the campground and trailhead 0.8 mile after turning on Zepher Road. The trailhead is at the southwest corner of the campground. There is parking for several cars at the trailhead. A fee is charged for camping. The elevation at the trailhead is 2,060 feet. GPS: N47 37.855'/W117 03.512'

If you plan to use the lower portion of this trail during the winter or early spring (the higher country will probably be snowed in), the road from the park entrance booth to the campground may be closed. In this case, turn right at the entrance booth and drive a short distance to the parking area next to the playground equipment. From this parking area, walk south along the east side of the marshland on a path, passing a boardwalk, which leads to a viewing platform. The path soon joins a service road, which leads to the campground and trailhead. The added distance is only about 0.2 mile.

THE HIKE

This loop hike begins and ends on Liberty Creek Trail. Liberty Creek Trail begins at the south end of Liberty Lake County Park Campground. Before you begin your hike on the broad, gravel trail, stop and read the reader board, then pass through a gate and head south. Slightly over 0.1 mile from the trailhead, there is a path to the left. Hike straight ahead here, staying on the main trail. At the junction the trail surface becomes dirt.

Three-tenths of a mile from the trailhead, the loop portion of this hike begins at the junction with the Edith Hanson Cut-Off Trail. You can hike the loop in either direction, but this description is clockwise, so bear left (straight ahead to the south). Bikes are allowed on this side of the loop but horses are not. The track climbs very gently, heading south-southeast through the mixed forest. The trail splits a little over a mile from the trailhead. Take the left fork and cross a wooden bridge over Split Creek. The trails quickly rejoin each other after cross-ing the creek. In the mile from the Split Creek crossing to the Liberty Creek Cedar Forest, the route crosses a couple more small wooden bridges and traverses over wet areas on a couple of sections of boardwalk. Liberty Creek Cedar Forest, at 2,500 feet elevation, is the end of the gentle, broad trail for a while. Take the time to read the informational signs about the cedar forest.

At the cedar forest bear right, cross a wooden bridge over the creek, and start the steepest part of this hike. In the next 0.3 mile, the narrow and steep trail makes eleven switchbacks, climbing to a viewpoint at 2,790 feet elevation. To the north Liberty Lake dominates the view.

The track crosses a couple of tiny streams, which may be dry, after passing the viewpoint. Then you make a couple more switchbacks before crossing a wooden bridge just below a small waterfall. By the time you reach the bridge and waterfall, you are 3.1 miles from the trailhead and have climbed to 2,870 feet

Waterfall next to the trail

elevation. Past the waterfall the track continues to climb, and in the next 0.5 mile, you make fourteen more switchbacks. Then you cross the creek on a wooden bridge. The trail then leaves the creek behind and continues to climb. You will soon cross an abandoned roadbed with a sign next to it that states MORE HIKING. Continue straight ahead here and climb the short distance to the top of a rise, at 3,260 feet elevation. Then the tread passes a side trail that leads a short distance to an outhouse, before you descend the last few steps to Camp Hughes.

Camp Hughes is at 3,250 feet elevation and 3.7 miles from Liberty Lake County Park. At Camp Hughes there is a small cabin with a fireplace and bunks. As of this writing, the bunks are in poor condition. Outside the cabin is a fire pit.

Next to the cabin the Edith Hanson Riding Trail turns left. You will be following the Edith Hanson Riding Trail for the next 3.2 miles, so turn left and descend a short distance to a junction with an abandoned roadbed. This roadbed, which is open to stock, will serve as the trail much of the way back to the trailhead.

Turn left on the roadbed and start a very gentle downgrade. In 0.4 mile the broad trail crosses a tiny stream, and you begin to descend a little more steeply. The track crosses another small stream 1 mile farther along.

Another trail (abandoned roadbed) joins the one you are hiking on 2 miles from Camp Hughes. Continue straight ahead (northwest) here, descending gently. There are no signs at this junction.

You will reach a SCENIC OVERLOOK sign 0.1 mile after passing the unmarked junction, however, trees obstruct much of the view. There is another unmarked trail junction a couple tenths of a mile farther along. Bear slightly right, staying on the main trail, and walk a few yards downhill to the junction with the Scenic Trail. This signed junction is 6 miles from the trailhead where this hike started. At the junction with the Scenic Trail, you have descended to 2,690 feet elevation.

After you pass the junction with the Scenic Trail, the tread continues straight ahead and descends moderately. Liberty Lake comes into view ahead, through the trees, 0.2 mile farther along.

The course passes through a gate and flattens out in another 0.5 mile. In a short distance you reach the junction with the Edith Hanson Cut-Off Trail. A sign here commemorates Edith Hanson, for whom these trails were named. Hike straight ahead (northeast) on the Edith Hanson Cut-Off Trail. (The Edith Hanson Riding Trail turns to the left.) In a short distance the route turns to the east. You cross a couple of sluggish streams, then reach the junction with the Liberty Creek Trail, completing the loop. Turn left on the Liberty Creek Trail and retrace your steps the last 0.3 mile back to the trailhead.

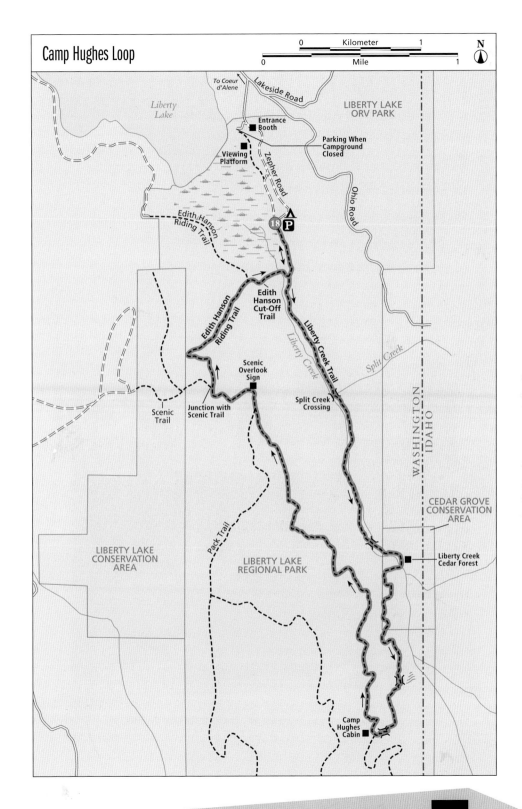

Camp Hughes Loop

To Coeur d'Alene

Lakeside Road

Liberty Lake

LIBERTY LAKE
ORV PARK

Entrance Booth

Parking When Campground Closed

Viewing Platform

Zepher Road

Ohio Road

Edith Hanson Riding Trail

18 P

Edith Hanson Cut-Off Trail

Edith Hanson Riding Trail

Liberty Creek Trail

Liberty Creek

Split Creek

Scenic Overlook Sign

Junction with Scenic Trail

Split Creek Crossing

Scenic Trail

WASHINGTON

IDAHO

CEDAR GROVE CONSERVATION AREA

LIBERTY LAKE CONSERVATION AREA

Pack Trail

LIBERTY LAKE REGIONAL PARK

Liberty Creek Cedar Forest

Camp Hughes Cabin

MILES AND DIRECTIONS

0.0 Hike south from the Liberty Lake County Park and Trailhead.

0.3 Hike straight ahead at the trail junction to begin the loop.

2.1 Turn right at the Liberty Creek Cedar Forest and begin to climb.

3.1 The trail crosses a bridge below a waterfall.

3.7 Turn left at Camp Hughes cabin.

6.0 Bear right at the junction with the Scenic Trail.

6.9 Hike straight ahead on the Edith Hanson Cut-Off Trail.

7.4 Arrive back at the Liberty Lake County Park and Trailhead.

Camp Hughes cabin

English Point East

The east side of the English Point Trail System consists of the Red Loop and the Gray Loop Trails. The Red Loop Trail is the longer route of the two. The Red and Gray Loops follow the same route for their first 0.4 mile and last 0.3 mile. Both loops offer easy hiking through second-growth forest. The Red Loop also features a couple of viewpoints. Either of these loops is great for all but the smallest children (unless they are in a kiddy pack).

Start: English Point Trailhead
Distance: Red Loop 1.6 miles, Gray Loop 0.8 miles; day hike
Hiking time: About 1 hour Red Loop, 0.5 hour Gray Loop
Difficulty: Easy
Best seasons: Spring, summer, and fall. These trails are open to cross-country skiing during the winter.
Canine compatibility / other trail users: Dogs are permitted but must be kept under control. These trails are open to hikers and skiers only; however, horse trails do cross them.
Fees and permits: None
Maps: The map on the reader board at the trailhead or the map in this book should be all that is needed. The USGS *Hayden Lake* 7½-min. quad covers the area.
Trail contact: USDA Forest Service, Coeur d'Alene River Ranger District, Fernan Office, 2502 E. Sherman Ave., Coeur d'Alene, ID 83814; (208) 664-2318

Finding the trailhead: Take exit 12 off I-90 in Coeur d' Alene. From the exit, drive north on US 95 for 6 miles to the junction with Lancaster. Turn right on Lancaster and go 3.5 miles east to the junction with English Point Road. Turn right on English Point Road and quickly turn left into the parking area at English Point Trailhead. Plenty of parking and restrooms are available at the trailhead. GPS: N47 47.250' /W116 42.619'

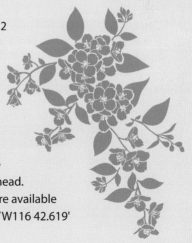

THE HIKE

Hike east from the parking area through the gate, then quickly bear left to start the loop. The gravel-surfaced trail is in excellent condition. Every few yards, rubber water bars cross the route to help prevent trail erosion. The course gently descends through the ponderosa pine (*Pinus ponderosa*) and Douglas fir (*Pseudotsuga menziesii*) forest. A quarter mile into the hike, a path to the left leads a few feet to a bench. Bear right, staying on the main trail.

Four-tenths of a mile from the trailhead, the route reaches the first junction with the Gray Loop. If you choose to take the shorter hike, on the Gray Loop, turn right here and hike 0.1 mile west to another junction with the Red Loop. Turn right on the Red Loop and hike the last 0.3 mile back to the trailhead.

To continue on the longer Red Loop, bear left at the first junction with the Gray Loop. The Red Loop heads south through the forest, which now includes grand fir (*Abies grandis*), lodgepole pine (*Pinus contorta*), western larch (*Larix occidentalis*), and quaking aspen (*Populus tremuloides*).

Three-tenths of a mile after leaving the junction with the Gray Loop, there is a viewpoint with benches to the left of the trail. There is another viewpoint to

Viewpoint overlooking Hayden Lake

the left of the trail, this one with a wooden platform and benches, a little farther along. The view is of Hayden Lake and the hills beyond. The second viewpoint is 0.9 mile from the trailhead.

To the right nearly across the trail from the second viewpoint is a dirt-surfaced horse-and-bike trail. There is also a hitching post here. Hike straight ahead to stay on the graveled Red Loop. The route crosses the horse trail and goes through a gate to prevent horse passage along the Red Loop, slightly over 0.1 mile past the viewpoint and platform. A short distance farther along, the trail becomes a boardwalk for a few yards. You soon pass another bench and reach another junction with a horse trail. Another gate here keeps horses off the Red Loop. Remember that the Red Loop is graveled, while the others, except for the Gray Loop, aren't.

The second junction with the Gray Loop is reached in few more yards. This junction is 1.3 miles into the hike. Bear left here and hike northwest on the now combined Red and Gray Loops. The tread crosses a horse trail again in a little over 0.1 mile. The horse trail shortly joins the combined Red and Gray Loops, and in 0.1 mile more you return to the English Point Trailhead.

MILES AND DIRECTIONS

Around the Red Loop

0.0 Hike east from the English Point Trailhead.

0.4 Bear left at the first junction with the Gray Loop Trail.

1.3 Bear left at the second junction with the Gray Loop Trail.

1.6 Arrive back at the English Point Trailhead.

Options

For a longer but also easy hike, try Hike 20, which is across English Point Road from the parking area.

> **🌱 Green Tip:**
> *Rechargeable (reusable) batteries reduce one source of toxic garbage.*

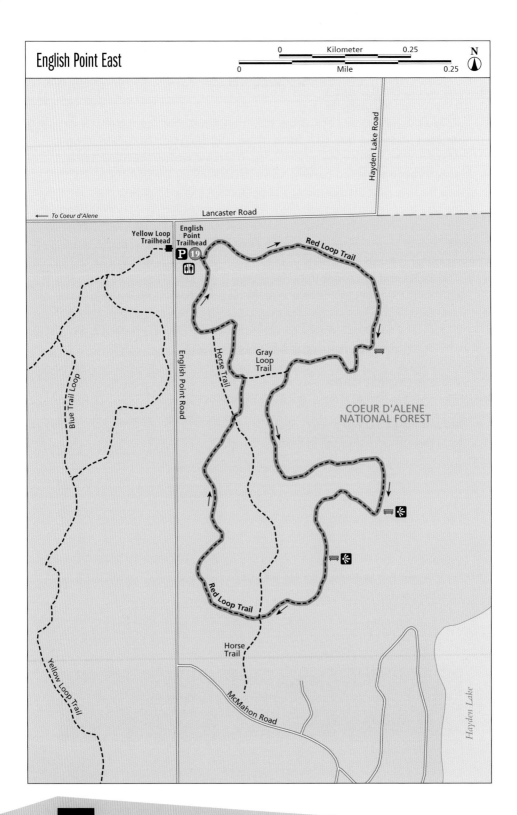

English Point East

Kilometer
0   0.25

Mile
0   0.25

N

← To Coeur d'Alene

Hayden Lake Road

Lancaster Road

Yellow Loop Trailhead

English Point Trailhead

P 19

Red Loop Trail

Horse Trail

Gray Loop Trail

Blue Trail Loop

English Point Road

COEUR D'ALENE NATIONAL FOREST

Red Loop Trail

Horse Trail

Yellow Loop Trail

McMahon Road

Hayden Lake

Quaking Aspen

Quaking aspen (*Populus tremuloides*) is so named because its leaves, at the end of the very slender and flattened stems, quiver with only the slightest breeze. Aspen leaves are nearly round with only a small point on the tip. They turn bright yellow and sometimes orange in the fall.

Aspens are medium-size trees up to about 90 feet tall. The bark is white to light greenish gray. Fairly fast growing and short lived, aspen trees grow at all elevations up to timberline. They mainly reproduce from root suckers. The wood of the aspen is used in a wide variety of products, including lumber, plywood, and matches. Beavers feed on the young shoots and bark of the aspen and cut many trees to construct their dams and lodges.

Aspens in fall color

English Point West

The trails in the English Point Trail System are on an isolated parcel of national forest land, somewhat unusual in this suburban setting. Because of the gentle grades of these routes and the opportunity to take one of the shorter loops if members of your party are getting tired, these hikes are good for families with kids. Each loop is marked with plastic diamonds that are colored to match the name of the loop.

Start: English Point West Side Trailhead, sometimes referred to as the Yellow Loop Trailhead

Distance: Yellow Loop 3.2 miles, Green Loop 1.8 miles, Blue Loop 0.8 mile; lollipop-loop day hikes

Hiking time: Yellow Loop about 1.5 hours, Green Loop 1 hour, Blue Loop 0.5 hour

Difficulty: Easy to moderate

Best seasons: Spring, summer, and fall

Canine compatibility / other trail users: Dogs are permitted but must be kept under control. These trails are open to hikers, equestrians, and mountain bikers. They are also marked cross-country-ski trails in the winter.

Fees and permits: None

Maps: The map on the reader board at the trailhead or the map in this book should be all that is needed. The USGS *Hayden Lake* 7½ min. quad covers the area.

Trail contact: USDA Forest Service, Coeur d'Alene River Ranger District, Fernan Office, 2502 E. Sherman Ave., Coeur d'Alene, ID 83814; (208) 664-2318

Finding the trailhead: Take exit 12 off I-90 in Coeur d'Alene. From the exit, drive north on US 95 for 6 miles to the junction with Lancaster Road. Turn right on Lancaster and go 3.5 miles east to the junction with English Point Road. Turn right on English Point Road and quickly turn left into the parking area at English Point Trailhead. Plenty of parking and restrooms are available at the trailhead. To find the West Side Trailhead for the Yellow, Blue, and Green Loops, cross English Point Road from the parking area, angling slightly north. GPS: N47 47.256' / W116 42.694'

THE HIKE

At the trailhead stop and check out the maps and signs. Then start your hike by heading southwest. For the first 0.5 mile, all three of the loop trails (Yellow, Green, and Blue) follow the same route. Diamonds on the trees beside the trail mark the way. The color of the diamond corresponds with the name of the trail (e.g., follow the yellow diamonds to stay on the Yellow Loop). Bear left in 0.1 mile at a trail junction, starting the loops. Hike southeast for a short distance, then turn south, close to English Point Road. Soon the trail turns southwest again. Five-tenths of a mile from the trailhead, you will reach the first junction with the Blue Loop.

Ponderosa pine

To hike the shortest of the three loops on the west side of the English Point Trail System, turn right on the Blue Loop. Hike north for 0.2 mile on the Blue Loop to another junction with the Yellow and Green Loops (the Yellow and Green Loops follow the same route here). Turn right again and hike northeast back to the trailhead, making a total of 0.8 mile for the loop.

To stay on the Yellow and Green Loops, bear left and continue to walk beneath the Douglas firs (*Pseudotsuga menziesii*) and ponderosa pines (*Pinus ponderosa*). Rosebushes beside the tread add a splash of color both with their blooms and their bright-orange hips. There is a poor trail to the left, a little less than 0.5 mile after leaving the junction with the Blue Loop; don't take it. A few more yards of hiking brings you to a trail junction with benches next to it. This junction, 1 mile from the trailhead, is where the Green Loop leaves the Yellow Loop.

To hike the Green Loop, turn right at the junction and hike northwest, then north for 0.5 mile to another junction with the Yellow Loop. Turn right at this junction and follow the combined Yellow and Green Loops, and later the Blue Loop back to the trailhead. The total distance around the Green Loop is 1.8 miles.

To hike the longer Yellow Loop, bear left at the junction and walk the boardwalk, passing a small pond.

For the next 1.9 miles, only yellow diamonds mark the route. One-half mile farther along, the route approaches a paved road. Hayden Lake is in view to the left, through the trees. Two and one-tenth miles into the hike, the track crosses a short wooden boardwalk. In another 0.2 mile the trail forks. Yellow diamonds mark both forks. Bear left and descend; the forks quickly rejoin each other. The route to the right is an easier way for cross-country skiers to ascend and descend here. Before long the course crosses a wooden bridge, and then you climb for a short distance. A little farther along there is a field to your left and a view of houses and mountains. After passing a large house, the trail soon crosses another bridge. The Yellow Loop rejoins the Green Loop 0.1 mile after crossing the bridge. At this junction you are 2.9 miles into the hike.

Turn left at the junction and hike north on the now combined Yellow and Green Loops. In slightly under 0.2 mile, you reach the second junction with the Blue Loop. Hike straight ahead here to the northeast. Now all three diamonds—blue, green, and yellow—mark the route. Soon you pass the junction where all the loops begin. In another 0.1 mile you are back at the English Point West Side Trailhead.

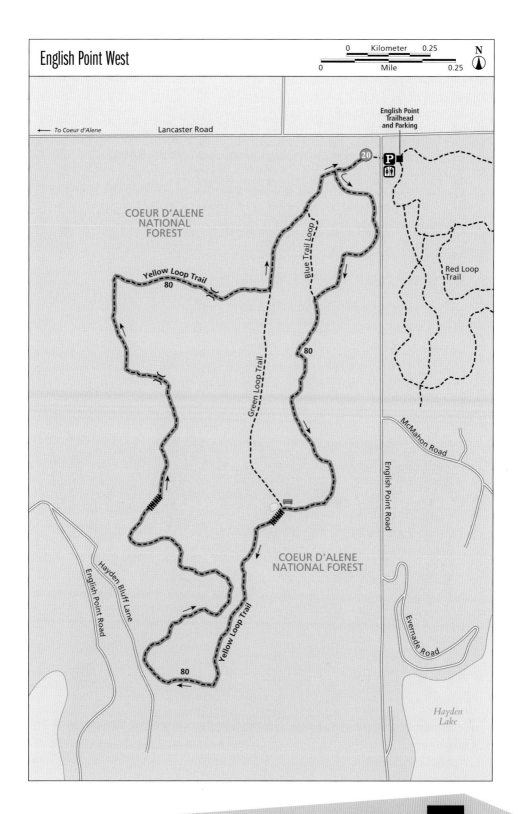

English Point West

0   Kilometer   0.25
0   Mile   0.25

N

English Point Trailhead and Parking

← To Coeur d'Alene   Lancaster Road

P

COEUR D'ALENE NATIONAL FOREST

Yellow Loop Trail
80

Blue Trail Loop

Green Loop Trail

Red Loop Trail

McMahon Road

English Point Road

80

COEUR D'ALENE NATIONAL FOREST

Hayden Bluff Lane

English Point Road

Yellow Loop Trail

80

Evernade Road

Hayden Lake

Around the Yellow Loop

0.0 Cross English Point Road, then hike southwest from the trailhead.

0.1 Turn left at the trail junction to start the loop portion of these hikes.

0.5 Pass the junction of the Yellow, Green, and Blue Loops.

1.0 Pass the junction of the Yellow and Green Loops.

2.3 The trail forks. Bear left and descend a short distance.

2.9 Pass the junction of the Yellow and Green Loops.

3.1 Pass the junction of the Yellow, Green, and Blue Loops.

3.2 Arrive back at the English Point Trailhead.

Options

The Red and Gray Loop trails on the other side of English Point Road make excellent additional hikes to enjoy while you are at English Point. See Hike 19.

Rose hips along the trail

Tubbs Hill Loop

Hike around the east, south, and west sides of Tubbs Hill along the shoreline of beautiful Lake Coeur d'Alene. Then return to the trailhead across the hills forested north slope.

Start: East Tubbs Hill Park Trailhead

Distance: 2.8-mile lollipop-loop day hike (including side trip to Corbin Point)

Hiking time: About 1 to 1.5 hours

Difficulty: Easy

Best seasons: Spring, summer, and fall. Flowers abound in the spring and early summer.

Canine compatibility / other trail users: These are hiker-only trails. Bikes, smoking, camping, fires, and fireworks are prohibited. Dogs must be on a leash and cleaned up after.

Fees and permits: None

Maps: *Tubbs Hill Nature Trails,* produced by the Coeur d'Alene Parks Department and Tubbs Hill Foundation. The map on the reader board at the trailhead is also accurate and easy to read.

Trail contact: Coeur d'Alene Parks Department, 710 E. Mullan Ave., Coeur d'Alene, ID 83814; (208) 769-2252; www.cdaidparks.org

Finding the trailhead: Take exit 12 off I-90 in Coeur d' Alene. From the exit, drive south on US 95 for 0.9 mile to Northwest Boulevard. Head southeast (left) on Northwest Boulevard for 1 mile to Sherman Avenue. Turn left on Sherman Avenue and follow it to Ninth Street. Turn right on Ninth Street and follow it to Mullan. Turn left and go 2 blocks east on Mullan, then turn right on 10th Street and head southeast for 0.3 mile to Eastside Park, which is the trailhead. The total distance from I-90 is about 3 miles. GPS: N47 40.022' /W116 46.316'

THE HIKE

From the reader board at the East Tubbs Hill Park Trailhead, hike south on the paved trail. Shortly the pavement ends as you continue south, climbing slightly, with the marina to your left. If you're here around June 1, bluedicks (*Brodiaea douglasii*) will be blooming beside the trail. A little farther along there is a path to the left that drops to the shoreline and a small beach. Two-tenths of a mile from the trailhead, you will reach the junction with the main trail that circles Tubbs Hill. Turn left at the junction to begin the loop portion of this hike and quickly cross a bridge.

A little more than 0.1 mile past the bridge, there is a path to the left that leads to a viewpoint overlooking the lake. A few yards farther along, there is another trail junction. Hike straight ahead to the southwest, then west, passing several more viewpoints. Arrowleaf balsamroot flourishes along this sunny slope in late spring, as do lupines (*Lupinus*) and desert parsleys (*Lomatium*).

After passing several more paths to viewpoints overlooking the lake, the course passes a shallow cave in the rocks to the right of the trail. Another 0.2 mile of hiking along this ponderosa pine (*Pinus ponderosa*)–covered slope brings you to the junction with the 0.1-mile-long side trail to Corbin Point. Really there are several side paths here that lead to the point. This junction is 1 mile from the East Tubbs Hill Park Trailhead. It's worth the time to hike the short distance to Corbin

Lake Coeur d'Alene

Point and back before continuing your loop hike. The rocks on the point make it a great place to relax for a while.

Back on the main loop trail, hike north along the shoreline, passing a trail to the right in 0.1 mile. The track passes several paths to the left that lead to viewpoints. Soon the Coeur d'Alene Resort comes into view ahead. Now the slope faces a little more to the northwest and the timber changes to mostly Douglas fir (*Pseudotsuga menziesii*). The track becomes a little rough and rocky in spots here. At 0.7 mile from the junction with the path to Corbin Point, a side trail descends to the left, reaching the Third Street Trailhead in a short distance. The Third Street Trailhead is one of the two primary entrances to the Tubbs Hill Trail system. Unless you want to go to the resort, bear right (east) on the now braided trail. In a short distance the braids in the trail come back together as you begin to traverse the north slope of Tubbs Hill.

The northern slopes of Tubbs Hill are mostly covered with medium-age Douglas fir trees. Dogtooth violets (*Erythronium grandiflorum*; aka glacier lilies) grow in abundance on the forest floor on this shady slope. The peak of their bloom is in late April. In a little more than 0.1 mile, you will reach another trail junction. Bear right here and climb. The route crosses a paved road in another 0.2 mile. Signs here point out the trail. Quickly you will pass two more trail junctions. Bear left at both, staying on the main trail.

Three-tenths of a mile after crossing the paved road, the track crosses a gravel service road. A short distance after crossing the service road, there is another trail junction. This one has signs pointing back the way you came to the Third Street Trailhead and to the left to the 10th Street Trailhead. If you wish to shorten your hike a little, turn left and descend to the 10th Street Trailhead, which is also known as the East Tubbs Hill Park Trailhead (the place where you started this hike).

To continue on the loop, bear right (nearly straight ahead) and hike southeast. In 0.1 mile the course descends some steps, then passes a couple of side paths, one to the left and one to the right. To your left and below, the 11th Street Marina comes into view. The track crosses a bouncy suspension bridge, passes a couple more side paths to the left, then reaches the trail junction where the loop portion of this hike began. This junction is 0.8 mile from the path to the Third Street Trailhead and 2.6 miles into the hike. Turn left at the junction and retrace your steps for 0.2 mile to the East Tubbs Hill Park Trailhead.

MILES AND DIRECTIONS

0.0 Begin at the East Tubbs Hill Park Trailhead.

0.2 Turn left at tail junction and cross a bridge.

0.4 At the trail junction, hike straight ahead to the southwest.

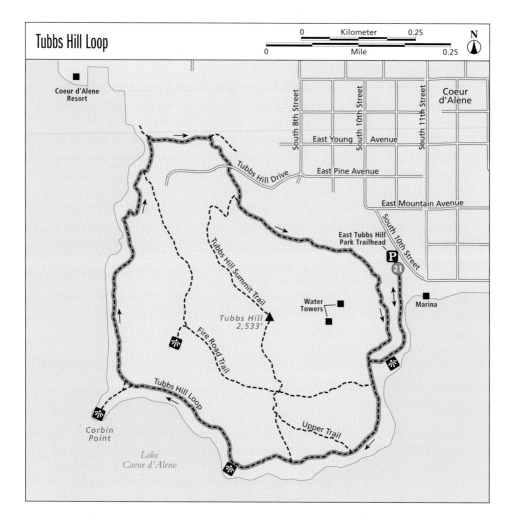

1.0 The path to the left goes 0.1 mile to Corbin Point.

1.9 The path to the left descends to the Third Street Trailhead. Hike straight ahead.

2.1 Cross the paved road.

2.6 Turn left at the trail junction.

2.8 Arrive back at the East Tubbs Hill Park Trailhead.

Options

This trail can easily be hiked in either direction. The numbered spots on the *Tubbs Hill Nature Trail Guide* correspond to the numbered blocks beside the trail and travel around Tubbs Hill in a counterclockwise direction (the opposite of the route described above).

Hike to the 2,533-foot-high summit of Tubbs Hill (Hike 22) on the same trip, taking in the views along the way.

Arrowleaf Balsamroot

Often called a sunflower, the arrowleaf balsamroot (*Balsamorhiza sagittata*) is widespread in the inland Northwest. It prefers well-drained slopes and ridgetops, with lots of exposure to direct sun. The mostly basal leaves are shaped like a large arrowhead, giving the perennial plant its name. Arrowleaf balsamroot grows up to 2 feet tall from a woody taproot. In spring its large, showy flowers turn many a hillside bright yellow. The plant—especially its young shoots—are relished by deer and elk.

Glacier lilies

Tubbs Hill Summit

Hike to the summit of Tubbs Hill and take in the view of beautiful Lake Coeur d'Alene.

Start: East Tubbs Hill Park Trailhead

Distance: 2.8-mile lollipop-loop day hike

Hiking time: About 1.5 hours

Difficulty: Moderate

Best seasons: Spring, summer, and fall. Flowers abound in the spring and early summer.

Canine compatibility / other trail users: These are hiker-only trails. Bikes, smoking, camping, fires, and fireworks are prohibited. Dogs must be on a leash and cleaned up after.

Fees and permits: None

Maps: *Tubbs Hill Nature Trails,* produced by the Coeur d'Alene Parks Department and Tubbs Hill Foundation. The map on the reader board at the trailhead is also accurate and easy to read.

Trail contact: Coeur d'Alene Parks Department, 710 E. Mullan Ave., Coeur d'Alene, ID 83814; (208) 769-2252; www.cdaidparks.org

Finding the trailhead: Take exit 12 off I-90 in Coeur d'Alene. From the exit, drive south on US 95 for 0.9 mile to Northwest Boulevard. Head southeast (left) on Northwest Boulevard for 1 mile to Sherman Avenue. Turn left on Sherman Avenue and follow it to Ninth Street. Turn right on Ninth Street and follow it to Mullan. Turn left and go 2 blocks east on Mullan, then turn right on 10th Street and head southeast for 0.3 mile to East Tubbs Hill Park Trailhead. The total distance from I-90 is about 3 miles. The elevation at the trailhead is 2,150 feet. GPS: N47 40.022' / W116 46.316'

THE HIKE

H ike south from the reader board at the East Tubbs Hill Park Trailhead, on the paved trail. The pavement quickly ends; continue south, climbing slightly. In a short distance there is a path to the left that drops to a small beach on the shore of Lake Coeur d'Alene. You will reach the junction with the Tubbs Hill Loop Trail 0.2 mile from the trailhead. The loop trail circles Tubbs Hill close to the lake level. Turn left at the junction and hike south, quickly crossing a wooden bridge.

Seventy-five yards after crossing the bridge, there is an unmarked trail junction. Don't take it, but rather continue hiking south on the main trail. Slightly less than 0.2 mile after crossing the bridge, you will reach the junction with Upper Trail. There are signs at the junction, but unfortunately they are easily seen only when coming from the other direction.

Turn right at the junction and climb to the north, through the ponderosa pine (*Pinus ponderosa*) forest, on Upper Trail. On the forest floor beneath the pines, Arrowleaf Balsamroot (*Balsamorhiza sagittata*) brings forth its cheerful yellow flowers in late spring. There is an unmarked trail junction a little less than 0.2 mile after heading up Upper Trail. Bear right here and continue to climb. Watch the ground here for white mariposa lilies (*Calochortus*). The track crosses a narrow dirt road a little farther up the hill. This roadbed will be your return route,

Coeur d'Alene Resort from Tubbs Hill

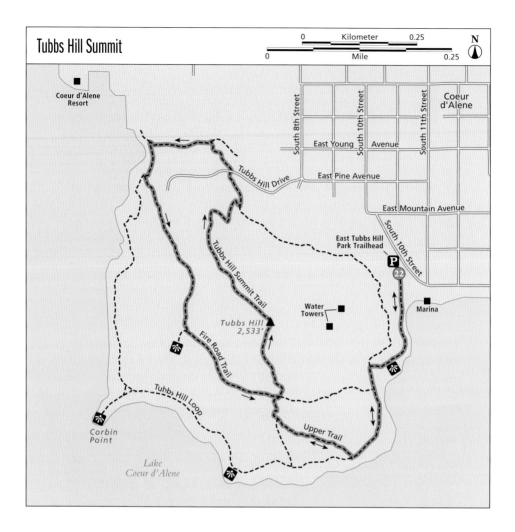

but for now cross it and continue to climb north. In 0.2 mile you will reach the 2,533-foot-high summit of Tubbs Hill. A small rock outcrop at the summit makes a good place for a break and maybe a snack.

Leaving the summit the route descends to the northwest along a semi-open ridge. Balsamroot and larkspur sprout in the openings, and ninebark (*Physocarpus malvaceus*) crowds the track in places. As the route steepens, the Coeur d'Alene Resort soon comes into view ahead. There is a trail junction 0.25 mile after leaving the summit. Turn right here, staying on the main trail and continuing to descend. The route heads down through the Douglas fir (*Pseudotsuga menziesii*) woods for 0.1 mile to another junction with the loop trail. Turn left on the loop trail and hike north-northwest, quickly crossing a paved road. There is another trail junction shortly after crossing the paved road. Bear left at this junction, staying on the main trail.

In a little less than 0.2 mile, you reach the junction with the trail that leads a short distance to the Third Street Trailhead. This junction is 1.6 miles into the hike. The trail is braided for a short distance close to this junction. Unless you want to go to the resort, turn left here and hike south for about 100 yards to another unmarked trail junction. Turn left at this junction, leaving the loop trail. The track is a little rough and rocky here as you climb a short distance to another trail junction, where you bear right. There is a house to your left as you walk a short distance southeast to a junction with a narrow dirt fire road. Bear right on the fire road and continue southeast, soon passing another trail junction.

To your right 0.2 mile after getting on the fire road, there is a short path to the right that leads to a viewpoint that overlooks Lake Coeur d'Alene from 250 feet above the water level. After taking in the view, return to the fire road and continue hiking southeast, quickly passing another trail junction. Stay on the fire road, and in a little more than 0.1 mile, you will reach the junction with your inbound route. This junction is 2.1 miles into the hike and you have 0.7 mile to go to return to the East Tubbs Hill Park Trailhead. Turn right at the junction and descend as you came for 0.3 mile to the junction with the Tubbs Hill Loop Trail. Turn left here and retrace your steps back to the East Tubbs Hill Park Trailhead.

MILES AND DIRECTIONS

0.0   Hike south from East Tubbs Hill Park Trailhead.

0.2   At the junction with Tubbs Hill Loop Trail, turn left.

0.4   Turn right, leaving Tubbs Hill Loop Trail.

0.7   Cross the dirt roadbed (return route).

0.9   At the summit of Tubbs Hill, descend northwest.

1.3   At the junction with Tubbs Hill Loop Trail, turn left.

1.5   At the trail to Third Street Trailhead, bear left.

1.6   Turn left, leaving Tubbs Hill Loop Trail.

2.1   Turn right at the junction.

2.8   Arrive back at the East Tubbs Hill Park Trailhead.

Options
Hike the Tubbs Hill Loop Trail (Hike 21) on the same trip. A few short sections of these two trails follow the same route.

Cougar Bay Nature Conservancy Preserve

Hike along the marsh at the head of Cougar Bay on the northwest shore of Lake Coeur d'Alene. Then climb a short distance up the forested north-facing slope above it for your return trip. Take your time and watch for waterfowl, shorebirds, and other wildlife, which could even include a moose.

Start: Cougar Bay Nature Conservancy Preserve parking area
Distance: 1.1-mile loop day hike
Hiking time: About 1 hour
Difficulty: Easy
Best seasons: Spring, summer, and fall, or any time when there is little or no snow cover
Canine compatibility / other trail users: Hikers only; dogs must be under close control
Fees and permits: None
Maps: The map at the kiosk,100 yards from the trailhead, is adequate for this hike, as is the one in this book. The National Geographic *Washington* topo on CD-ROM, disk 4, covers the area and shows only a small portion of this route (as an unimproved roadbed).
Trail contact: The Nature Conservancy, Ball Creek Field Office, (208) 267-9629
Special considerations: At present this is the only route open to hikers on the Cougar Bay Preserve. The route, at this time, is marked with blue paint spots on trees beside the trail. In the future there will be more trails open to hikers in this preserve.

Finding the trailhead: From exit 12 on I-90 in Coeur d'Alene, drive south on US 95 for about 3 miles. Turn left into the Cougar Bay Nature Conservancy Preserve parking area. A sign points you to the preserve parking area. There is room for only about three vehicles at the parking area, and there are no other facilities. The elevation at the parking area is 2,140 feet. GPS: N47 39.592' /W116 50.150'

THE HIKE

Follow the roadbed south from the small parking area, crossing a wooden bridge as you walk. In about 100 yards you will reach the junction where the loop begins. Turn left and take a couple of minutes to check out the postings on the informational kiosk to your right. From the kiosk, the route follows a long-abandoned roadbed along the edge of the marshland, heading northeast.

In a short distance the track passes an informational reader board that discusses the marsh-edge habitat. To the right of the trail, 0.2 mile from the parking area, a bench has been placed beneath a large cottonwood tree. This is a good place to sit quietly and watch the activities of the marsh. A short distance farther

Black cottonwood

along, you will pass another informational reader board, this one about nature's water filter.

The route makes a turn at two more reader boards 0.4 mile into the hike. Turn right here and climb south, through the Douglas fir (*Pseudotsuga menziesii*), grand fir (*Abies grandis*), and ponderosa pine (*Pinus ponderosa*) forest. Soon the track climbs some rock steps and reaches a vague and unmarked trail junction. Bear right here, staying on the main trail. The trail then makes two climbing switchbacks, before reaching a junction with an abandoned roadbed. At this junction you are 0.7 mile into the hike and have climbed to 2,270 feet elevation, the highpoint of this loop. This junction is a place where it is very easy to take the wrong trail. The trail appears to angle across the roadbed, but this will put you on the wrong route. Turn right on the grass-covered roadbed and hike west.

The tread soon turns south, then west and reaches a junction with another abandoned roadbed in a little over 0.1 mile. Hike straight ahead (west) at this junction and continue your gradual descent for another 0.2 mile to the junction where you started the loop. From here hike north, retracing your steps to the parking area.

Black Cottonwood

The black cottonwood (*Populus trichocarpa*) is a very fast-growing tree, one of, if not the, fastest growing of our native trees. When mature it can reach a height of 150 feet or more and have a trunk 3 feet thick. The cottonwood generally lives on moist sites at low to middle elevations. Its large leaves, 3 to 5 inches long, are dark shiny green on top, silvery beneath, and suspended by a slender round stem. The leaves are broad and sharp pointed with fine teeth on their margins and conspicuous veins. The bark on a young black cottonwood is ashy gray to greenish yellow. It is dark gray, deeply furrowed, and may be 2 inches thick on older trees. Hairy catkins appear on the twigs early in the spring, well before the leaves emerge. Small, round, green capsules form on these catkins. Inside the capsules are the tiny cottony seeds that give the tree its name.

Native Americans found the cottonwood tree to be very useful. The sweet inner bark and cambium tissues were eaten in the spring and early summer. These parts had to be eaten quickly after harvest; if left too long, they would ferment. The terminal buds of the cottonwood are very sticky with a sweet resin. These resinous buds had many medical uses, from curing baldness and sour throats to treating rheumatism. Gum from the resin was used as glue to hold feathers onto arrow shafts. The fibers of the inner bark were

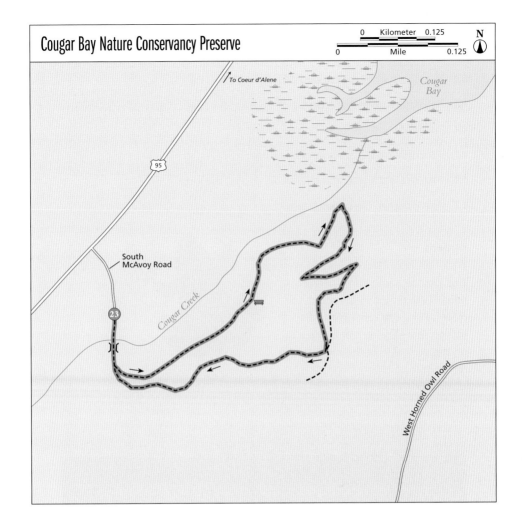

used to strengthen other plant fibers when making cloth. Cottonwood trunks were sometimes used to make dugout canoes, and the wood was used as fuel for smoking fish.

The wood of the black cottonwood is presently used for lumber, plywood, veneer, and box making. It is light, straight grained, and moderately strong but not very durable. It works easily and takes a good finish.

Bees collect the resin and use it to seal over invaders, like mice, that have been killed in their hives. This sealing prevents decay and protects the hive from the organisms that would invade the decaying bodies and cause danger of infection for the hive.

MILES AND DIRECTIONS

0.0 Hike south from the parking area.

0.1 Turn left to begin the loop.

0.4 Turn right and climb, leaving the marsh.

0.7 Turn right on the abandoned roadbed.

1.0 Hike straight ahead at the junction, ending the loop.

1.1 Arrive back at the parking area.

Options

Walk the short Blackwell Island Wetland Trail on the same trip. To reach it, drive north on US 95 for about 1.5 miles to the Blackwell Island Recreation Area. The recreation area is on the west side of the highway 1.4 miles south of I-90.

🌿 **Green Tip:**
When hiking in a group, walk single file on established trails to avoid widening them. If you come upon a sensitive area, spread out so you don't cut one path through the landscape. Don't create new trails where there were none before.

Mineral Ridge Trail System

The Mineral Ridge Trail System makes for a very pleasant hike with great views. There is also mining history to be learned about, as well as natural history. The hike climbs to the ridgeline of Mineral Ridge, then a side trip takes you up the ridgeline to more views and the out-of-the-way Lost Man Trailhead. After returning from the Lost Man Trailhead, you continue down Mineral Ridge and complete the loop before returning to the Mineral Ridge Trailhead. The upgrades on the Mineral Ridge Trail System are generally moderate, and several benches along the way make pleasant rest stops, if you are so inclined.

Start: Mineral Ridge Trailhead
Distance: 4.4-mile lollipop-loop day hike, including 2 side trips
Hiking time: About 2.5 to 3.5 hours, including side trips
Difficulty: Moderate
Best seasons: Late spring, summer, and early fall
Canine compatibility / other trail users: Leashed dogs are permitted on these hiker-only trails.
Fees and permits: None
Maps: The one in this book is more than adequate for this hike. If there are some available at the trailhead, pick up a BLM *Mineral Ridge Trail Guide*. The numbered spots along the Mineral Ridge Trail correspond to the map and information in the *Mineral Ridge Trail Guide*.
Trail contact: United States Department of the Interior, Bureau of Land Management, Coeur d'Alene Field Office, 3815 Schreiber Way, Coeur d'Alene, ID 83815; (208) 769-5000
Special considerations: Don't leave valuables in your car at this trailhead The rock outcrop next to the Bluebird Viewpoint presents a fall hazard especially during wet weather. If you have children along, keep a close watch on them here.

Finding the trailhead: From Coeur d'Alene, drive 10 miles east on I-90 to exit 22. Take SH 97 south and west from I-90 for 2.2 miles. The Mineral Ridge Trailhead is on the left side of SH 97. There is parking for about fifteen cars and restrooms at the trailhead. The elevation at the trailhead is 2,150 feet. GPS: N47 36.920' / W116 40.713'

Take the time to read the reader board that is next to the parking area and pick up a *Mineral Ridge Trail Guide* booklet. Then climb the steps and follow the trail, heading to the west. The route quickly makes three climbing switchbacks before reaching a trail junction. This junction is the beginning of the loop portion of the hike. Hike nearly straight ahead to the east, beneath the forest canopy of ponderosa pine (*Pinus ponderosa*) and Douglas fir (*Pseudotsuga menziesii*) trees. Continuing to climb, the route makes a couple more switchbacks. Two-tenths of a mile after starting the loop, the tread crosses an abandoned roadbed.

A sign next to the trail reads "RADIO ELEVATION 2,705" 0.25 mile farther along. The sign refers to the Radio Mining Company, which had some underground tunnels in the area, rather than anything to do with radios or your present elevation.

You will reach a junction with a spur trail to the left 0.2 mile after passing the RADIO sign. The spur trail leads to an abandoned prospect. This junction is 0.9 mile from the trailhead and you have climbed to 2,550 feet elevation. A sign at the junction states that it's 400 feet to the abandoned prospect, however, it is really slightly farther than that. For a short side trip, follow the spur trail to the

Prospect Hole

prospect hole. Once you have checked out the diggings, and maybe sat on the bench beside them and took in the view, return to the main trail. Then turn left and continue your hike up Mineral Ridge.

The route reaches the 2,780-foot-high ridgeline of Mineral Ridge slightly over 0.4 mile farther along. On the ridge you will find a water fountain and the junction with the Wilson Trail. To the right the Wilson Trail and its continuation, the Lost Man Trail, connect the Mineral Ridge National Recreation Trail with the Lost Man Trailhead on Elk Mountain Road (FR 1575) atop Mineral Ridge. These trails make an excellent 1.6-mile (1 to 1.5 hours) out-and-back side trip from the Mineral Ridge Trail.

To make this side trip, turn right at the junction onto the Wilson Trail. This part of the Wilson Trail was once a road and is still shown as such on some maps. The old roadbed is reverting nicely to a trail. In a little less than 0.2 mile, the route bears slightly to the left, leaving the ridgeline and the abandoned roadbed. For the next 0.2 mile, the track traverses the steep semi-open slope to Bluebird Viewpoint and the junction with the Lost Man Trail. Bluebird Viewpoint, which is 20 feet to the left at the junction, is the end of the Wilson Trail. The elevation at the Bluebird Viewpoint is approximately 2,900 feet.

Caribou Cabin

A bench at the viewpoint makes this a great place to spend a few minutes and enjoy the view. Just past the bench is a rock outcrop that hikers often step up on to get a slightly better view. If you step up onto this rock, be very careful as the rock can be slippery, especially when it's wet, and there is some exposure to the north and east. A fall could be serious. If you have children (of any age) along, watch them carefully here.

Once you are finished admiring the view, step back to the junction and turn left. You are now on the Lost Man Trail, which climbs fairly steeply to the south. The course makes three switchbacks as you climb the 120 vertical feet to the Silver Wave Viewpoint. There is a bench here and a good view to the east and the north. After passing the Silver Wave Viewpoint, the trail makes six more switchbacks and climbs nearly 200 more feet to the Lost Man Trailhead on Elk Mountain Road. This trailhead, at 3,180 feet elevation, is 2.3 miles from the Mineral Ridge Trailhead. This is your turnaround point (Unless you have arranged for a high-clearance-vehicle shuttle to this trailhead. See the options below), so retrace your steps for 0.8 mile back to the junction with the Mineral Ridge Trail.

Bear right (nearly straight ahead) at the junction and walk a short distance west to the Caribou Cabin. Check out the cabin and the view to the north, then continue your hike by heading west along the ridgeline. The trail reaches the Gray Wolf Viewpoint in a little over 0.3 mile. Gray Wolf Viewpoint offers an excellent view of Lake Coeur d'Alene. Continue down the ridge from the Gray Wolf Viewpoint. The Silver Tip Viewpoint 0.25 mile farther west along the trail offers an even better view of Lake Coeur d'Alene.

The route begins to descend fairly steeply once you are past the Silver Tip Viewpoint. You leave the ridgeline of Mineral Ridge and make eleven switchbacks in the next 0.8 mile. You also lose a little over 500 feet of elevation in that distance before you reach the junction ending the loop. At the junction turn right and retrace your steps for the 0.2 mile back to the Mineral Ridge Trailhead.

MILES AND DIRECTIONS

0.0 Leaving the trailhead, climb the steps, then head west.

0.2 Bear right at a trail junction and start the loop.

0.9 Turn left at a junction and head for the abandoned prospect.

1.0 Turn around after inspecting the prospect.

1.1 Return to the main trail and turn left.

1.5 Turn right at the junction onto the Wilson Trail.

1.9 At the Bluebird Viewpoint, head south on the Lost Man Trail.

Mineral Ridge Trail System

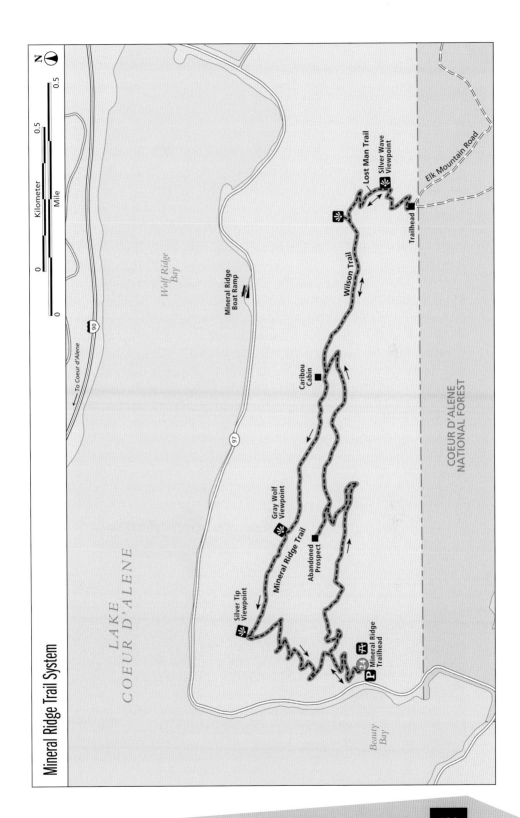

N

Kilometer
0   0.5   0.5

Mile
0

LAKE COEUR D'ALENE

Wolf Ridge Bay

Beauty Bay

To Coeur d'Alene

90

97

Mineral Ridge Boat Ramp

Gray Wolf Viewpoint

Silver Tip Viewpoint

Mineral Ridge Trail

Abandoned Prospect

Caribou Cabin

Mineral Ridge Trailhead

P   24

Wilson Trail

Lost Man Trail

Silver Wave Viewpoint

Trailhead

Elk Mountain Road

COEUR D'ALENE NATIONAL FOREST

2.3 Turn around at the Lost Man Trailhead.

3.1 Return to the Mineral Ridge Trail, bear right, and hike west.

3.4 Pass the Gray Wolf Viewpoint.

4.2 Reach the trail junction that ends the loop and turn right.

4.4 Arrive back at the Mineral Ridge Trailhead.

Options

To make this a shorter (2.8-mile) loop, turn left at the junction with the Wilson Trail 1.5 miles into the hike. From there continue on the Mineral Ridge Trail back to the trailhead.

If you wish, you could make this a one-way 2.3-mile uphill hike (requiring a vehicle shuttle) to the Lost Man Trailhead. To make the vehicle shuttle to that trailhead from the Mineral Ridge Trailhead, drive 0.2 mile farther south on SH 97. Turn left off SH 97 onto FR 438 and go 0.4 mile to the junction with FR 1575 (Elk Mountain Road). Turn left on Elk Mountain Road and drive approximately 3.8 miles to the unmarked trailhead. The trailhead is at the point where Elk Mountain Road crosses Mineral Ridge. There is a wide parking area at the trailhead but no other facilities and at present no sign. The elevation at the trailhead is 3,180 feet, and the GPS coordinates are N47 36.805' /W116 39.427'. A GPS receiver may be a big help with finding this out-of-the-way trailhead. FR 1575 is often deeply rutted—a high-clearance vehicle will probably be necessary to reach this trailhead safely.

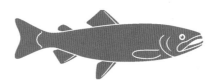

🌿 Green Tip:
*When you just have to go, dig a hole 6–8 inches deep
and at least 200 feet from water, camps, and trails.
Carry a zip-lock bag to carry out toilet paper, or use
a natural substitute such as leaves instead (but not poison
ivy!!!). Fill in the hole with soil and other natural
materials when you're done.*

Mount Coeur d'Alene

TRAIL 79

Make the fairly strenuous climb up Caribou Ridge on the Caribou Ridge National Recreation Trail, passing several viewpoints along the way. At 4.6 miles from the Beauty Creek Campground and Trailhead, the route crosses FR 439 and passes Mount Coeur d'Alene Picnic Area and Trailhead. Then you continue to climb another 0.8 mile on the Mount Coeur d'Alene Trail through the mountain forest to a cabin at the summit of Mount Coeur d'Alene. The lower 2.6 miles of this trail is generally rougher, rockier, narrower, and steeper than is the rest of the course.

Start: Beauty Creek Campground and Trailhead

Distance: 10.9-mile out-and-back day hike or backpack

Hiking time: About 6 to 7.5 hours round-trip

Difficulty: Strenuous

Best seasons: Summer and early fall

Canine compatibility / other trail users: Dogs are permitted but must be under control. The route is open to hikers only up to the junction with Trail 227 (5.1 miles from the Beauty Creek Trailhead and 0.5 mile from the Mount Coeur d'Alene Picnic Area and Trailhead). Above there, horses are allowed, as are 2-wheeled vehicles at certain times of the year.

Fees and permits: None

Maps: *Coeur d'Alene Mountain* USGS quad covers the area. Montana Mapping & GPS LLC's Hunting and GPS maps on CD-ROM and the National Geographic *Idaho* topo on CD-ROM cover the area but show this trail somewhat inaccurately, as does the USDA Forest Service *Idaho Panhandle / Coeur d'Alene National Forest Map.* The Forest Service map is very small-scale and not very good as a hiking map.

Trail contact: USDA Forest Service, Idaho Panhandle National Forests, Coeur d'Alene River Ranger District, Fernan Office, 2502 E. Sherman Ave., Coeur d'Alene, ID 83814; (208) 664-2318

Special considerations: There is some exposure in places so children must be kept well under control. There is no water available except at the Beauty Creek Campground and the Mount Coeur d'Alene Picnic Area and Trailhead.

THE HIKE

This hike to the summit of Mount Coeur d'Alene starts on the Caribou Ridge National Recreation Trail 79. Leaving the trailhead, hike south across the grassy creek bottom. As you leave the bottomland, the track begins to climb. The route soon makes a switchback to the left as you climb the slope through a forest of Douglas fir (*Pseudotsuga menziesii*) and western red cedar (*Thuja plicata*). The trail makes another switchback, this one to the right about 0.3 mile into the hike. At 2,400 feet elevation and 0.5 mile from the trailhead, there is a view of the Beauty Creek Valley through the trees. At 0.1 mile farther along, the tread makes a switchback to the left, where there is a good view of Beauty Bay (an arm of Lake Coeur d'Alene). There is another switchback 0.5 mile farther up the trail. The course is fairly narrow in places and somewhat exposed in this area.

The route makes a steep switchback to the left 1.8 miles into the hike. A path goes straight ahead to the southwest here, but don't take it. After you make the switchback, it's 0.2 mile more to the Beauty Creek Overlook. There is a good view of Beauty Creek Valley here, but no sign to mark the overlook. You have climbed to 2,950 feet elevation by the time you reach the Beauty Creek Overlook.

You will reach a junction with an abandoned four-wheel-drive road 0.6 mile after passing the overlook. Like the overlook, there are no signs at this junction. At the junction you have climbed to 3,160 feet elevation and are 2.6 miles from the trailhead.

Turn left on the abandoned four-wheel-drive road and continue to climb up Caribou Ridge. Soon the roadbed disappears and you are back on a trail. As you ascend, the track makes several more switchbacks. You will reach another trail junction 0.9 mile further up the ridge. Bear to the right here, staying on the main trail. There is no sign at this junction either. A few yards farther along, turn around and look back at the junction to make a mental note of what it will look like coming back down. It would be fairly easy here to take the wrong trail on the return trip. The course bears right off the ridgeline 4.2 miles from the Beauty Bay Trailhead (0.8 mile above the last trail junction). You now head west for 0.4 mile, crossing the forested slope, to the junction with FR 439 at the Mount Coeur d'Alene Picnic Area and Trailhead. At the Mount Coeur d'Alene Picnic Area and Trailhead, you have climbed to 4,030 feet elevation.

To continue your hike to the summit of Mount Coeur d'Alene, angle to the right (west) as you cross FR 439 and pick up the trail on the other side of the road. After crossing the road, Trail 79, which is now the Mount Coeur d'Alene Trail, heads west-southwest. At 0.2 mile from the Mount Coeur d'Alene Picnic Area and Trailhead, you make a sweeping turn to the left and head southeast. The track climbs gently and passes a few western white pines (*Pinus monticola*) mixed in with the other conifers. A little over 0.5 mile from the Mount Coeur d'Alene Picnic Area and Trailhead, you reach the junction with Trail 227, at 4,260 feet elevation.

Bear left at the junction and climb gently to the east. Slightly less than 0.3 mile from the junction with Trail 227, you come to a junction with a four-wheel-drive road. The summit cabin is a short distance to the right on the road. The metal skin of the cabin has shotgun holes through it and it's in generally poor condition. At the summit cabin you are slightly more than 5.4 miles from the Beauty Creek Trailhead, at 4,398 feet elevation. This is you turnaround point so retrace your steps back to the trailhead.

Mount Coeur d'Alene Cabin

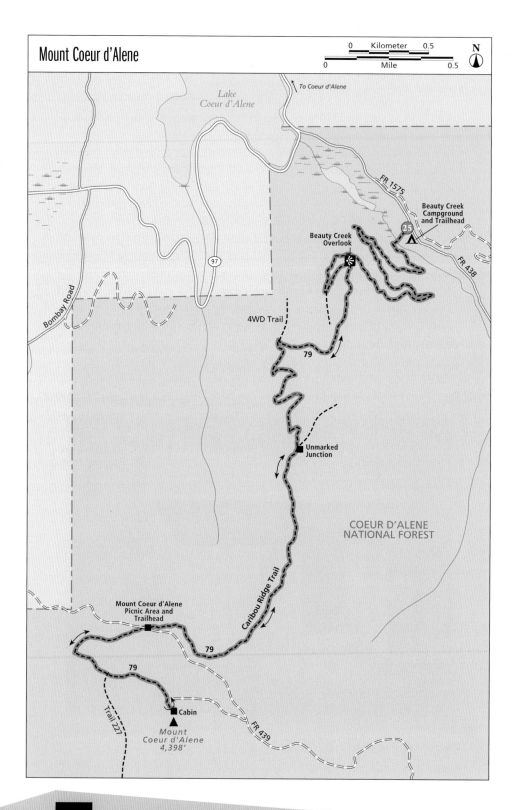

0   Kilometer   0.5

0   Mile   0.5

N

*Lake
Coeur d'Alene*

To Coeur d'Alene

FR 1575

Beauty Creek
Campground
and Trailhead

25

Beauty Creek
Overlook

FR 438

97

4WD Trail

79

Bombay Road

Unmarked
Junction

COEUR D'ALENE
NATIONAL FOREST

Caribou Ridge Trail

Mount Coeur d'Alene
Picnic Area and
Trailhead

79

79

Trail 221

Cabin

FR 439

*Mount
Coeur d'Alene
4,398'*

0.0 Hike southwest from the trailhead.

2.6 Turn left at a junction with a four-wheel-drive road.

4.6 Angle right (west) across FR 439.

5.1 Bear left at the junction with Trail 227.

5.4 Reach the summit of Mount Coeur d'Alene and turn around.

10.9 Arrive back at the Beauty Creek Campground and Trailhead.

Options

The hike to the summit of Mount Coeur d'Alene can be shortened to 1.6 miles round-trip by driving to the Mount Coeur d'Alene Trailhead and Picnic Area. This is a much easier way to reach the summit but not nearly as much fun or exercise.

To reach the Mount Coeur d'Alene Picnic Area and Trailhead from the Beauty Creek Campground and Trailhead, go back out to FR 438 and turn right (southeast). Follow FR 438 for 3.8 miles to the junction with FR 453. Turn right on FR 453 and drive 2.4 miles to the end of the pavement and the junction with FR 439. Turn right on FR 439 and go 2.3 miles to the trailhead. Be sure to bear right 0.1 mile after leaving FR 453 and stay on FR 439. The other road looks better here than does FR 439. FR 439 is a dirt road and it's a little rough and rutted in places, but it can generally be navigated with a standard passenger car with a little caution. A high-clearance vehicle makes it much easier. There is somewhat limited parking, water, and a restroom at the Mount Coeur d'Alene Picnic Area and Trailhead.

Green Tip:
If at all possible, camp in established sites. If there are none, then camp in an unobtrusive area at least 200 feet (70 paces) from the nearest water source.

Bald eagle overlooking Lake Pend Oreille

About 23 miles northeast of Coeur d'Alene, on the shore of beautiful Lake Pend Oreille, is Farragut State Park. The 4,000 acres of land that is now the park was a World War II–era military base. The park has an extensive trail system, much of which follows roadbeds that were once traversed by rumbling military jeeps and equipment. The routes in Farragut State Park that are covered here are all south of SH 54 and are open to pedestrian and bicycle traffic only, with no horses or motorized vehicles allowed.

Hike 26 is really a trail system that connects the visitor center with the town of Bayview. It also connects with all the other trails in Farragut State Park that are covered here. Hike 27 is a self-guided nature trail through widely varied woodland. Hikes 28 and 29 climb south of the state park on easements across timber company land to ridgetop viewpoints overlooking the deep-blue waters of Lake

Pend Oreille. Hikes 30, 31, and 32 are loops that are close to the lake's shoreline. South of Farragut State Park on national forest land, Hike 33 leads to open summits with great views. All of the hikes in Farragut State Park interconnect.

Just south of Fourth of July Pass, 16 miles east of Coeur d'Alene, hikes 34 and 35 traverse heavily wooded terrain where moose are fairly common. These routes are also used as cross-country-ski trails during the winter season.

Thimbleberry, Hike 29

Lynx Trail

More than just a single trail, the Lynx Trail is a system of trails that link most points in the southern part of Farragut State Park. The description here is of the main loop of the Lynx Trail system. Some of the connecting trails are covered in the options. All of the trails in Farragut that are described in this book interconnect.

Start: Farragut State Park Visitor Center

Distance: 6.3-mile lollipop-loop day hike

Hiking time: About 3 hours

Difficulty: Easy

Best seasons: Spring, summer, and fall. Parts of this route are also groomed for cross-country skiing during the winter.

Canine compatibility / other trail users: The Lynx Trail is open to pedestrians and cyclists only. Dogs must be on a leash.

Fees and permits: Day-use permit or annual pass, purchased at the visitor center. A camping permit no longer covers day-use parking.

Maps: The *Farragut State Park Trail Guide* available at the visitor center is adequate for hiking the trails within the park.

Trail contact: Farragut State Park, 13550 E. Highway 54, Athol, ID 83801; (208) 683-2425; www.parksandrecreation.idaho.gov (state parks link; Farragut); far@idpr.idaho.gov

Special considerations: Most of the trail junctions in Farragut State Park are marked with numbers on guideposts. These numbers correspond with the numbers on the *Farragut State Park Trail Guide* map.

Finding the trailhead: From I-90 (exit 12) in Coeur d'Alene, drive north on US 95 for 18.7 miles to the junction with SH 54 in Athol. Turn right (east) on SH 54 and go 4.5 miles to the Farragut State Park Visitor Center. There is plenty of parking and restrooms at the visitor center. The trailhead is on the northeast side of the visitor center. The elevation at the visitor center is 2,410 feet. GPS: N47 57.105' / W116 36.153'

THE HIKE

Hike east from the Farragut State Park Visitor Center and in a bit less than 0.2 mile, reach the junction with Ranger Road. Turn left on Ranger Road, and walk a few yards to the junction with Residence Road. Cross Residence Road and continue east on the Lynx Trail. In 0.2 mile there is a trail junction. Turn right, following the Lynx Trail. Turn left at another junction in 0.1 mile and quickly turn left again at another junction, staying on the main trail. A short distance more brings you to Junction #42, slightly over 0.5 mile from the visitor center. Hike straight ahead (northeast) at Junction #42 and reach Junction #43 in 0.1 mile. Junction #43 is very close to the Highpoint Trailhead. Hike straight ahead at Junction #43, continuing northeast.

The wide gravel roadbed that is the Lynx Trail here parallels South Road through the young forest for almost 0.5 mile to Junction #64. Turn left, then quickly turn right at another junction and continue to parallel South Road, heading northeast. The Lynx Trail crosses the access road to Squirrel Cache Trailhead in 0.3 mile, and in another 0.3 mile it crosses the Gilmore Campground access road. About 0.1 mile past the Gilmore Campground access road, the trail begins

Bernard Peak above the Lynx Trail

to veer away from South Road and soon crosses Buttonhook Road. Junction #96 is 100 yards south of the crossing point on the Buttonhook Road. Just after crossing Buttonhook Road, the track passes beneath some power lines.

Beaver Bay Road is crossed 0.2 mile after crossing the Buttonhook Road. The route then follows power lines through the woods, still heading northeast for 0.6 mile to the junction with the trail leading to the Whitetail Campground, which is located to the right (see options below). At this junction you are 2.7 miles from the visitor center.

Hike straight ahead (east) at the junction and reach the Whitetail Campground access road in 0.25 mile. The route crosses Boat Launch Road 0.1 mile farther along. Just after crossing Boat Launch Road, turn left at a trail junction and angle across South Road to the Snowberry Campground access road. Straight ahead (east), this junction leads to the Sunrise Day Use Area (see options below). Head north along the access road and quickly reach Junction #82. Continue north past Junction #82, then bear left (really straight ahead), leaving the paved roadway, at the extra vehicle parking area. The broad gravel trail continues north for a short distance then turns to the left, soon paralleling Locust Grove Road as you hike west. At this point you are in the disc golf course.

In 0.3 mile the track reaches another trail junction. The signs say that the Lynx Trail goes all ways at this junction. Hike straight ahead to the west. In a little over 0.1 mile the trail crosses Kinglet Road. Bennion East Trailhead and parking is at the crossing. Junction #89 is reached a little less than 0.2 mile past Bennion East Trailhead along the wide, paved trail. See the options below. Hike straight ahead at Junction #89, heading west, and pass a grove of young western white pines (*Pinus monticola*). In 0.3 mile you'll reach the junction with the Bennion Historic Trail. Straight ahead to the southeast, the Bennion Historic Trail reaches a trailhead on South Road in a little less than 0.2 mile. Turn right at the junction, leaving the pavement, and hike west through the young lodgepole pines (*Pinus contorta*). In a little more than 0.5 mile, the route crosses Brig Road. At the junction with Brig Road, you are 4.6 miles into this loop hike.

The course turns south as you cross a paved road 0.2 mile farther along. You'll soon come to Waldron Campground on the right. As you reach the south side of the campground, the trail turns right and heads southwest to another trail junction. Hike west at the junction, crossing the Waldron Campground access road at Junction #65. Continue west and southwest from Junction #65, through the young pines. In 0.7 mile the trail crosses South Road. After crossing South Road walk a short distance south-southwest on Ranger Road. Then turn right on the Lynx Trail and hike west for a little less than 0.2 mile, retracing your steps to the visitor center.

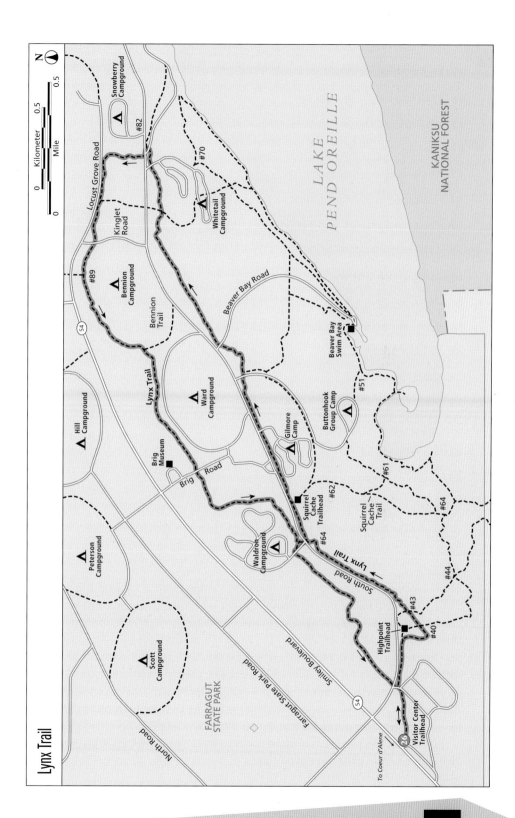

Lynx Trail

MILES AND DIRECTIONS

0.0 Hike east from visitor center.

0.5 Hike straight ahead at Junction #42.

0.6 Hike northeast from Junction #43.

1.1 Turn left at Junction #64.

1.4 Cross the Squirrel Cache Trailhead access road.

1.7 Cross the Gilmore Campground Access Road.

1.9 Cross Buttonhook Road.

2.1 Cross Beaver Bay Road.

2.7 At the junction with the side trail to Whitetail Campground, hike east.

3.0 Turn left next to Boat Launch Road and cross South Road.

3.1 Pass Junction #82.

3.6 Cross Kinglet Road.

3.8 Hike straight ahead at Junction #89.

4.1 Turn right at the junction with the Bennion Historic Trail.

4.6 Cross Brig Road.

5.4 Cross the Waldron Campground access road at Junction #65.

6.1 Cross South Road.

6.3 Arrive back at the visitor center.

Options

At the junction with the side trail to Whitetail Campground, 2.7 miles from the visitor center, the trail to the right (south) reaches the campground in 0.2 mile. At the east end of the campground, the route connects with Beaver Bay Shoreline Loop (Hike 30).

To the left (north) at the same junction, the side trail reaches the north side of the Lynx Trail Loop in 0.4 mile. This side trail could be used to shorten the loop hike.

At the junction next to Boat Launch Road, 3 miles from the visitor center, the trail that goes straight ahead (east) leads to the Sunrise Day-Use Area in about 0.6 mile. From the day-use area, you can access the Willow Lakeview Loop (Hike 32).

From Junction #89, the trail to the north connects the main loop of the Lynx Trail with the town of Bayview in 0.7 mile.

Squirrel Cache Trail

Hike through mostly young to medium-age forest on a self-guided nature trail. This is a good hike on which to take small children as it's fairly short and there are interesting trees and a rock formation.

Start: Squirrel Cache Trailhead
Distance: 1.5-mile lollipop loop
Hiking time: About 1 hour
Difficulty: Easy
Best seasons: Late spring, summer, and early fall
Canine compatibility / other trail users: Pets must be on a leash at all times. As with all the trails in Farragut State Park south of SH 54, this trail is open to pedestrian and bicycle traffic only.
Fees and permits: Day-use permit or annual pass, purchased at the visitor center. A camping permit no longer covers day-use parking.

Maps: *Farragut State Park Trail Guide* available at the visitor center is adequate for hiking most of the trails within the park. Most of the trail junctions in Farragut State Park are marked with numbers on guideposts. These numbers correspond with the numbers on the *Farragut State Park Trail Guide* map.
Trail contact: Farragut State Park, 13550 E. Highway 54, Athol, ID 83801; (208) 683-2425; www.parks andrecreation.idaho.gov (state parks link; Farragut); far@idpr .idaho.gov

Finding the trailhead: From I-90 (exit 12) in Coeur d'Alene, drive north on US 95 for 18.7 miles to the junction with SH 54 in Athol. Turn right (east) on SH 54 and go 4.6 miles to the junction with South Road. The junction is just past (east of) the Farragut State Park Visitor Center. Turn right on South Road and drive 1.1 miles to the Squirrel Cache Trailhead, which is on the right. The elevation at the trailhead is 2,310 feet. GPS: N47 57.466' / W116 34.961'

S tart the Squirrel Cache Trail by hiking southeast from the trailhead on a blocked but paved roadway. Quickly pass a trail junction; continue on the paved roadway, heading southeast. A trail shelter and sign on the right, 0.1 mile from the trailhead, mark Junction #68, where you leave the paved roadway. Turn right at the junction and head south on the well-maintained trail, through the forest of Douglas fir (*Pseudotsuga menziesii*) and grand fir (*Abies grandis*).

The trail forks at Junction #62, 0.1 mile after leaving the pavement. Bear right here and start the loop portion of the Squirrel Cache Trail. Hike south-southwest, passing a bench in 0.1 mile and reaching Junction #63 in another 0.4 mile. At Junction #63 a short trail to the right leads to a junction with the Highpoint Trail in about 60 yards. Turn left (east then northeast) at this junction to continue on the Squirrel Cache Trail. Between Junctions #63 and #61, the Squirrel Cache Trail and the Buttonhook Bay Trail follow the same route.

In a little less than 0.2 mile, there are signs on several large trees identifying them. The species include western white pine (*Pinus monticola*), western red cedar (*Thuja plicata*), western larch (*Larix occidentalis*; aka tamarack), western hemlock (*Tsuga heterophylla*), and Douglas fir.

Trail shelter along Squirrel Cache Trail

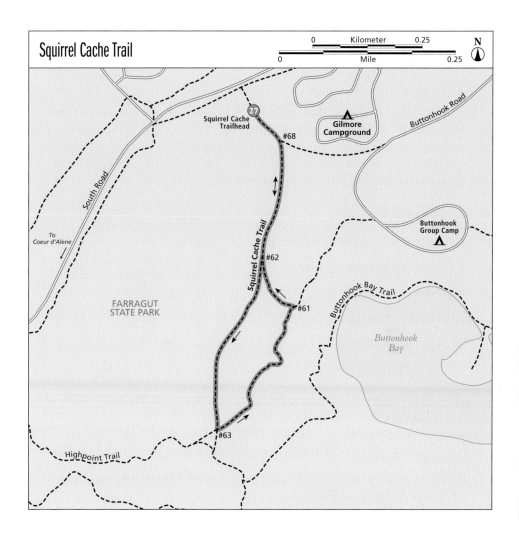

0   Kilometer   0.25
0   Mile   0.25

N

Squirrel Cache
Trailhead

#68

Gilmore
Campground

Buttonhook Road

Buttonhook
Group Camp

South Road

To
Coeur d'Alene

Squirrel Cache Trail

#62

#61

Buttonhook Bay Trail

FARRAGUT
STATE PARK

Buttonhook
Bay

#63

Highpoint Trail

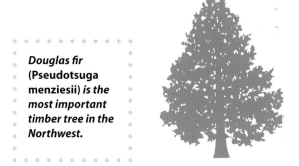

Douglas fir
(Pseudotsuga
menziesii) *is the*
most important
timber tree in the
Northwest.

At 0.1 mile farther along, the course reaches Peek Hole Rock. The rock is on the left with an explanatory sign on the right. Shortly after passing Peek Hole Rock, Lake Pend Oreille comes into view through the trees to the right. A little farther along is an informational sign, next to a bench overlooking the lake. A few more yards brings you to Junction #61. Turn left at Junction #61 and climb gently to the northwest, passing an informational sign about woodpeckers. In 0.25 mile you will reach Junction #62 and end the loop portion of the hike. Turn right and retrace your steps for 0.2 mile to the Squirrel Cache Trailhead.

MILES AND DIRECTIONS

0.0 Begin at the Squirrel Cache Trailhead.

0.1 Turn right at the trail shelter.

0.2 Bear right to start loop.

0.7 Turn left at the trail junction #63.

0.9 Pass Peek Hole Rock.

1.0 Turn left at Junction #61.

1.3 Turn right at Junction #62, ending the loop.

1.5 Arrive back at the Squirrel Cache Trailhead.

Options
To make a longer and more challenging loop, combine this trail with the southern part of the Highpoint Trail (Hike 29).

Peek Hole Rock

Bernard Peak / Scout Trail

The Scout Trail to Bernard Peak is one of the longest described in this book. With great viewpoints along the way, this challenging trip climbs through richly diverse coni-fer forest nearly all the way to the 5,150-foot-high summit of Bernard Peak. Grouse and white-tailed deer are common and often found along this route. There is also a chance of seeing a bear as I did when I last made this hike.

Start: Highpoint Trailhead

Distance: 17.4-mile out-and-back day hike, including the short side trip to a lake viewpoint

Hiking time: About 8 to 10 hours

Difficulty: Strenuous, because of distance and total elevation gain. Most trail grades are moderate.

Best seasons: Summer and early fall

Canine compatibility / other trail users: Pets must be on a leash at all times. This trail is open to pedestrian and bicycle traffic only.

Fees and permits: Day-use permit or annual pass, purchased at the visitor center. A camping permit no longer covers day-use parking.

Maps: Montana Mapping & GPS LLC's Hunting and GPS maps are good topos of the area as is the National Geographic *Idaho* topo on CD-ROM. However, both show this trail somewhat inaccurately, as does the USDA Forest Service *Idaho Panhandle/ Coeur d'Alene National Forest Map.* The Forest Service map is very small-scale for hiking purposes. *Farragut State Park Trail Guide,* available at the visitor center, covers this trail.

Trail contact: Farragut State Park, 13550 E. Highway 54, Athol, ID 83801; (208) 683-2425; www.parks andrecreation.idaho.gov (state parks link; Farragut); far@idpr .idaho.gov

Special considerations: Note the yellow arrows that mark this route at many but not all junctions. A portion of this trail follows an easement through private land— please stay on the trail. This is a long hike with a total elevation gain and loss of over 3,000 feet. Be sure the entire party is up to it.

Finding the trailhead: From I-90 (exit 12) in Coeur d'Alene, drive north on US 95 for 18.7 miles to the junction with SH 54 in Athol. Turn right (east) on SH 54 and go 4.6 miles to the junction with South Road. The junction is just past (east of) the Farragut State Park Visitor Center, where you need to stop and purchase a day-use or annual pass. Turn right on South Road and drive 0.4 mile to the Highpoint Trailhead, which is on the right. The elevation at the trailhead is 2,400 feet. GPS: N47 57.110' / W116 35.537'

THE HIKE

Walk a few feet south from the trailhead and turn right (west). Shortly you will reach Junction #49. Turn left at Junction #49 and head south, through the young conifer forest, which is quite dense in spots. In about 0.2 mile the trail turns east, and 0.5 mile from the trailhead you reach Junction #45. Turn right at Junction #45 and head southeast for another 0.2 mile to Junction #40. Bear right (nearly straight ahead) at Junction #40 and pass through a gate, leaving Farragut State Park.

Just past the gate there is another junction, where you will turn left. Now the route, which has not gained or lost much elevation so far, begins to climb. Yellow arrows now mark the sometimes rough and rocky course. Junction #37 is reached at about 2,640 feet elevation, 0.6 mile after passing through the gate. This is the last numbered junction along this route. At this junction the rough route to the Highpoint Viewpoint is to the left. Bear right at the junction and continue the climb toward Bernard Peak, passing a signboard about forest resource management.

The track tops a rise 0.25 mile from Junction #37. Then you descend slightly to pass a pond, before climbing between some rock outcrops. The route reaches another junction 0.8 mile from Junction #37. Turn left here, following the yellow arrow, and descend about 150 vertical feet, where the trail flattens out again. Soon the course begins to climb gently again, through the mixed forest, which now includes some western red cedars (*Thuja plicata*).

At 1.4 miles from Junction #37 and 2.7 miles from the trailhead, the route turns left on a dirt roadbed. A yellow arrow points the way here. In a short distance you cross a small stream and reach the junction with the side trail to a lake viewpoint. Hike straight ahead here for a little less than 0.1 mile to the viewpoint, at 2,820 feet elevation. The view includes Lake Pend Oreille, Idaho's largest and deepest lake. When you are finished admiring the view, return to the junction and turn left (east).

The route continues to climb to the east after leaving the junction with the side trail to the lake viewpoint, topping a rise in 0.3 mile. Then you descend for a short distance to a saddle, at 3,000 feet elevation. A dirt road leads right from the saddle; don't take it. There is another path to the right 0.1 mile past the saddle. Hike straight ahead here to the southeast. In another 0.2 mile you will reach the junction with the Twete Road Trail (bike). Turn left and head southeast, crossing a small creek lined with cedars in 0.3 mile. The route continues to climb and crosses another creek 0.4 mile farther along. This creek crossing is 4.4 miles from the Highpoint Trailhead.

The tread climbs, soon making a switchback to the right. Ahead 0.2 mile the track crosses another small stream, which flows beneath it in a culvert. Shortly after crossing the creek, you pass mile marker 4.8. The course makes a switchback to the left 0.4 mile farther along, and another 0.8 mile brings you to a switchback to the right. At this switchback there is a path that leads a few yards to the left to a viewpoint overlooking Lake Pend Oreille and the town of Bayview. The elevation at this viewpoint is about 4,100 feet and you are 6 miles from the Highpoint Trailhead.

Lake Pend Oreille from viewpoint

Bernard Peak / Scout Trail

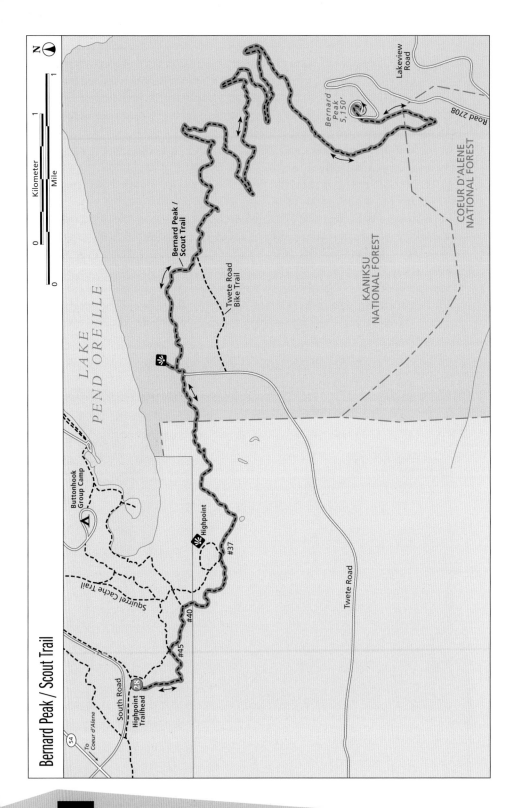

Past this viewpoint the route continues to climb through the forest. The track makes three more long switchbacks before crossing a road, at 5,080 feet elevation, 2.7 miles above the viewpoint. Once across the road the tread climbs steeply for a little less than 0.1 mile to a flat area with a campsite near the summit of Bernard Peak. The road also reaches this site.

To reach the very top, turn right at the campsite and walk a short distance to the summit and the concrete blocks that were once the foundation for a lookout tower. At the 5,150-foot-high summit, you are 8.8 miles into this hike, including the side trip to the lake viewpoint. Across the campsite area to the north is another set of foundation blocks. Trees generally obstruct the view from the summit area. After spending some time exploring the summit area, retrace your route back to the Highpoint Trailhead, saving about 0.2 mile by not taking the side trail to the lake viewpoint.

MILES AND DIRECTIONS

0.0   Hike south and west from Highpoint Trailhead.

0.5   Turn right at Junction #45.

0.7   Bear right at Junction #40.

1.3   Bear right at Junction #37.

2.8   Turn around and return to the main trail from the lake viewpoint.

8.8   Turn around at the summit of Bernard Peak.

17.4 Arrive back at the Highpoint Trailhead.

Highpoint Trail

Hike to Highpoint Viewpoint overlooking Buttonhook Bay at the southwest end of spectacular Lake Pend Oreille. Watch for the many white-tailed deer that are common in this area.

Start: Highpoint Trailhead
Distance: 3.2-mile figure 8 loop day hike
Hiking time: About 1.5 to 2.5 hours
Difficulty: Strenuous
Best seasons: Late spring, summer, and fall
Canine compatibility / other trail users: Pets must be on a leash at all times. As with all the trails in Farragut State Park south of SH 54, this trail is open to pedestrian and bicycle traffic only.
Fees and permits: Day-use permit or annual pass, purchased at the visitor center. A camping permit no longer covers day-use parking.
Maps: *Farragut State Park Trail Guide* available at the visitor center covers this trail. Montana Mapping & GPS LLC's Hunting and GPS maps are good topos of the area as is the National Geographic *Idaho* topo on CD-ROM. However, both show this trail somewhat inaccurately, as does the USDA Forest Service *Idaho Panhandle / Coeur d'Alene National Forest Map.* The Forest Service map is very small-scale for hiking purposes.

Trail contact: Farragut State Park, 13550 E. Highway 54, Athol, ID 83801; (208) 683-2425; www.parks andrecreation.idaho.gov (state parks link; Farragut); far@idpr .idaho.gov
Special considerations: Unlike most places where trails are numbered, at Farragut State Park, most of the trail junctions are numbered and so marked on guideposts. These numbers correspond with the numbers on the *Farragut State Park Trail Guide* map. The 0.5-mile-long outer loop of this hike is very rough and steep. It contains one short scramble that may be quite difficult for many hikers. If this section seems to be too much for your party, return to Junction #37 and follow the southern side of the inner loop (part of the Bernard Peak / Scout Trail) back to the Highpoint Trailhead.

Finding the trailhead: From exit 12 on I-90 in Coeur d'Alene drive north on US 95 for 18.7 miles to the junction with SH 54 in Athol. Turn right (east) on SH 54 and go 4.6 miles to the junction with South Road. The junction is just past (east of) the Farragut State Park Visitor Center, where you need to stop and purchase a day-use or annual pass, if you don't already have one. Turn right on South Road and drive 0.4 mile to the Highpoint Trailhead, which is on the right. The elevation at the trailhead is 2,400 feet. GPS N47 57.110' / W116 35.537'

THE HIKE

The inner loop of this hike is in a clockwise direction and the outer loop is counterclockwise. Hike southeast from the trailhead, quickly crossing the Lynx Trail (roadbed) at Junction #43. Past Junction #43 the track continues south through the young forest of Douglas fir (*Pseudotsuga menziesii*), grand fir (*Abies grandis*), western larch (*Larix occidentalis*), western white pine (*Pinus monticola*), ponderosa pine (*Pinus ponderosa*), and lodgepole pine (*Pinus contorta*). Beneath the trees are Oregon grape (*Mahonia aquifolium*), ocean spray (*Holodiscus discolor*), and patches of bracken fern (*Pteridium aquilinum*). In 0.25 mile the route reaches Junction #44, where you bear left to head east.

You pass a few western red cedars (*Thuja plicata*) in the next 0.2 mile to Junction #48. To the left here is a short connector trail to Junction #63 and the Squirrel Cache Trail. Bear right (nearly straight ahead) to continue on the Highpoint Trail. In 0.1 mile you will reach Junction #47. Hike straight ahead here and cross a small wooden bridge over a tiny creek. Across the bridge the course climbs slightly and passes a patch of thimbleberry (*Rubus parviflorus*) bushes. Soon the route begins to climb more steeply and becomes rough and rocky in places. In 0.2 mile you will reach an unmarked trail junction where you turn left. You are now outside of Farragut State Park but still on state land.

The rough and steep track continues to climb. In a little less than 0.2 mile, there is another unmarked trail junction. Bear slightly left (nearly straight ahead) and hike a bit less than 0.2 mile to yet another unmarked trail junction. This junction, at 2,580 feet elevation and 1.1 miles from the Highpoint Trailhead, is the start of the outer loop of this hike. Turn right at this junction and hike southeast, crossing a ridgeline, and reach the Bernard Peak / Scout Trail in 0.1 mile.

Turn left on the Scout Trail and go a few yards to Junction #37. There is a sign at the junction pointing to Highpoint Viewpoint. Turn left at Junction #37 and climb the steep, rough, boulder-strewn trail. The next 0.1 mile is the most difficult part of this hike. If it seems to be too difficult for your party, turn around, return to Junction #37, and follow the southern side of the inner loop (part of the Bernard Peak / Scout Trail) back to the Highpoint Trailhead. The trail really becomes a vague scrambling route for a short distance, then moderates as you near the ridgeline about 0.2 mile northeast of Junction #37. At the ridgeline you are at 2,805 feet elevation and 1.5 miles from the Highpoint Trailhead.

Leaving the top of the ridge, the trail soon bends around to the west and descends to a viewpoint overlooking Buttonhook Bay, at the southwest end of Lake Pend Oreille. The viewpoint is at the end of a path, a few feet to the right of the trail. Continue to descend the very steep, rocky trail for a short distance past the viewpoint path to an unmarked trail junction. Bear left at this junction and descend a short distance farther to the unmarked junction where you started the outer loop.

Rough section of Highpoint Trail

Highpoint Trail

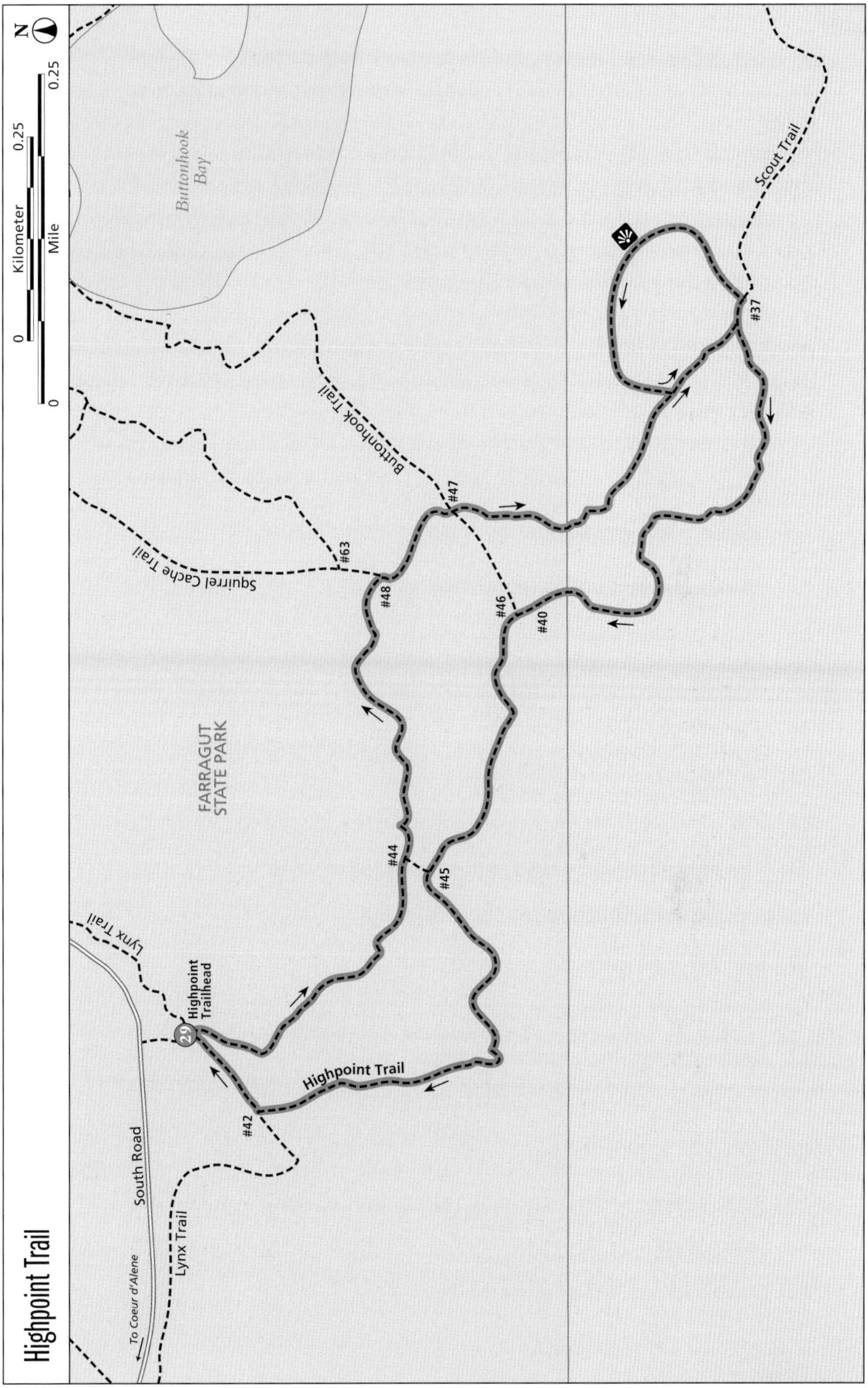

Buttonhook Bay

Buttonhook Trail

Squirrel Cache Trail

Scout Trail

FARRAGUT
STATE PARK

#37

#47

#63

#48

#46

#40

#44

#45

Highpoint
Trailhead

29

Highpoint Trail

#42

Lynx Trail

South Road

Lynx Trail

To Coeur d'Alene

Kilometer

Mile

0   0.25

N

Turn left at the junction and retrace your earlier steps for 0.1 mile to the junction with the Bernard Peak / Scout Trail. Turn right on the steep, rough, and rocky Scout Trail. In a little more than 0.1 mile, the track passes a small spring. Beyond the spring the trail is still rough but the grade moderates. In another 0.4 mile the route flattens out as you leave the sloping side hill. Soon you will cross a small stream and reach Junction #40 at 2,360 feet elevation. Turn right at Junction #40 and go through a gate to Junction #46, where you bear left. When you go through the gate, you reenter Farragut State Park.

From Junction #46, hike northwest for 0.3 mile to Junction #45. Turn left here and hike southwest, then west, before turning north-northwest toward Junction #42, which you will reach in a little less than 0.5 mile. Before reaching Junction #42, the timber begins to thin out. Watch for white-tailed deer, which are common along this section of the trail. Turn right at Junction #42 and reach Junction #43 in 0.1 mile. Turn left here and walk the last few feet to the Highpoint Trailhead.

MILES AND DIRECTIONS

0.0   Hike southeast from the Highpoint Trailhead.

0.3   Bear left at Junction #44.

0.5   Bear right at Junction #48.

0.6   Hike straight ahead at Junction #47.

0.8   Turn left at the unmarked trail junction.

1.0   Bear slightly left (nearly straight ahead) at the unmarked trail junction.

1.1   Turn right at the unmarked trail junction.

1.2   Turn left at the junction with the Scout Trail.

1.3   Turn left at Junction #37.

1.5   Pass Highpoint Viewpoint.

1.7   Turn left at the unmarked trail junction.

1.8   Turn right at the junction with the Scout Trail.

2.3   Turn right at Junction #40.

2.6   Turn left at Junction #45.

3.0   Turn right at Junction #42.

3.2   Arrive back at the Highpoint Trailhead.

Beaver Bay Shoreline Loop

Hike along the shoreline of Idlewilde Bay, which is part of beautiful Lake Pend Oreille.

Start: Trailhead at the northeast end of Whitetail Campground

Distance: 2.2-mile loop

Hiking time: About 1.5 hours

Difficulty: Easy

Best seasons: Late spring, summer, and early fall

Canine compatibility / other trail users: Pets must be on a leash at all times. As with all the trails in Farragut State Park south of SH 54, this trail is open to pedestrian and bicycle traffic only.

Fees and permits: Day-use permit or annual pass, purchased at the visitor center. A camping permit no longer covers day-use parking.

Maps: *Farragut State Park Trail Guide,* available at the visitor center,

is adequate for hiking most of the trails within the park. Montana Mapping & GPS LLC's Hunting and GPS maps are good topos of the area as are National Geographic maps on CD-ROM.

Trail contact: Farragut State Park, 13550 E. Highway 54, Athol, ID 83801; (208) 683-2425; www.parks andrecreation.idaho.gov (state parks link; Farragut); far@idpr .idaho.gov

Special considerations: Most but not all of the trail junctions in Farragut State Park are marked with numbers on guideposts. These numbers correspond with the numbers on the *Farragut State Park Trail Guide* map.

Finding the trailhead: From I-90 (exit 12) in Coeur d'Alene, drive north on US 95 for 18.7 miles to the junction with SH 54 in Athol. Turn right (east) on SH 54 and go 4.6 miles to the junction with South Road. The junction is just past (east of) the Farragut State Park Visitor Center. Turn right on South Road and drive 2.3 miles to the entrance for Whitetail Campground. Turn right and go 0.3 mile to the trailhead, which is on the right, at the east end of the south (lower) loop of the Whitetail Campground. The elevation at the trailhead is 2,180 feet, and there is parking for two or three cars. GPS: N47 57.831'/W116 33.349'

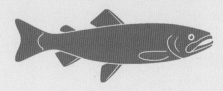

30

THE HIKE

H ike southeast from the trailhead for a short distance to a trail junction with the Beaver Bay Shoreline Loop at Junction #70. Turn right at the junction and begin the loop, heading southwest on the abandoned roadbed. The second-growth forest here is made up of medium-age trees, mostly Douglas fir (*Pseudotsuga menziesii*). Slightly less than 0.2 mile from the trailhead, Junction #56 is reached. To the right at the junction is the campground program area and to the left a trail descends to the trail along the lakeshore, which will be your return route. Hike straight ahead (southwest) at the junction with Lake Pend Oreille, visible through the trees to your left.

Lake Pend Oreille

In 0.3 mile you will pass Junction #57, and a little farther along, Junction #58. Hike straight ahead to the southwest at both of these junctions. Eight-tenths mile from the trailhead is Junction #59, very close to the east end of the Beaver Bay Beach parking area. Turn left at Junction #59, then quickly turn left again on the Shoreline Trail, at Junction #53. Junctions #59 and #53 are very close together, and this almost seems like you are making a U-turn.

Now the route heads northeast along the shoreline of Idlewilde Bay, which is part of Lake Pend Oreille. The course shortly bears slightly left at another junction, then follows a roadbed for 100 yards or so to Junction #54. This section of the route is a little rocky in spots as you follow the lakeshore northeast. Lupine, asters, and a few rosebushes brighten the trailside beneath the ponderosa pines (*Pinus ponderosa*) and Douglas firs. The track reaches an unmarked junction 0.3 mile from Junction #54. Hike straight ahead, continuing to the northeast along the sparkling lake, and reach Junction #55 in another 0.1 mile. Junction #55 is 1.4 miles into the hike and very close to the level of Lake Pend Oreille, at 2,060 feet elevation.

After a little over 0.5 mile more of hiking along the lake, and taking in the view across it, the trail reaches an unsigned junction (labeled #72 on *Farragut State Park Trail Guide* map). Bear left at this junction. (Another trail follows the lakeshore northeast. See options below.) Climb a short distance to Junction #71, which is not on the *Farragut State Park Trail Guide* map, but it is marked on the trail. Turn left again at Junction #71 and walk west for 0.25 mile to Junction #70, ending the loop. Turn right at Junction #70 and walk the short distance northwest to the trailhead.

MILES AND DIRECTIONS

0.0 Hike southeast from the trailhead. Then proceed southwest at Junction #70.

0.8 Turn left at Beaver Bay Beach parking area.

1.4 Pass Junction #55.

1.9 Turn left at Junction #71.

2.2 Arrive back at the trailhead.

🌿 Green Tip:
Avoid sensitive ecological areas. Hike, rest, and camp at least 200 feet from streams, lakes, and rivers.

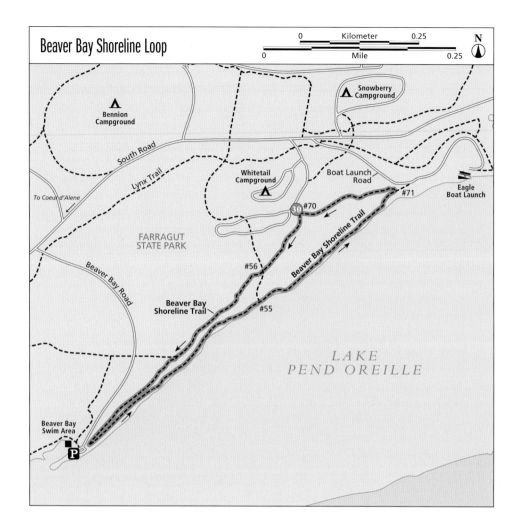

Options

Combine this route with the Buttonhook Bay Loop (Hike 31) at the Beaver Bay Beach parking area to lengthen the hike to 4.9 miles.

To add 1.4 miles to your hike, connect with the Willow Lakeview Loop (Hike 32) from the unsigned junction (labeled #72 on *Farragut State Park Trail Guide* map). Hike generally east for about 0.3 mile around the boat launch area to Junction #74 at the southwest end of the Willow Lakeview Loop. From here you can follow that loop for 0.8 mile back to Junction #74. Then retrace your route back to unsigned Junction #72 and continue on the Beaver Bay Shoreline Loop.

Buttonhook Bay Loop

Hike the shoreline of Lake Pend Oreille, passing the site of historic Pend Oreille City and around Buttonhook Bay. Then return through the second-growth transitional-zone forest, which abounds with white-tailed deer, passing Peek Hole Rock along the way.

Start: Beaver Bay Beach parking area

Distance: 2.7-mile lollipop-loop day hike

Hiking time: About 2 hours

Difficulty: Easy

Best seasons: Late spring, summer, and early fall

Canine compatibility / other trail users: Pets must be on a leash at all times. As with all the trails in Farragut State Park south of SH 54, this trail is open to pedestrian and bicycle traffic only.

Fees and permits: Day-use permit or annual pass, purchased at the visitor center. A camping permit no longer covers day-use parking.

Maps: *Farragut State Park Trail Guide* available at the visitor cen-

ter is adequate for hiking most of the trails within the park. The National Geographic *Idaho* map on CD-ROM is a good topo of the area. Montana Mapping & GPS LLC's Hunting and GPS maps are good maps for your GPS unit.

Trail contact: Farragut State Park, 13550 E. Highway 54, Athol, ID 83801; (208) 683-2425; www.parks andrecreation.idaho.gov (state parks link; Farragut); far@idpr .idaho.gov

Special considerations: Most of the trail junctions in Farragut State Park are marked with numbers on guideposts. These numbers correspond with the numbers on the *Farragut State Park Trail Guide* map.

Finding the trailhead: Take exit 12 off I-90 in Coeur d'Alene and drive north on US 95 for 18.7 miles to the junction with SH 54 in Athol. Turn right (east) on SH 54 and go 4.6 miles to the junction with South Road. The junction is just past (east of) the Farragut State Park Visitor Center. Turn right on South Road and drive 1.5 miles to the Beaver Bay access road. Turn right on the Beaver Bay access road and go 0.6 mile to the Beaver Bay Beach parking area. Restrooms and showers are available next to the parking area. GPS: N47 57.305' /W116 34.095'

Leaving the parking area, you descend the steps on the right side of the restrooms and showers. Then turn right and walk a few steps northwest, bearing right at another unsigned junction, to a sign pointing out the Shoreline Trail. This junction is shown as Junction #99 on the *Farragut State Park Trail Guide* map. Bear left at the sign on the Shoreline Trail, and hike west through the medium-age ponderosa pine (*Pinus ponderosa*) and Douglas fir (*Pseudotsuga menziesii*) woods. Below to your left is the Beaver Bay swimming area. The route passes an unmarked junction with a trail that leads down to the swimming area in about 0.1 mile. This side trail continues back to the unmarked junction you passed before reaching the sign that pointed out the Shoreline Trail, and may be used as an alternate return route to the parking area if you choose. To continue on the Buttonhook Bay Loop, hike straight ahead at this unmarked junction.

You will reach Junction #51 and the start of the loop portion of this hike 0.25 mile from the parking area. Bear left here, beginning the loop, and quickly hike straight ahead past another unmarked junction. The route soon passes between a building and the lake, then reaches yet another unmarked junction with a path and a roadbed. At this junction the docks in Buttonhook Bay are straight ahead. The path to the left crosses a wooden bridge to an island, where the path quickly

Beaver Bay swimming area

deteriorates. The area around this junction was once the site of Pend Oreille City.

Head up the roadbed to the right, then turn left at a sign marking the Shoreline Trail. In a little less than 0.4 mile, the trail bears to the right, leaving the shoreline of Buttonhook Bay. The rough, rocky, and eroded trail climbs. In 0.25 mile there is a flat area above the trail to the left. A short path leads to the flat area, where there is an informational sign that discusses Buttonhook Bay and Pend Oreille City. Past the flat spot the tread continues to climb gently alongside a tiny creek. White-tailed deer can sometimes be seen in this area as well as several other spots along the trail.

The route reaches trail Junction #47 0.2 mile after passing the flat area and sign. Turn right at the junction and hike northwest for 0.1 mile to Junction #48. Turn right again at Junction #48 and walk a few yards north to Junction #63. From this junction to Junction #61, the Buttonhook Bay Loop and the Squirrel Cache Trail (Hike 27) follow the same route. Turn right at Junction #63 and hike northeast. There are signs on several large trees identifying them in a little less than 0.2 mile. The course passes Peek Hole Rock 0.1 mile farther along. The rock is on the left with an explanatory sign on the right. Lake Pend Oreille comes into view through the trees to the right, shortly after passing Peek Hole Rock. A little farther along is an informational sign about the steamboat *Mary Moody,* and a few yards' more hiking brings you to Junction #61.

Junction #61 is 0.3 mile from Junction #63 and 1.8 miles into this hike. Turn right at Junction #61 and continue to head northeast. In 0.2 mile there is an unsigned trail junction. Hike straight ahead on the main trail and quickly reach Junction #76, where you turn right on a paved roadway through the Buttonhook Group Camp. Hike straight ahead at a road junction passing the restrooms. After following the paved road for 0.2 mile, you reach Junction #60. Turn right at the junction and descend, leaving the paved roadway. Quickly you will reach another junction with a much less used trail. Bear left here, staying on the main trail. Slightly less than 0.2 mile after leaving the paved road, you will reach Junction #51, ending the loop part of this hike. Turn left and retrace your steps for the 0.25 mile to the Beaver Bay Beach parking area. If you like, you can take the side route to the left a short distance ahead. This route descends and leads past the swimming area before returning to the main route close to the restrooms and showers.

MILES AND DIRECTIONS

0.0 Hike northwest from Beaver Bay Beach parking area.

0.3 Bear left at Junction #51 to start loop.

0.5 Bear left off of the roadbed.

1.4 Turn right at Junction #47.

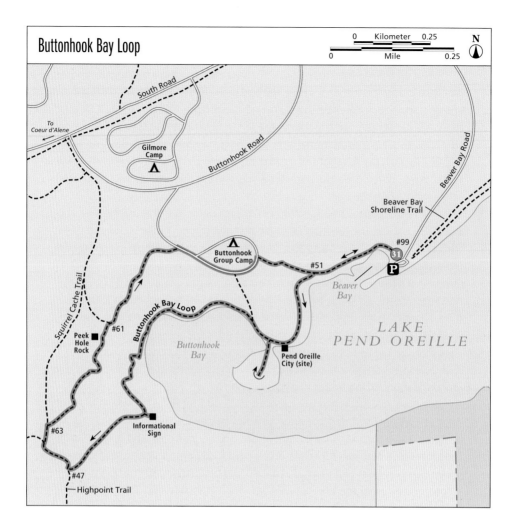

0   Kilometer   0.25
0   Mile   0.25
N

South Road

To
Coeur d'Alene

Gilmore
Camp

Buttonhook Road

Beaver Bay Road

Beaver Bay
Shoreline Trail

#99

31

P

Buttonhook
Group Camp

#51

Beaver
Bay

Squirrel Cache Trail

Buttonhook Bay Loop

LAKE
PEND OREILLE

#61

Peek
Hole
Rock

Buttonhook
Bay

Pend Oreille
City (site)

#63

Informational
Sign

#47

Highpoint Trail

1.5 Turn right at Junction #63.

1.8 Turn right at Junction #61.

2.1 Turn right on the paved road.

2.4 Turn left at Junction #51, ending the loop.

2.7 Arrive back at the Beaver Bay Beach parking area.

Options

Combine this hike with the Squirrel Cache Trail (Hike 27) and/or the Beaver Bay
Shoreline Loop (Hike 30) for a longer hike.

Willow Lakeview Loop

Hike along the shore of Lake Pend Oreille. Along the way you will pass an abandoned anti-aircraft battery, part of the World War II–era Farragut Military Base.

Start: Viewpoint and turnaround at the east end of South Road

Distance: 1.3-mile lollipop loop

Hiking time: About 1 hour

Difficulty: Easy

Best seasons: Late spring, summer, and early fall

Canine compatibility / other trail users: Pets must be on a leash at all times. As with all the trails in Farragut State Park south of SH 54, this trail is open to pedestrian and bicycle traffic only.

Fees and permits: Day-use permit or annual pass, purchased at the visitor center. A camping permit no longer covers day-use parking.

Maps: *Farragut State Park Trail Guide* available at the visitor cen-

ter is adequate for hiking most of the trails within the park. Montana Mapping & GPS LLC's Hunting and GPS maps are good topos of the area as are National Geographic *Idaho* maps on CD-ROM.

Trail contact: Farragut State Park, 13550 E. Highway 54, Athol, ID 83801; (208) 683-2425; www.parks andrecreation.idaho.gov (state parks link; Farragut); far@idpr .idaho.gov

Special considerations: Most of the trail junctions in Farragut State Park are marked with numbers on guideposts. These numbers correspond with the numbers on the *Farragut State Park Trail Guide* map.

Finding the trailhead: From I-90 exit 12 in Coeur d'Alene, drive north on US 95 for 18.7 miles to the junction with SH 54 in Athol. Turn right (east) on SH 54 and go 4.6 miles to the junction with South Road. The junction is just past (east of) the Farragut State Park Visitor Center. Turn right on South Road and drive 3 miles to the viewpoint and turnaround at the east end of South Road. GPS: N47 58.220' / W116 32.397'

THE HIKE

ike north from the viewpoint and turnaround past the boulders that block the road to motor vehicle traffic. In about 100 yards you will reach Junction #85. Turn right at the junction, leaving the roadbed, and descend steeply to the northeast. Shortly you will reach another junction, which is unmarked. Turn right again here on the broad trail. A little over 0.1 mile more brings you to an informational sign about Lake Pend Oreille and Junction #84, where the loop portion of this hike begins.

Bear left at Junction #84 and descend slightly. The track passes an abandoned anti-aircraft battery in 0.1 mile, where you can stop and read the sign explaining the purpose of these gun emplacements. In another 0.2 mile there is another unmarked junction, where you will hike straight ahead to the southwest, staying on the main trail. Soon you will pass another unmarked junction. Continue southwest on the main trail. A few more steps brings you to Junction #74, 0.7 mile from the viewpoint and turnaround. From here you may want to make a side trip to the boat launch and restroom, which are a couple hundred yards to the west. This is also the route that connects with the Beaver Bay Shoreline Loop. See the options below for more information.

Mountain goat

32

To continue on the Willow Lakeview Loop, turn right at Junction #74 on the paved trail and quickly pass the junction with the Lynx Trail. Hike straight ahead (northeast), passing the shelters and a playground. In a short distance you will reach the junction with the road that leads to the rental cabins and the mountain-goat-viewing spot. Mountain goats (*Oreamnos americanus*) can sometimes be seen on the cliffs across the lake. Follow the road past the cabins and a restroom to Junction #83, then get back on the trail, heading northeast. In a little less than 0.2 mile you will reach Junction #84, ending the loop. From Junction #84, retrace the route back to the viewpoint and turnaround at the east end of South Road.

Mountain Goat

The mountain goat (*Oreamnos americanus*) is a pure-white animal except for its hooves, eyes, nose, and horns, which are shiny black. The agile climbers are 3 to 3½ feet tall at the shoulders and billies (males) can weigh up to 300 pounds. Like cattle and deer, mountain goats are cud-chewing animals. They are often seen lying on a tiny ledge, resting and chewing their cuds.

Mountain goats range from Oregon, Washington, Idaho, and Montana northward through Canada and southeast Alaska, with transplanted herds also living in South Dakota, Nevada, and Colorado. Being high in the mountains is not a necessity for mountain goats, but rugged cliffs are. A productive heard lives in the depths of Hells Canyon on the Oregon-Idaho border.

MILES AND DIRECTIONS

0.0   Hike north from the viewpoint at the east end of South Road.

0.3   Bear left at Junction #84, starting the loop.

0.7   Turn right at Junction #74.

0.9   Leave the paved road at Junction #83.

1.3   Arrive back at the viewpoint.

Options

You can add 2.9 miles of easy hiking by combining the Willow Lakeview Loop with the Beaver Bay Shoreline Loop (Hike 30). To do this, hike the short distance west from Junction #74 to the Eagle Boat Launch. Close to the shoreline on the

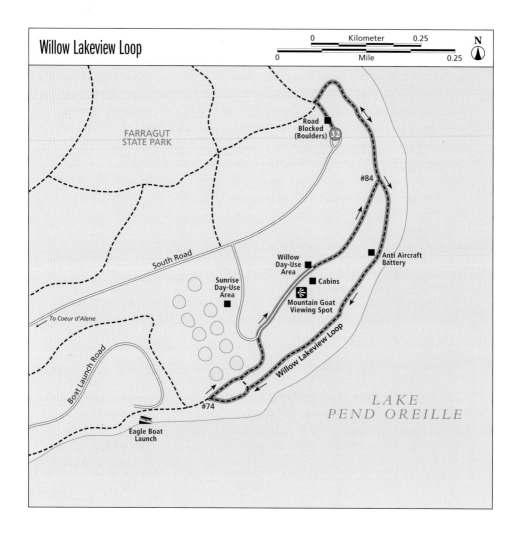

Kilometer

Mile

FARRAGUT
STATE PARK

Road
Blocked
(Boulders) 32

#84

South Road

Willow
Day-Use
Area

Sunrise
Day-Use
Area

Cabins

Mountain Goat
Viewing Spot

Anti Aircraft
Battery

To Coeur d'Alene

Willow Lakeview Loop

Boat Launch Road

#74

LAKE
PEND OREILLE

Eagle Boat
Launch

west side of the launch is an unmarked trail that follows the shore west for 0.3 mile to unmarked Junction #72 and the Beaver Bay Shoreline Loop (Hike 30). The Beaver Bay Shoreline Loop can be hiked in either direction but if you want to follow the directions in Hike 30, turn right at this junction.

To make an even longer hike, adding another 2.7 miles for a total of 6.9 miles of easy hiking, you can add on the Buttonhook Bay Loop (Hike 31) west of the Beaver Bay Shoreline Loop.

Chilco Mountain National Recreation Trail

Hike from a remote trailhead to the ridgeline of Chilco Mountain. Then follow the ridge south to the open subalpine summit of North Chilco Peak, with its great view of Lake Pend Oreille. Continue south from the north peak to Chilco Saddle, then ascend South Chilco Peak.

Start: Chilco Mountain Trailhead

Distance: 9.9-mile out-and-back day hike or backpack

Hiking time: About 5 hours

Difficulty: Moderate to strenuous; some route-finding skill is required

Best seasons: Summer and early fall

Canine compatibility / other trail users: Dogs that are under close control are allowed. Besides hikers, most of this route is open to mountain bikes, horses, and 2-wheel motor vehicles.

Fees and permits: None

Maps: Montana Mapping & GPS LLC's Hunting and GPS maps are good topos of the area as is the National Geographic *Idaho* topo on CD-ROM. However, both show this trail somewhat inaccurately, as does the USDA Forest Service *Idaho Panhandle / Coeur d'Alene National Forest Map.* The Forest Service map is very small-scale for hiking purposes.

Trail contact: USDA Forest Service, Coeur d'Alene River Ranger District, Fernan Office, 2502 E. Sherman Ave., Coeur d'Alene, ID 83814; (208) 664-2318

Special considerations: Route finding can be difficult for a short distance on the south side of the north peak. A GPS unit can be of help here. This hike involves about 3,000 feet of elevation gain and loss round-trip, so be sure all party members are up for this hike. There is no water along this route, so if you want to backpack, prepare for a dry campsite.

Finding the trailhead: Take exit 12 off I-90 in Coeur d'Alene. Then drive north on US 95 for 15.5 miles to the junction with Bunco Road. The junction with Bunco Road is next to the Silverwood Amusement Park. Turn right on Bunco Road, which becomes FR 332, and drive for 13.2 miles to the Chilco Mountain Trailhead. The trailhead is in a saddle next to the junction with FR 385. The elevation at the trailhead is 4,130 feet. GPS: N47 54.340' / W116 30.795'

THE HIKE

The Chilco Mountain National Recreation Trail climbs fairly steeply to the southwest as you leave the trailhead. After a few yards, walk around the metal barrier and continue to ascend the wide trail, which was once a roadbed. The mixed conifer woods here are made up of western white pine (*Pinus monticola*), lodgepole pine (*Pinus contorta*), western larch (*Larix occidentalis*), western hemlock (*Tsuga heterophylla*), Douglas fir (*Pseudotsuga menziesii*), and grand fir (*Abies grandis*). The course makes a switchback to the right, leaving the roadbed 0.25 mile after passing the barrier. This is the first of eight ascending switchbacks that take you up approximately 600 feet. Above the last switchback, 1.1 miles into the hike, the track continues to climb to the southwest.

There is a dry campsite a few steps to the right of the trail, 1.7 miles from the trailhead. From the campsite, which is on a ridgeline above a talus slope, there is a great view to the west. Just past the campsite there is a trail junction at about 5,420 feet elevation. The main trail, which will be your return route, turns to the right. The route to the right may be used both ways if you don't feel comfortable descending the south slope of North Chilco Peak.

Lake Pend Oreille from North Chilco Peak

To continue to the summit of North Chilco Peak, bear left at the junction and climb to the south. In less than 0.1 mile, the tread leaves the timber. The talus slopes here have a scattering of mountain ash (*Sorbus scopulina*) bushes and small groves of other subalpine trees. The section of trail crossing the talus is rough, so watch your step to avoid twisting an ankle. A little less than 0.4 mile from the junction, you will reach the summit of North Chilco Peak, at 5,635 feet elevation. The remains of a fire lookout lie on the ground close to the summit sign. To the north and far below are the deep-blue waters of Lake Pend Oreille. This is a great place to stop for lunch and take in the 360-degree view.

The next 0.2 mile of this route follows a faint path. If you don't feel comfortable following a hard-to-see trail or if your means of transportation is other than hiking, return to the junction 0.4 mile back. Turn left at the junction and follow the main trail as it traverses around the west side of North Chilco Peak. This will add about 0.8 mile to your hike but will be easier for some hikers.

If the short stretch of faint trail doesn't bother you, descend fairly steeply through the talus to the south. Soon the vague route enters a grassy slope. At the edge of the timber at the bottom of the grassy slope, turn to the right and head west. Soon the track bears left (southwest) and descends the short distance through the timber. You soon rejoin the main trail at 5,420 feet elevation, on the southwest slope of North Chilco Peak. A GPS receiver as well as an altimeter may be helpful on this section of the route. The GPS coordinates where you rejoin the main trail are N47 53.399' / W116 32.061'.

Turn left at the junction with the main trail and hike southwest, descending moderately for 0.7 mile to Chilco Saddle at 4,900 feet elevation. Many maps show a road reaching Chilco Saddle. This was once the case, but the road is now so overgrown that it is impassable. Unless you are looking for this long-abandoned road, you will probably not even see it. There is a possible dry campsite in the saddle.

Past the saddle the trail quickly begins to climb to the south-southwest. The route makes ten switchbacks in the next 1.2 miles. Then you turn left on the ridgeline and hike the last 0.7 mile to the summit of South Chilco Peak. There is no sign at the 5,670-foot-high summit. The area is covered with subalpine timber, with beargrass (*Xerophyllum tenax*) covering the ground beneath the trees.

The summit of South Chilco Peak is the turnaround point for this hike. When you're ready, retrace the route back for 2.6 miles, through Chilco Saddle and up to the junction on the southwest side of North Chilco Peak. Bear left at the junction, staying on the main trail, and begin the traverse along the western slope of North Chilco Peak. The route descends slightly to pass beneath the talus on the west slope of the peak. You hike through a small but pretty grove of aspen trees (*Populus tremuloides*) growing at the base of the talus slope. After passing the aspens the track ascends via two switchbacks to the junction north of the

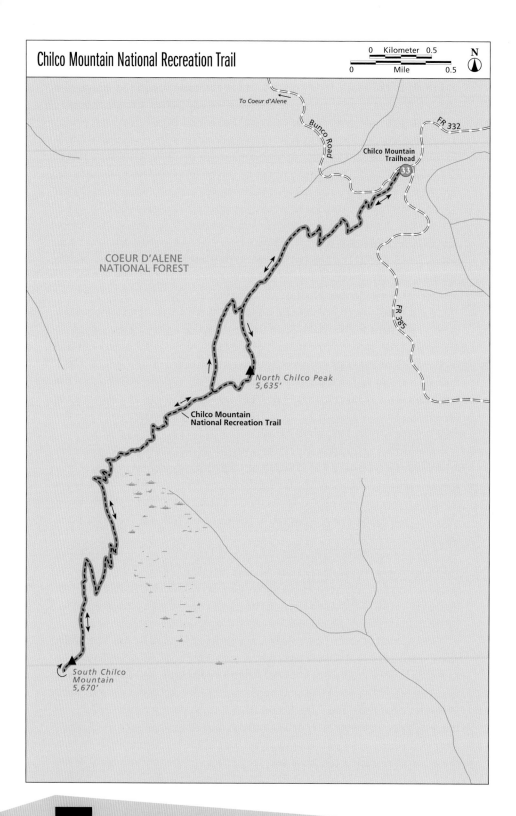

Chilco Mountain National Recreation Trail

0   Kilometer   0.5

0   Mile   0.5

N

To Coeur d'Alene

Bunco Road

FR 332

Chilco Mountain
Trailhead

33

COEUR D'ALENE
NATIONAL FOREST

FR 385

*North Chilco Peak
5,635'*

Chilco Mountain
National Recreation Trail

*South Chilco
Mountain
5,670'*

peak. Traversing the 0.6 mile around the west side of North Chilco Peak is slightly farther than hiking over the top, but it is an easier route. Turn left at the junction and follow your inbound course back to the trailhead.

MILES AND DIRECTIONS

0.0 Climb southwest from Chilco Trailhead.

1.7 Bear left at the junction.

2.1 Descend southwest from North Chilco Peak.

2.3 Return to main trail and turn left.

3.0 Hike through Chilco Saddle.

4.9 Turn around at South Chilco Peak.

7.5 Bear left to traverse around North Chilco Peak.

8.2 Return to the junction north of North Chilco Peak and turn left.

9.9 Arrive back at the Chilco Trailhead.

Options

Shorten your hike by 5.6 miles by returning as you came from the summit of North Chilco Peak. The best views are from the north peak.

🌿 Green Tip:
Pack out what you pack in, even food scraps because they can attract wild animals.

Fourth of July Pass Inner Loop

This route is a very pleasant hike through the woodlands close to Fourth of July Pass. This entire hike follows roadbeds that are closed to motor vehicles and kept widely cleared for cross-country skiers.

Start: Fourth of July Park Ski and Snowshoe parking area

Distance: 5.2-mile lollipop-loop day hike

Hiking time: About 3 hours

Difficulty: Easy hiking, but close attention needs to be paid to maps and signs

Best seasons: Summer and fall for hiking

Canine compatibility / other trail users: Under-control dogs are OK in the summer and fall. Mountain bikers also use these trails. There are moose in this area, and they may not take to kindly to barking dogs.

Fees and permits: None in the summer. A parking fee is charged during the ski season.

Maps: Detailed maps of this area seem to be hard to find. The best one I have found is on the map

board 1.2 miles along the trail from the parking area. The map in this book, however, should be more than adequate for this hike. Montana Mapping & GPS LLC's Hunting and GPS maps are good topos of the area for your GPS unit.

Trail contact: USDA Forest Service Coeur d'Alene River Ranger District, Fernan Office, 2502 E. Sherman Ave., Coeur d'Alene, ID 83814; (208) 664-2318

Special considerations: Moose (*Alces alces*) inhabit this area. Keep a watch for one of these huge animals. If you see one, don't approach or challenge it in any way. Some moose have a poor attitude; all of them are unpredictable and potentially dangerous. As with all wildlife, getting too close is not the thing to do.

Finding the trailhead: Drive east from Coeur d'Alene on I-90 for 16 miles to exit 28. Leave the freeway, go southwest for 0.2 mile, and turn right into the Fourth of July Park Ski and Snowshoe parking area. A large sign marks the entrance. The trail begins at the northwest end of the parking area. There may be no signs marking the trail here. GPS: N47 37.260' / W116 31. 885'

THE HIKE

As you leave the parking area, the trail (which is a roadbed that is closed to motorized vehicles) leads northwest, quickly passing a gate. A short distance into the hike, the Jeanette's Jaunt Trail turns to the right at a signed junction. Continue straight ahead here, passing another gate, and hike first northwest then west along the roadbed. The route reaches the Panhandle Hut, which is a Nordic ski shelter, 0.2 mile from the trailhead. The well-maintained hut is just to the right of the trail. Past the Panhandle Hut the track continues through the dense forest of western red cedar (*Thuja plicata*), western hemlock (*Tsuga heterophylla*), Douglas fir (*Pseudotsuga menziesii*), and grand fir (*Abies grandis*). If you're here in the spring (around June 1), watch the ground for fairy slippers (*Calypso bulbosa*) blooming at the trailside.

The course climbs very gently, passing a small shed 0.4 mile from the Panhandle Hut. As the route swings around onto a drier, west-facing slope, the composition of the woods changes somewhat. Now ponderosa pine (*Pinus ponderosa*) makes up a larger percentage of the timber, and a few western white pines (*Pinus monticola*) show up. Beneath the pines grow Rocky Mountain

Panhandle Hut

maples (*Acer Glabrum*). The tread passes the ¾-mile marker, then descends very gently to the 1-mile marker. These markers indicate the distance from the trailhead. Slightly more than 0.2 mile after passing the 1-mile marker, there is a trail (roadbed) junction. This junction is the beginning of the loop portion of this hike.

Take the time to look at the map board next to the junction, then turn left and climb gently up the Loose Moose Trail. Follow the Loose Moose Trail for 0.5 mile to the junction with the Skateaway Trail and the High Road Trail. Bear right at the junction (almost straight ahead) and hike west and northwest along the High Road Trail. Along the High Road you pass the "2 mile" marker and enter a forest restoration area. Below the track to your right, the slope has been planted with western white pines to aid in the study of a disease that affects these beautiful trees. Watch for elk (*Cervus canadensis*) on this semi-open slope. The roadbed that can be seen at the bottom of the slope is part of your return route.

The junction with the Spencer's S Trail is reached in another 0.3 mile. Bear right here, staying on the High Road Trail. Three-tenths of a mile farther, you reach another trail (roadbed) junction. To your left a short distance along the Elderberry Trail are a picnic shelter and restroom. Directly across from the picnic shelter is the western terminus of the Jeanette's Jaunt Alternate Trail, the eastern

Fairy slipper

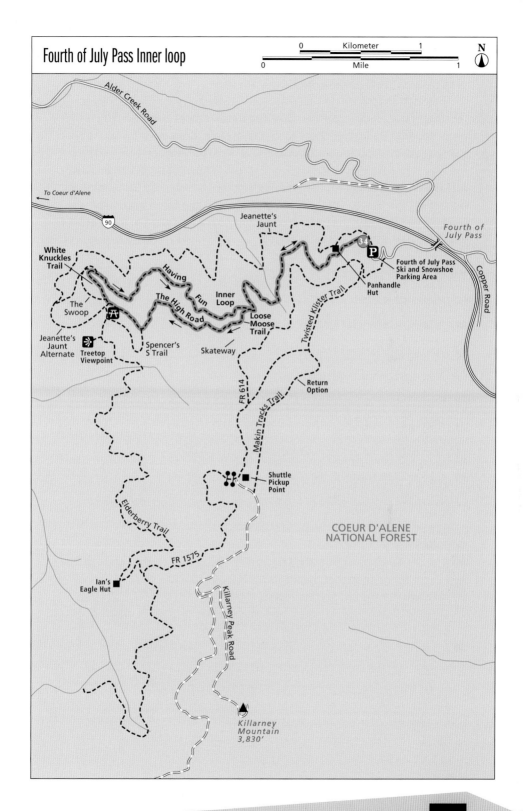

Fourth of July Pass Inner loop

0 ——— Kilometer ——— 1
0 ——— Mile ——— 1

N

Alder Creek Road

To Coeur d'Alene

90

Jeanette's Jaunt

Fourth of July Pass

White Knuckles Trail

Having Fun

The Swoop

The High Road

Inner Loop

Loose Moose Trail

Jeanette's Jaunt Alternate

Treetop Viewpoint

Spencer's S Trail

Skateway

Fourth of July Pass Ski and Snowshoe Parking Area

34

P

Panhandle Hut

Twisted Klister Trail

Copper Road

FR 614

Makin Tracks Trail

Return Option

Elderberry Trail

Shuttle Pickup Point

COEUR D'ALENE NATIONAL FOREST

FR 1575

Ian's Eagle Hut

Killarney Peak Road

Killarney Mountain 3,830'

end of which you passed just after leaving the parking lot. The picnic shelter is a good place to take a break or maybe have lunch.

Hike northwest from the junction with the Elderberry Trail and quickly reach yet another trail junction, this one with the White Knuckles Trail. Turn right on the White Knuckles Trail and descend following the blue diamond cross-country-ski trail markers. In slightly under 0.2 mile, you come to the junction with the Having Fun Trail. Turn right on the Having Fun Trail and follow it southeast, then northeast, then southeast again to the junction with the Loose Moose Trail, ending the loop. Along the Having Fun Trail, you pass beneath the forest restoration area. From the junction with the Loose Moose Trail, retrace your steps to the Fourth of July Park Ski and Snowshoe parking area.

MILES AND DIRECTIONS

0.0 Hike northwest from the Fourth of July Park Ski and Snowshoe parking area.

0.2 Pass the Panhandle Hut.

1.2 Turn left on the Loose Moose Trail.

1.7 Bear right on the High Road Trail.

2.0 Bear right at the Junction with the Spencer's S Trail.

2.3 Hike straight ahead at the junction with the Elderberry Trail.

2.6 Turn right at the junction with the Having Fun Trail.

4.0 Hike straight ahead on the junction Loose Moose Trail.

5.2 Arrive back at the Fourth of July Park Ski and Snowshoe parking area.

Options
For a longer hike leaving from the same trailhead, try Hike 35, the Fourth of July Pass Outer Loop. Check out the Mullan Military Road while you are at Fourth of July Pass. See "Honorable Mentions."

Fourth of July Pass Outer Loop

Hike mostly on abandoned roadbeds that are reverting nicely to trails, through the dense and diverse midmountain forest just south of Fourth of July Pass. Grouse are common along this route and there are elk and moose sign nearly everywhere.

Start: Fourth of July Park Ski and Snowshoe parking area (aka Fourth of July Hiking, Mountain Biking & Horseback Riding Area)
Distance: 9.8-mile loop or 7.6-mile shuttle day hike
Hiking time: About 3 to 4 hours shuttle, 4 to 5 hours loop
Difficulty: Moderate
Best seasons: Summer and fall for hiking. This is a cross-country-ski route in the winter.
Canine compatibility / other trail users: Under-control dogs are allowed in the summer and fall, however, there are moose in this area that may not be friendly to dogs. Mountain bikers also use these trails.
Fees and permits: None in the summer. There is a parking fee charged during the ski season.
Maps: The map in this book should be more than adequate for this hike. There is a good map on the map board 1.2 miles along the trail from the parking area. Detailed maps of the area can be found on the Panhandle Nordic Clubs website at panhandlenordic club.com. Montana Mapping & GPS LLC's Hunting and GPS maps are good topos of the area for your GPS unit.
Trail contact: USDA Forest Service, Coeur d'Alene River Ranger District, Fernan Office, 2502 E. Sherman Ave., Coeur d'Alene, ID 83814; (208) 664-2318
Special considerations: Keep a watch for moose (*Alces alces*), which inhabit this area. If you encounter one, don't challenge or approach it. Moose are very unpredictable and potentially dangerous. As with all wildlife, getting too close is not the thing to do. This is not a good hike to take when it's raining or shortly thereafter. In many places bushes and small trees crowd the track, and if they are wet, you will be too.

Finding the trailhead: Drive east from Coeur d'Alene on I-90 for 16 miles to exit 28. Leave the freeway and go southwest for 0.2 mile on FR 614, then turn right into the Fourth of July Park Ski and Snowshoe parking area. A large sign marks the entrance. The trail (which is a closed to motor vehicles) roadbed begins at the northwest end of the parking area. There may be no signs marking the trail here. The elevation at the parking area is 3,130 feet. GPS: N47 37.260'/W116 31. 885'

To reach the junction of FR 1575 and FR 614 for a shuttle pickup, continue southwest on FR 614 for 2 miles.

THE HIKE

Hike northwest from the parking area on the closed roadbed, quickly passing a gate. A few more steps bring you to the junction with the Jeanette's Jaunt Trail. Turn to the right at the signed junction on Jeanette's Jaunt. Jeanette's Jaunt is a designated snowshoe trail in the winter and is therefore marked with yellow diamond snowshoe trail markers. The tread descends through the dense cedar, fir, and hemlock forest, soon making a couple of switchbacks. Soon the trail is following an overgrown roadbed. The course crosses a couple of small wooden bridges as you hike generally west. There is a signpost and map on the right of the trail 1.1 miles from the trailhead. A bit less than 0.2 mile farther along, the trail crosses a small creek without the benefit of a bridge. The track crosses two more small streams in the next 0.8 mile as you gradually descend to 2,780 feet elevation. A couple tenths of a mile after crossing the third creek, there is another signpost (marker "3") and map next to the trail. Just past the signpost the route passes a metal gate and begins to climb very gently.

The track crosses another bridgeless creek 0.3 mile farther along. Another 0.7 mile of hiking brings you to the junction with the Jeanette's Jaunt alternate route. Turn left here and climb. In 0.25 mile the tread crosses a roadbed that is marked with blue diamond cross-country-ski trail markers. Continue a few more yards to another roadbed and turn right. In a little less than 0.2 mile, you will reach another junction, this one with the Swoop Ski Trail. At this point you have climbed back up to 3,030 feet elevation. A short distance farther southeast is the junction with the Elderberry Trail. This junction is 3.7 miles into this hike. Straight ahead, across the Elderberry Trail, is a picnic shelter. To the left a few feet is the junction of the High Road Trail and the Elderberry Trail.

Turn right on the Elderberry Trail and head south, quickly passing the junction with the Spencer's S Trail. The junction with the Tree Top Trail is reached in another 300 yards. The short (only 5 minutes round-trip) Tree Top Trail leads to a viewpoint looking across the wooded ridges to the west. After checking out the viewpoint, resume your hike by continuing southeast on the Elderberry Trail.

The course goes into and out of three draws in the next 1.5 miles. Then you reach a rest spot with benches on the left side of the trail (roadbed). There is also a trail map posted here. The route crosses a couple more creeks in the remaining 0.5 mile to Ian's Eagle Hut. Ian's Eagle Hut is a cross-country-ski shelter. The elevation at the hut is 3,100 feet and you are 6.1 miles into this hike.

A few feet past the hut, the trail turns left, leaving the roadbed. There is a sign here that states UP TO FSR 1575 (FSR is an abbreviation for Forest Service Road). The route is marked with yellow diamonds, indicating this is a snowshoe trail. The track climbs, making a couple of switchbacks in the 0.3 mile to the junction with FR 1575 at 3,260 feet elevation. Turn left on the roadbed and hike east. The route

Ian's Eagle Hut

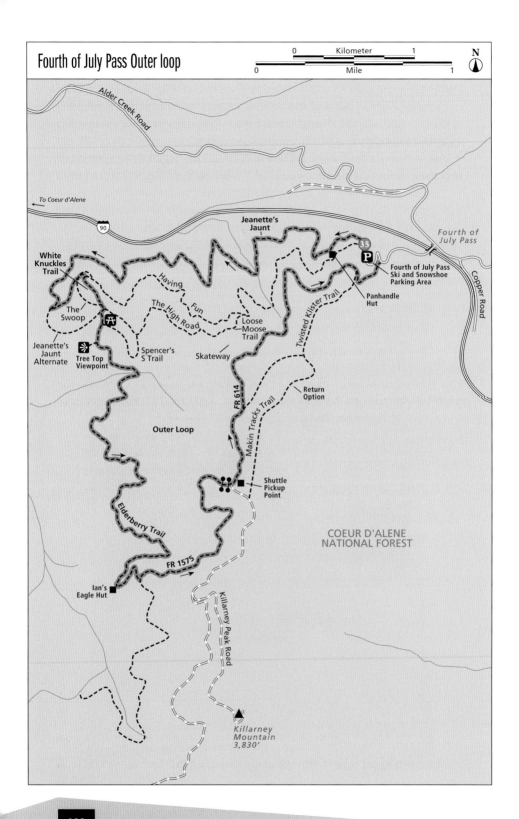

Fourth of July Pass Outer loop

0   Kilometer   1

0   Mile   1

N

Alder Creek Road

To Coeur d'Alene

90

Jeanette's Jaunt

Fourth of July Pass

White Knuckles Trail

Having Fun

The High Road

The Swoop

Loose Moose Trail

Jeanette's Jaunt Alternate

Tree Top Viewpoint

Spencer's S Trail

Skateway

Twisted Kilster Trail

Fourth of July Pass Ski and Snowshoe Parking Area

Panhandle Hut

Copper Road

35

P

FR 614

Makin Tracks Trail

Return Option

Outer Loop

Shuttle Pickup Point

Elderberry Trail

FR 1575

COEUR D'ALENE NATIONAL FOREST

Ian's Eagle Hut

Killarney Peak Road

Killarney Mountain 3,830'

follows FR 1575 for 1.1 miles to a pair of metal gates that block it to motor vehicle traffic. A short distance past the gates is the junction with FR 614. At this junction you have climbed to 3,500 feet elevation and have hiked 7.6 miles from the parking area. This is the end of your hike if you have arranged for a shuttle back to the Fourth of July Park Ski and Snowshoe parking area.

If you are going to make this a loop hike, you have 2.2 more easy miles to walk back to the Fourth of July Park Ski and Snowshoe parking area. This road (FR 614) is lightly traveled, making it a pleasant, mostly downhill hike. To continue hiking, turn left on FR 614 and hike north. In 0.3 mile there is a junction, where you will keep left, staying on FR 614. Another 0.7 mile brings you to another road junction. The road to the left is blocked by a gate and is the Skateaway Ski Trail in the winter. Continue on FR 614 still heading north. Seven-tenths mile farther along there is another road junction, keep left here. The road passes through a metal gate in another 0.1 mile and reaches a pipeline crossing 0.2 mile farther along. Turn left next to the pipeline and descend the steep trail for about 0.1 mile to the access road for Fourth of July Park Ski and Snowshoe parking area. This trail is the steepest part of this hike. (If you would rather not take this trail, it is only a couple of tenths of a mile farther to follow FR 614 to the access road.) Turn left on the paved road and follow it the short distance to the parking area, completing the loop.

MILES AND DIRECTIONS

0.0   Hike northwest from Fourth of July Park parking area.

3.7   Turn right on the Elderberry Trail.

6.1   Pass Ian's Eagle Hut.

7.6   End shuttle hike or turn left on FR 614.

9.8   Arrive back at the Fourth of July Park Ski and Snowshoe parking area.

Options

If you would like a slightly shorter hike, try Hike 34, Fourth of July Pass Inner Loop.

You can make a slightly longer return hike from the junction of FR 1575 and FR 614 over trails that are closed to motorized traffic. To make this return trip, first hike southeast (right) on FR 614 for about 250 yards. Then turn left on FR 918 and quickly turn left again on Makin Tracks Trail. Follow Makin Tracks Trail for about a mile, then bear right on Twisted Klister Trail. In another mile Twisted Klister Trail rejoins FR 614. Turn right on FR 614 and it's about 0.4 mile to the parking area.

While you are at Fourth of July Pass, check out the short, Mullan Military Road Trail. See "Honorable Mention" below.

C. *Honorable Mention*

Mullan Military Road

Hike a short section of the historic Mullan Military Road. The Mullan Military Road trailhead is on the north side of I-90 adjacent to Fourth of July Pass. Coming from Coeur d'Alene, leave I-90 at exit 28 and cross the overpass over the freeway. Turn right on the far side, and drive a short distance east to the trailhead. This section of the Mullan Military Road is an interpretive trail that describes how and why the road was built, and why this area is called Fourth of July Pass.

Bull moose next to the Trail of the Coeur d'Alenes

Two large Idaho state parks lay a short distance to the south of Coeur d'Alene. All the hikes described here are within these parks, with the exception of Hike 36. Hike 36 is the longest hike described in this book, but the broad paved path is one of the easiest to hike despite its distance.

Hikes 37 through 40 are within 5,744-acre Heyburn State Park. Hikes 37 and 38 climb above Chatcolet Lake, which is really a southern extension of Lake Coeur d'Alene. Both of these hikes offer viewpoints and wildlife-viewing possibilities. Hike 39 is a self-guided nature trail that leaves from the same trailhead as Hikes 37 and 38. Hike 40 follows the shoreline of Chatcolet Lake. This hike also includes a boardwalk trail out into a marsh before climbing away from the shore and traversing wooded slopes back to its starting point. The boardwalk offers good waterfowl-viewing opportunities. All of the hikes in Heyburn State Park interconnect, allowing for lots of route possibilities.

South and west of Heyburn State Park is the 5,412-acre Mary Minerva McCroskey State Park. These two parks are managed jointly. Mary Minerva McCroskey State Park contains hikes 41 through 43. Hike 41 climbs to a hilltop campground, passing through excellent white-tailed deer and wild turkey habitat as you ascend. Hike 42 climbs along a ridgeline to another hilltop campground. Hike 43 traverses a slope that is managed to mimic natural conditions with fire and thinning, from a ridgetop campground to a viewpoint overlooking the farm country of the Idaho Palouse Prairie. As you may have noticed, all three of the campgrounds in Mary Minerva McCroskey State Park are on ridgelines or hilltops, and they are also free of charge.

White-tailed doe, Hike 37

Trail of the Coeur d'Alenes

This description covers the western section of the Trail of the Coeur d'Alenes, the part that is closest to the Spokane–Coeur d'Alene area. The 42-mile length of this route is too long for a day hike, and backpacking possibilities are limited because of the lack of campsites close to the trail. For these reasons, the best way to hike this trail is with a support shuttle from a base camp or other lodging close to the route. Good places for shuttle pickup and drop-off are mentioned in the hike description as shuttle points. Much of the land along this part of the Trail of the Coeur d'Alenes is within a wildlife management area. Take your time along this easy trail and enjoy the wildlife. There are interpretive signs at most of the waysides that are well worth reading.

Start: Cataldo Trailhead
Distance: 42-mile multiday shuttle
Hiking time: About 20 to 25 hours total hiking time
Difficulty: Moderate only because of length; the grades are easy
Best season: Year-round, depending on the type of footwear you use—boots, snowshoes, skis, etc.
Canine compatibility / other trail users: Dogs are welcome but must be on a short leash. Biking, inline skating, cross-country skiing, and snowshoeing are also allowed. The Trail of the Coeur d'Alenes is accessible for visitors with physical challenges.
Fees and permits: None
Maps: *Trail of the Coeur d'Alenes*, published jointly by the Coeur d'Alene Tribe and Idaho Department of Parks and Recreation. *Recreational Trails of the Idaho Panhandle* by Friends of the Coeur d'Alene Trails. Either of these maps is adequate for this trip. The *Recre-ational Trails of the Idaho Panhandle* by Friends of the Coeur d'Alene Trails shows the roads leading to the trailheads more clearly. Either of these maps should be used in conjunction with a good Idaho road map.
Trail contacts: Coeur d'Alene Tribe Project Coordinator, P.O. Box 408, Plummer, ID 83851; (208) 686-7045; cdatribe-nsn.gov. Idaho Department of Parks and Recreation, Trail Manager, Coeur d'Alene's Old Mission State Park, P.O. Box 30, Cataldo, ID 83810; (208) 682-3814; old@idpr.state.id.us.
Special considerations: For safety, yield to bicycle traffic (even though this is not a legal requirement). Expect mostly bicycle traffic on some sections of this trail, however, other parts may have more walkers than cyclists. Give moose all the room they want and don't challenge them in any way.

Finding the trailhead: Drive east from Coeur d'Alene on I-90 for 28 miles to exit 40. Leave the freeway and drive the short distance into the town of Cataldo (on the north side of I-90). The trailhead and parking area are on your left as you enter the town. The elevation at the trailhead is 2,150 feet. GPS: N47 32.901'/W116 19.795'

To reach the Hn'ya')pqi'nn Trailhead where this hike (or series of hikes) ends, take exit 12 off I-90 in Coeur d'Alene. From the exit, head south on US 95 for 31 miles. The trailhead is on your right just before entering the town of Plummer.

THE HIKE

Heading southwest from the Cataldo Trailhead, the broad paved trail quickly passes beneath I-90. The route crosses a bridge over a creek 1 mile from the trailhead, as you come close to the Coeur d'Alene River. In another 0.8 mile the tread crosses Latour Creek and reaches the Latour Creek Scenic Rest Area. There is a picnic table at the rest area if you want to take a break.

The course crosses a gravel road next to milepost 39. Here you are close to the river again. Another 0.4 mile brings you to the River Bend Scenic Wayside, where there is a restroom and tables. River Bend Scenic Wayside is 3.4 miles from the Cataldo Trailhead. Two and two-tenth miles after passing the River Bend Scenic Wayside is the Dudley Scenic Wayside.

The Cedar Grove Scenic Wayside is reached 1.5 miles past the Dudley Scenic Wayside. Here a path leads a few feet left to a picnic table situated beneath the Cedar Grove. The western red cedars that make up the grove are closely spaced, so that no direct sunlight reaches the ground between them. This leaves the ground beneath the grove devoid of undergrowth. None of these cedars are very large; most of the cedars in this area were cut for shakes, posts, and lumber years ago.

Western Red Cedar

The western red cedar (*Thuja plicata*) was as important to Native Americans as it is to our culture today, maybe even more so. The native people used the cedar bark to make mats, baskets, ropes, and in some cases robes. The wood was used to make dugout canoes as well as many other things.

Leaving the Cedar Grove Scenic Wayside, continue southwest for 1.4 miles to the Bull Run Lake Trailhead, which is 8.5 miles from Cataldo. There is easy access to the Bull Run Lake Trailhead from SH 3, so you may want to use it as a shuttle point.

To reach Bull Run Lake Trailhead, drive south on SH 3 from exit 34 on I-90 for 3.3 miles to the junction with Bull Run Road. Turn left on Bull Run Road and follow it for 0.3 mile to the trailhead. Signs lead the way to the trailhead, where there is adequate parking, benches, a picnic table, and restrooms.

The trail heads west between the Coeur d'Alene River and Bull Run Lake as you leave the Bull Run Lake Trailhead. Ponderosa pines (*Pinus ponderosa*), cottonwoods (*Populus trichocarpa*), and a few western white pines (*Pinus monticola*) flank the route. Douglas fir (*Pseudotsuga menziesii*) and aspen (*Populus tremuloides*) groves add to the variety of flora. Beneath the trees bracken fern (*Pteridium aquilinum*) covers the ground in spots. After you pass milepost 32, there is a lily pad–covered lake on the left. Soon after, there is marshland on both sides of the route. The trail crosses the bridge 1.7 miles from the Bull Run Lake Trailhead. Spirea (*Spiraea douglasii*) grows from the banks below both sides of the trail in this area. The course leaves the marsh 0.4 mile after crossing the bridge. The Coeur d'Alene River is now to the right of the trail again. Another 0.1 mile brings you to

Chatcolet Bridge

the junction with the side trail to the Black Rock Trailhead. The trailhead, which also makes a good shuttle point, is a short distance to the right.

Past the Black Rock Trailhead junction, the route passes beneath SH 3 and continues west-southwest. By the time you reach milepost 31, there is marsh on both sides of the trail. The track crosses a bridge at milepost 30. When I went past this spot, there was a great blue heron (*Ardea herodias*) standing on the trail near the bridge. The course reaches the Lane Scenic Wayside 1.6 miles from the Black Rock Trailhead. A table and restroom are available at the wayside. Watch for moose (*Alces alces*) in the marshland on the sides of the route between here and the Medimount Trailhead 3.8 miles ahead. The Medimont Trailhead, which is 5.4 miles from the Black Rock Trailhead and 16.2 miles from the Cataldo Trailhead, is another good shuttle point. To reach the Medimont Trailhead, drive south on SH 3 from exit 34 on I-90 for 12.3 miles, turn right, and proceed 1.5 miles to the trailhead.

Next the route traverses another 1.6 miles between marshes to the Cave Lake Wayside, which has a restroom and table. At 3.5 miles past the Cave Lake Wayside, you reach the Grays Meadow Wayside, which also has a picnic table. About 1 mile after passing the Grays Meadow Wayside, the route skirts a steep

Cedar grove

hillside next to the Coeur d'Alene River. Then about a mile past the hillside, you reach the Cottonwood Wayside. Back along the marshes it's another 0.3 mile to the Springston Trailhead. A restroom and picnic table are available at the Springston Trailhead. The Springston Trailhead is 7.5 miles from the Medimount Trailhead and 23.7 miles from the Cataldo Trailhead. The Springston Trailhead can be reached by car from SH 97, 2 miles north of Harrison via Blue Lake Road.

Continuing southwest from the Springston Trailhead, it's 1.7 miles through the marshland to the Anderson Lake Wayside. Just past the wayside the trail passes beneath SH 97, and 1.3 miles from the wayside is the Harrison Marina Trailhead, another good shuttle point. Harrison is located 28 miles south of I-90 exit 22. It can also be easily reached from SH 3. Lodging and several restaurants are available in Harrison as well as a city campground.

Leaving Harrison, the Trail of the Coeur d'Alenes follows the shoreline south, soon passing the Steamboat Landing Wayside at milepost 15. The track follows the shoreline closely for the next 2.9 miles to the Sqwe'mu'lmkhw Wayside, where restrooms and a table are available. Another 2.1 miles along the beautiful lakeshore is the Hndarep Wayside, which also has a restroom and table. The route follows the shoreline for about 1.5 miles more. Then you make a turn to the right and head west on the causeway leading to the historic Chatcolet Bridge.

The Chatcolet Bridge was once a drawbridge spanning the St. Joe River. The Post Falls Dam raised the level of Lake Coeur d'Alene in 1906, flooding the valley here. Trees growing through the water's surface outline some of the old riverbank. The route crosses the Chatcolet Bridge to the Chatcolet Trailhead in Heyburn State Park. The Chatcolet Trailhead is 8 miles from Harrison and is an excellent shuttle point. To reach the Chatcolet Trailhead, drive east from Plummer on SH 5 for 6.3 miles to the entrance to Heyburn State Park. Turn left and go 50 yards to the visitor center. Turn left again and drive 2.4 miles, following the signs to the Chatcolet Trailhead.

After crossing the bridge the route follows the western shoreline of Chatcolet Lake for 1.2 miles to the side trail to the Plummer Point Trailhead. This junction is just before reaching milepost 6. Chatcolet Lake and Lake Coeur d'Alene have merged because of the raised water level behind Post Falls Dam. There may be no sign on the trail marking the Plummer Point Trailhead, which is to the left.

From Plummer Point the Trail of the Coeur d'Alenes begins its climb gently to the west. The average grade from here to the Hn'ya')pqi'nn Trailhead at Plummer is only about 2 percent. A short distance up the grade, the Indian Cliffs Trailhead is on the right just after you cross Chatcolet Road. The Indian Cliffs Trailhead serves several hiking trails besides the Trail of the Coeur d'Alenes. The Heyburn State Park Visitor Center and Hawley's Landing Campground are 1.1 miles to the southeast as you cross Chatcolet Road, next to the Indian Cliffs Trailhead.

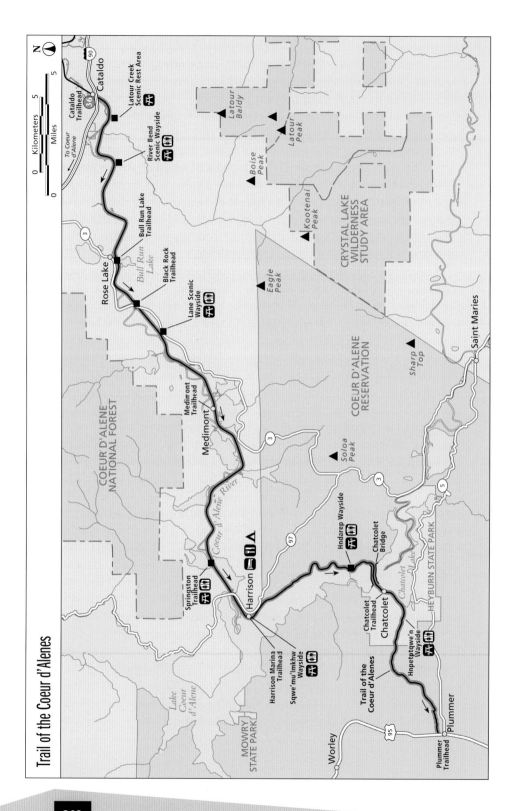

Trail of the Coeur d'Alenes

The course continues its gentle climb to the west, reaching the Hnpetptqwe'n Wayside in about 1 mile, at milepost 5. Restrooms and a bench are available here. The route passes junctions with two side trails 1 mile above the Hnpetptqwe'n Wayside. There is also a restroom at the Hntsaqaqn Wayside 1.6 miles past the junctions. Next to the wayside the route crosses a bridge over Plummer Creek.

The Trail of the Coeur d'Alenes climbs on to the west, crosses a road, then passes beneath US 95. Shortly after going under the highway, the route reaches its end at the Hn'ya')pqi'nn (Plummer) Trailhead. The elevation at the Hn'ya') pqi'nn Trailhead is 2,750 feet, and you have come 42 miles from the Cataldo Trailhead.

MILES AND DIRECTIONS

0.0 Head southwest from the Cataldo Trailhead.

8.5 Pass the Bull Run Trailhead.

10.7 Pass the Black Rock Trailhead junction.

16.2 Pass the Medimont Trailhead.

26.7 Pass the Harrison Marina Trailhead.

34.8 Pass the Chatcolet Trailhead.

42.0 Reach the Hn'ya')pqi'nn (Plummer) Trailhead.

Options

Make this a five-day trip with shuttle pickups and deliveries at the Bull Run Lake, Medimont, Harrison Marina, and Chatcolet Trailheads. If you are camping, a base camp could be set up at Heyburn State Park. Lots of indoor lodging is also available close to the Trail of the Coeur d'Alenes.

Check out *Trail of the Coeur d'Alenes Unofficial Guidebook* (Gray Dog Press, 2013), available at many outdoor stores and the Heyburn State Park Visitor Center, for the wide variety of places to stay.

Whitetail–Shoeffler Butte Loops

The Whitetail Loop is aptly named. White-tailed deer are common all along the way, as are bear tracks and sign. Generally following easy grades, the route traverses the open forests typical of the inland Northwest. By adding the Shoeffler Butte Loop to the trip, you climb to the highest point in Heyburn State Park, with its better views. Much of this hike follows primitive fire roads.

Start: Indian Cliffs Trailhead

Distance: 10.7-mile double-loop day hike

Hiking time: About 5 to 6 hours

Difficulty: Moderate

Best season: Late spring through early fall

Canine compatibility / other trail users: Open to hikers, mountain bikers, and equestrians. Dogs are prohibited.

Fees and permits: A day-use fee is charged; camping fees no longer cover day use. Get your Day-Use Permit at the visitor center.

Maps: *Heyburn State Park Trail System,* available free at the visitor center, covers the trails in Heyburn State Park but has very limited detail. Montana Mapping & GPS LLC's Hunting and GPS maps are good topos of the area as are National Geographic maps on CD-ROM.

Trail contact: Heyburn State Park Manager, 57 Chatcolet Rd., Plummer, ID 83851; (206) 686-1308; fax (206) 686-0171; hey@idpr.idaho .gov; www.parksandrecreation .idaho.gov

Finding the trailhead: Leave I-90 at exit 12 in Coeur d'Alene, then drive south on US 95 for 31 miles to Plummer. From Plummer drive east (left) on SH 5 for 6.3 miles to the entrance to Heyburn State Park. Turn left and go 50 yards to the visitor center. Turn left again and drive 1.1 miles to the Indian Cliffs Trailhead, which is on your left. The trailhead and parking area are located just after crossing the Trail of the Coeur d'Alenes. The elevation at the trailhead is 2,190 feet. GPS: N47 21.622' / W116 46.786'

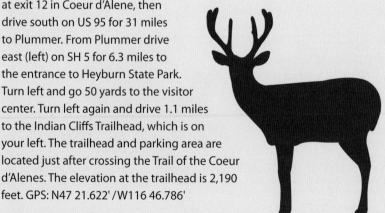

THE HIKE

Hike west from the west end of the parking area at the Indian Cliffs Trailhead. The trail, which is really a fire road, passes a gate, which blocks it to vehicle traffic. Continue westerly through the open ponderosa pine (*Pinus ponderosa*) forest. In a short distance the track passes the junction with a trail to the left that leads south to an equestrian trailhead. Hike straight ahead (west) at the junction. In places the paved Trail of the Coeur d'Alenes is visible below to the south. Wild roses and lupine line the route, and white-tailed deer (*Odocoileus virginianus*) are often seen in this area.

The track crosses a creek in a draw 0.5 mile from the trailhead. Another 0.4 mile of hiking brings you to the trail junction that begins the first loop section of this hike. Hike straight ahead (northwest) at the junction. The tread crosses another draw 0.2 mile past the junction. In the draw the woods becomes mostly Douglas fir (*Pseudotsuga menziesii*) with a brushy understory that includes Rocky Mountain maple (*Acer glabrum*).

The course enters another draw 0.5 mile farther along. You first climb along the east slope of this draw, then you cross the bottom at a little over 2,600 feet

Whitetail Loop Trail

elevation. The trace continues to climb for another 300 yards along the west slope of the draw. Then you descend slightly, reaching the junction with the Plummer Creek Fire Trail, slightly over 0.3 mile after crossing the bottom of the draw. This junction is 2.2 miles from the Indian Cliffs Trailhead at 2,620 feet elevation.

Hike straight ahead (west-northwest) at the junction with the Plummer Creek Fire Trail, and start to climb. In 0.1 mile the route turns north along a fence line. This fence line is Heyburn State Park's western boundary and the line between Benewah and Kootenai Counties. The Whitetail Loop follows the fence line north for 0.6 mile. Then you turn right, at 2,780 feet elevation, and hike east through the open woods of ponderosa pine, Douglas fir, and western larch (*Larix occidentalis;* aka tamarack). This area has been partially cut at sometime in the past. After hiking through the partial cut for about 0.9 mile, the course enters denser timber. The track follows the edge of another partial cut 0.5 mile farther along. You will reach the junction with the Shoeffler Butte Loop 1.6 miles after leaving the fence line. This junction, 4.5 miles from the Indian Cliffs Trailhead, is at 2,920 feet elevation. The Mullan Military Road also reaches this junction from the east. See "Options" below.

Turn left at the junction and climb to the northwest on the Shoeffler Butte Loop. This part of the Shoeffler Butte Loop is also an abandoned roadbed. The track climbs gently at first, then steepens slightly, making a sweeping switch-back to the right 1 mile from the junction. Then you continue to climb, heading east-northeast and generally following a ridgeline. In about 0.5 mile the route becomes steeper, and another 0.2 mile brings you to the summit of Shoeffler Butte. The summit is at 3,366 feet elevation (a sign says 3,320) and you are 6.2 miles into this hike. This is a good place to take a break, have a snack or lunch, and look at the scenery. For better or worse, there is good cell phone service at the summit of Shoeffler Butte.

When you are ready to continue your hike, the track, which is now a trail rather than a roadbed, descends to the southeast. The route is a little vague as you start down. Three hundred yards from the summit, there is a post on the left side of the trail, marking the state park boundary. The trail remains within the state park and continues to descend. In slightly over 0.5 mile, you reach the junction with the Mullan Military Road, the Whitetail Loop, and another roadbed.

At the junction hike straight ahead (south), crossing the roadbed. You are now back on the Whitetail Loop. In 0.1 mile the trail intersects another roadbed. Turn right on the rocked roadbed and continue south. After about 0.1 mile the road is no longer rocked. Follow the dirt road along a poorly defined ridgeline for 0.4 mile. Then the route bears left off the rounded ridge. About 200 yards farther along, bear right (there is a vague trail to the left here), staying on the main route. There will soon be a view of Chatcolet Lake below to your left. The route has now become a singletrack trail.

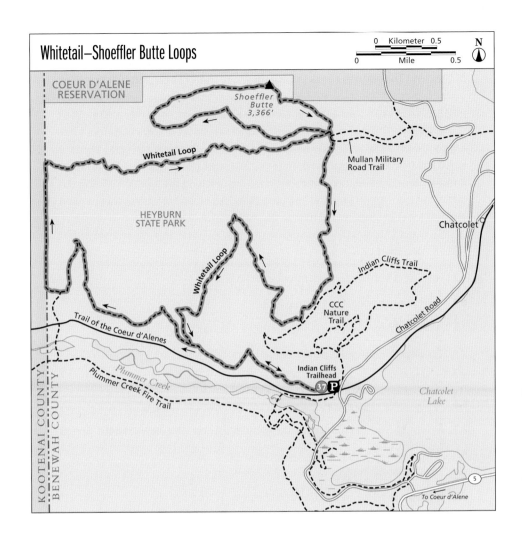

0   Kilometer   0.5

0   Mile   0.5

N

COEUR D'ALENE RESERVATION

Shoeffler Butte 3,366'

Whitetail Loop

Mullan Military Road Trail

HEYBURN STATE PARK

Chatcolet

Whitetail Loop

Indian Cliffs Trail

CCC Nature Trail

Chatcolet Road

Trail of the Coeur d'Alenes

Plummer Creek

Plummer Creek Fire Trail

Indian Cliffs Trailhead

37 P

Chatcolet Lake

KOOTENAI COUNTY

BENEWAH COUNTY

5

To Coeur d'Alene

🍃 **Green Tip:**
Don't take souvenirs home with you. This means natural materials such as plants, rocks, shells, and driftwood as well as historic artifacts such as fossils and arrowheads.

The course reaches the signed junction with the Indian Cliffs Trail 0.2 mile farther along. Really this is a junction with a very short connecting trail that joins with the Indian Cliffs Trail. The GPS coordinates at this junction are N47 21.919' / W116 47.019'. Bear right at the junction. The tread soon descends a semi-open slope. Then you hike northwest, crossing three very small side draws before turning southwest as you cross the head of a major draw. The track traverses a brushy slope and leaves the major draw. Then you descend a semi-open rounded ridgeline and slope, making two switchbacks before reaching the junction ending the Whitetail Loop. At this junction you have hiked 9.8 miles. Turn left at the junction and retrace your steps for 0.9 mile to the Indian Cliffs Trailhead.

MILES AND DIRECTIONS

0.0 Hike west from Indian Cliffs Trailhead.

0.9 Hike straight ahead to start the loop.

2.2 At the junction with the Plummer Creek Fire Trail, hike straight ahead.

2.9 Turn right, leaving the park boundary fence.

4.5 Turn left at the junction with Shoeffler Butte Loop.

6.2 At the summit of Shoeffler Butte, hike southeast.

6.7 Return to the junction with the Whitetail Loop and hike straight ahead (south).

9.8 Turn left at the trail junction, ending the loop.

10.7 Arrive back at the Indian Cliffs Trailhead.

Options

You can shorten your hike to 8.5 miles by omitting the Shoeffler Butte Loop and turning right at the junction 4.5 miles into the hike.

The Mullan Military Road Trail can also be used to access the Shoeffler Butte Loop. See "Honorable Mention" on page 235.

Indian Cliffs Trail

Hike to the semi-open, often flower-covered ridge above Chatcolet Lake. Take in the view from the viewpoint before descending again, down through the forest, to the Indian Cliffs Trailhead.

Start: Indian Cliffs Trailhead

Distance: 3.1-mile, lollipop-loop day hike

Hiking time: About 1.5 hours

Difficulty: Moderate

Best season: Late spring through early fall

Canine compatibility / other trail users: This trail is open to hikers only. Dogs are prohibited.

Fees and permits: A day-use fee is charged; camping fees no longer cover day use. Get your Day-Use Permit at the visitor center.

Maps: *Heyburn State Park Trail System*, available free at the visitor center, covers the trails in Heyburn State Park and is adequate for the hikes described in this book. Montana Mapping & GPS LLC's Hunting and GPS maps are good topos of the area for your GPS unit. The National Geographic *Idaho* map on CD-ROM is also a good topo. However, neither of these show all the trails.

Trail contact: Heyburn State Park Manager, 57 Chatcolet Rd., Plummer, ID 83851; (206) 686-1308; fax (206) 686-0171; hey@idpr.idaho .gov; www.parksandrecreation .idaho.gov

Finding the trailhead: Leave I-90 at exit 12 in Coeur d'Alene. Then drive south on US 95 for 31 miles to Plummer. Turn left on SH 5 in Plummer and drive east for 6.3 miles to the entrance to Heyburn State Park. Turn left and go 50 yards to the visitor center. Turn left again and drive 1.1 miles to the Indian Cliffs Trailhead, which is on your left. The elevation at the trailhead is 2,190 feet. GPS: N47 21.627' / W116 46.763'

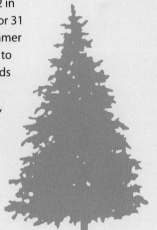

38

THE HIKE

The Indian Cliffs Trail and the CCC Nature Trail begin along the same route. As you leave the trailhead, the track first climbs three steps, then passes a reader board. The course crosses a small wooden bridge 0.2 mile from the trailhead. Just after crossing the bridge is the trail junction that starts the loop portion of this hike. Bear right (nearly straight ahead) at the junction and hike northeast, climbing moderately through the mixed conifer forest. Western white pine (*Pinus monticola*), Douglas fir (*Pseudotsuga menziesii*), grand fir (*Abies grandis*), and western larch (*Larix occidentalis*) make up the mix of trees. Another 0.1 mile brings you to a junction with an abandoned roadbed. Turn slightly left and follow the roadbed, continuing the northeasterly course. The track soon crosses another small wooden bridge over an often-dry stream.

Soon the roadbed becomes less distinct. The forest mix here also contains western red cedar (*Thuja plicata*) and pacific yew (*Taxus brevifolia*) trees in the damper spots. Bunchberry (*Cornus canadensis*) plants sprout beside the trail beneath the shade-producing forest canopy. The route begins to climb 0.6 mile after starting the loop. Soon a few ponderosa pines (*Pinus ponderosa*) show up in the slightly drier ground and an occasional mountain lady slipper (*Cypripedium*

Chatcolet Lake

montanum) graces the trailside. The tread makes a switchback to the left 1.1 miles from the trailhead. A bench sits beside the trail next to the switchback, which is at 2,450 feet elevation.

Past the switchback the trail climbs to the northwest, soon passing above a talus slope. The route flattens out at 2,690 feet elevation 0.4 mile past the switchback. The dry southeast-facing slope of this rounded ridgeline is covered with a semi-open ponderosa pine forest. The ground is covered with grass, arnica (*Arnica*), lupine (*Lupinus*), desert parsley (*Lomatium*), and arrowleaf balsamroot (*Balsamorhiza sagittata*). To the right, on top of and over the ridgeline, ninebark (*Physocarpus malvaceus*) brush covers the forest floor. Dark cliffs appear below to the left as you traverse along the ridgeline.

About 0.3 mile along the ridgeline, there is a trail junction. The trail to the left leads to a viewpoint overlooking the cliffs, with Chatcolet Lake far below to the southeast. The GPS coordinates at the viewpoint are N47 22.020' / W116 46.775'. After taking in the view, return to the main trail and hike west, descending the brushy west slope of the ridge. In a little less than 0.1 mile, the course makes a turn to the left and crosses another small wooden bridge over a usually dry stream. The tread then climbs gently, reaching the junction with a path to the right in another 0.3 mile. The path leads to the Whitetail Loop Trail in just a few yards. This junction at 2,670 feet elevation is 2.2 miles into the hike.

Hike straight ahead to the southwest from the junction, and quickly start descending a semi-open slope. There is a sign about the Indian Cliffs Fire next to the trail, 0.2 mile past the junction. Then the route passes a bench as you make a switchback to the left. Another 0.4 mile brings you to the junction with the CCC Nature Trail. Hike straight ahead here, staying on the Indian Cliffs Trail, and quickly reach the junction with the other end of the CCC Nature Trail. Continue straight ahead, cross another small wooden bridge, and reach the junction that ends the loop portion of this hike. Turn right at this junction and retrace your steps the 0.2 mile to the Indian Cliffs Trailhead.

MILES AND DIRECTIONS

0.0 Hike north from Indian Cliffs Trailhead.

0.2 At the trail junction, bear right (nearly straight ahead) to begin the loop.

1.8 A path to the left leads to a viewpoint.

2.2 Pass the path to the Whitetail Loop Trail.

2.8 At the junction with the CCC Nature Trail, hike straight ahead.

2.9 Turn right at a junction, ending the loop.

3.1 Arrive back at the Indian Cliffs Trailhead.

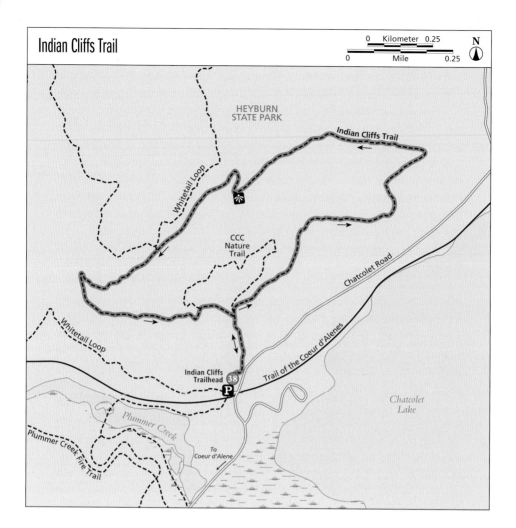

Indian Cliffs Trail

HEYBURN STATE PARK

Indian Cliffs Trail

Whitetail Loop

CCC Nature Trail

Chatcolet Road

Whitetail Loop

Indian Cliffs Trailhead 38

Trail of the Coeur d'Alenes

Chatcolet Lake

Plummer Creek

Plummer Creek Fire Trail

To Coeur d'Alene

Options

Hike the Civilian Conservation Corps (CCC) Nature Trail (Hike 39) on the same trip. They leave from the same trailhead.

Pine Species Identification

You can easily tell the species of pines apart by the number of needles that are bundled together as they come out of the branches. Western white pine is called a five-needle pine because it has five needles in a bundle. Lodgepole pine has two and ponderosa pine three.

CCC Nature Trail

Hike through the beautiful mixed conifer forest above Chatcolet Lake on a self-guided nature trail. The Civilian Conservation Corps (CCC) Company #1995 constructed the CCC Trail in 1937, at the height of the Great Depression.

Start: Indian Cliffs Trailhead
Distance: 1.2-mile lollipop-loop day hike
Hiking time: About 1 hour
Difficulty: Easy
Best seasons: Spring, summer, and fall
Canine compatibility / other trail users: This trail is open to hikers only. Dogs are prohibited.
Fees and permits: A day-use fee is charged; camping fees no longer cover day use. Get your Day-Use Permit at the visitor center.
Maps: *Civilian Conservation Corps Company #1995 Nature Trail,* available free at the visitor center, covers this trail and guides you to the fauna along the way. *Heyburn State Park Trail System,* available free at the visitor center, covers the trails in Heyburn State Park but has very limited detail.
Trail contact: Heyburn State Park Manager, 57 Chatcolet Rd., Plummer, ID 83851; (206) 686-1308; fax (206) 686-0171; hey@idpr.idaho.gov; www.parksandrecreation.idaho.gov
Special considerations: Be sure to pick up a copy of the *Civilian Conservation Corps Company #1995 Nature Trail* pamphlet at the visitor center before you start this hike. Not only is this pamphlet a guide to the flora at each of the nature trail markers, it also gives you an interesting overview of the Civilian Conservation Corps's contributions to Heyburn State Park.

Finding the trailhead: From Coeur d'Alene, drive south on US 95 for 31 miles to Plummer. Turn left and drive east from Plummer on SH 5 for 6.3 miles to the entrance to Heyburn State Park. Turn left and go 50 yards to the visitor center. Turn left again and drive 1.1 miles to the Indian Cliffs Trailhead, which is on your left. The elevation at the trailhead is 2,190 feet. GPS: N47 21.627' / W116 46.763'

THE HIKE

The CCC Nature Trail and the Indian Cliffs Trail begin along the same route, heading north from the Indian Cliffs Trailhead. As you leave the trailhead, the trail first climbs three steps, then passes a reader board. The course crosses a small wooden bridge 0.2 mile from the trailhead. Just after crossing the bridge is a trail junction, where you will bear left. The route quickly crosses another wooden boardwalk over a tiny stream, then reaches another trail junction.

Turn right at this junction and begin the loop portion of this hike by crossing another small wooden bridge. The course climbs moderately, passing nature trail marker #1, which is next to a large western white pine (*Pinus monticola*). The track passes markers #2, #3, and #4, then crosses another small wooden bridge over a tiny stream. Just after passing marker #5, the trail makes a turn to the left. At the turn you have climbed to 2,300 feet elevation and are a little less than 0.5 mile from the Indian Cliffs Trailhead. Soon you pass marker #6 next to a big ponderosa pine (*Pinus ponderosa*).

Now the route descends very gently as you pass markers #7, #8, and #9. Then you climb moderately, making a couple of switchbacks. At the second switchback there is a talus slope above to your right. The track crosses another tiny

Talus slope above the trail

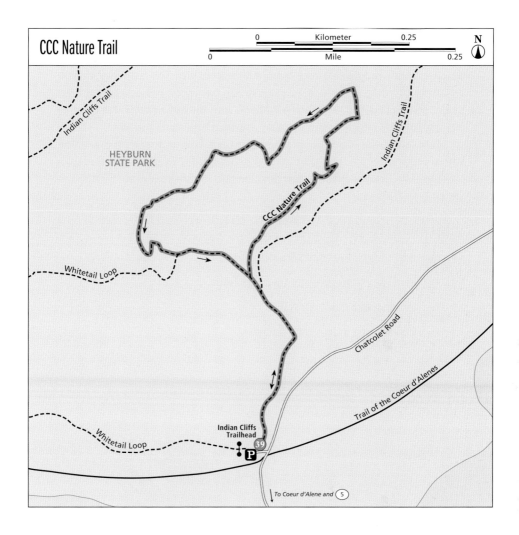

Kilometer

0   0.25

Mile

0   0.25

Indian Cliffs Trail

HEYBURN
STATE PARK

Indian Cliffs Trail

CCC Nature Trail

Whitetail Loop

Chatcolet Road

Trail of the Coeur d'Alenes

Whitetail Loop

Indian Cliffs
Trailhead

39

P

To Coeur d'Alene and 5

🌿 Green Tip:
*Observe wildlife from a distance. Don't interfere in their
lives—both of you will be better for it. Some wildlife
can be dangerous, especially moose.*

wooden bridge 0.7 mile into the hike. As you pass markers #10 and #11, the trail becomes a little rough and rocky, but not difficult to hike. This is the highest you get along this route at 2,340 feet elevation. The track soon passes a bench, then begins to descend. You will reach a junction with the Indian Cliffs Trail 0.1 mile after passing the bench. At this junction you are 0.9 mile into the hike.

Turn left at the junction on the Indian Cliffs Trail and reach the junction where you started the loop portion of the CCC Nature Trail in a little less than 0.1 mile. Hike straight ahead at this junction and retrace your route back to the Indian Cliffs Trailhead.

MILES AND DIRECTIONS

0.0 Hike north from Indian Cliffs Trailhead.

0.2 At the trail junctions bear left, then turn right.

0.9 Turn left on the Indian Cliffs Trail.

1.2 Arrive back at the Indian Cliffs Trailhead.

Options
Do Hike 37 or 38 on the same trip—they start from the same trailhead.

Lakeshore Loop Trail

Hike along the shoreline of Chatcolet Lake from Hawley's Landing Campground to the Indian Cliffs Trailhead. Along the way, make a side trip on the boardwalk out into Plummer Creek Marsh. Then return along the forested hillside above the lake.

Start: The Lakeshore Loop Trailhead in Hawley's Landing Campground

Distance: 5-mile loop day hike, with a short side trip

Hiking time: About 3 hours

Difficulty: Easy

Best seasons: Spring, summer, and fall

Canine compatibility / other trail users: Outbound (for the first 2.1 miles) this route is open to hikers and mountain bikers only. The return part of the course is also open to horses. Dogs are prohibited.

Fees and permits: A day-use fee is charged, camping fees no longer cover day use. Get your Day-Use Permit at the visitor center.

Maps: *Heyburn State Park Trail System,* available free at the visitor center, covers the trails in Heyburn State Park. This map's detail is limited but it is adequate for this hike.

Trail contact: Heyburn State Park Manager, 57 Chatcolet Rd., Plummer, ID 83851; (206) 686-1308; fax (206) 686-0171; hey@idpr.idaho.gov; www.parksandrecreation.idaho.gov

Special considerations: Take along your binoculars and possibly a bird-identification book. There are several species of waterfowl as well as many other birds along the shoreline and especially along the Plummer Creek Marsh boardwalk.

Finding the trailhead: Take exit 12 off I-90 in Coeur d'Alene. Then drive south on US 95 for 31 miles to Plummer. From Plummer, drive east on SH 5 for 6.3 miles to the entrance to Heyburn State Park. Turn left and go 50 yards to the visitor center. Then turn right into Hawley's Landing Campground. The trailhead is in Hawley's Landing Campground next to the walk-in tent sites. Parking is very limited at the trailhead, so park in the visitor center parking area and walk from there. GPS: N47 21.331'/W116 46.294'

THE HIKE

From the trailhead the route descends a short distance northwest to a trail junction. Turn left at the junction and hike southwest along the shoreline of Chatcolet Lake. In 0.1 mile the route passes between the lake and the visitor center. The track soon crosses two small wooden bridges as you hike between Chatcolet Road and Chatcolet Lake. Grand fir (*Abies grandis*), Douglas fir (*Pseudotsuga menziesii*), and western red cedar (*Thuja plicata*) line the trailside, with thimbleberry (*Rubus parviflorus*) and an occasional honeysuckle (*lonicera ciliosa*) beneath the tall timber. Bald eagles (*Haliaeetus leucocephalus*) can sometimes be seen soaring above the lake or sitting in the snags around it. You will pass a couple of benches and a reader board discussing the red-breasted nuthatch (*Sitta canadensis*).

The tread passes beneath some large cedars and western hemlocks (*Tsuga heterophylla*), crosses two more small wooden bridges, and passes another bench before reaching the parking area at the Plummer Creek Marsh Interpretive Area. The interpretive area is just over 1 mile from the Lakeshore Loop Trailhead. Next to the parking area are picnic tables, a viewing blind, restrooms, and a kiosk. Take

Plummer Creek

the time to make a side trip here by following the trail past the kiosk and blind and on to the boardwalk, which extends into the marsh. Two viewing platforms in the marsh are great places to enjoy the local wildlife. The entire side trip into the marsh is only about 0.5 mile round-trip.

After enjoying the marsh, return to the parking area and hike northwest, quickly crossing Chatcolet Road. You are now on the Plummer Creek Trail. After crossing the road the trail leads northwest, between a gravel road and Plummer Creek. A sign here points to the Indian Cliffs Trailhead. The route reaches a trail junction in 0.4 mile. To the left is a trail that connects with Plummer Creek Fire Trail. This connector trail will be your return route, but for now hike straight ahead, staying on the Plummer Creek Trail. The tread turns northeast and soon crosses a bridge over Plummer Creek. A short distance farther along is the junction with the Appaloosa Trail. Turn right at this junction. In 0.2 mile the trail forks. Turn right here (horse traffic goes straight ahead). In a short distance the trail reaches an abandoned roadbed. Turn left, staying just left of the roadbed, and soon cross the paved Trail of the Coeur d'Alenes. Just after crossing the Trail of the Coeur d'Alenes, you will reach the Indian Cliffs Trailhead, which is your

Honeysuckle

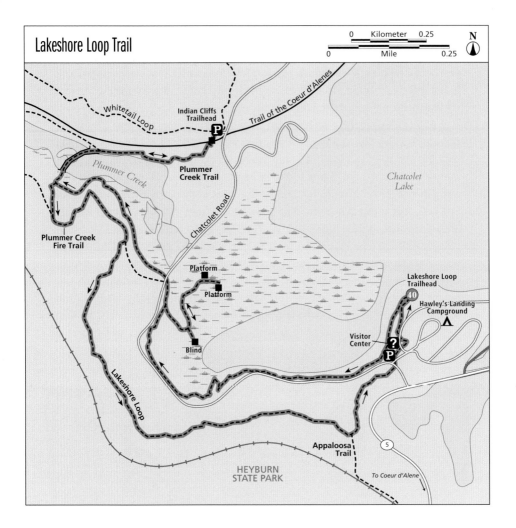

turnaround point. The Whitetail Loop, Indian Cliffs Trail, and CCC Nature Trail all start at the Indian Cliffs Trailhead, making lengthening your hike possible. The elevation at the Indian Cliffs Trailhead is 2,190 feet.

To continue on the Lakeshore Loop hike, retrace your route for 0.5 mile back across the Plummer Creek Bridge to the junction with the connector trail to the Plummer Creek Fire Trail. Turn right at the junction and climb through the western hemlock forest for a little over 0.1 mile to the junction with the Plummer Creek Fire Trail. Turn left on the Plummer Creek Fire Trail, which is a dirt road-bed, and hike east. The mixed conifer forest along the fire trail includes grand fir, Douglas fir, western hemlock, western larch (*Larix occidentalis*), and western white pine (*Pinus monticola*).

In 0.3 mile you will come to a junction with the gravel road that is part of the Lakeshore Loop. Turn right on the roadbed and climb fairly steeply to the south-southwest, soon reaching a water-treatment plant. Bear left here, leaving the road and going around the fenced lagoon. The trail becomes a dirt two track on the far side of the lagoon. This roadbed follows an underground cable. The route ungulates gently for the next 0.9 mile to another junction with the Appaloosa Trail. This junction is 4.6 miles into the hike (including side trips). Hike straight ahead at the junction (soon heading northeast). In about 250 yards you will pass a gate. Bear right here and soon reach the paved road that is the access to the visitor center. Turn left on the road, then right into Hawley's Landing Campground, or left into the visitor center parking area if your car is parked there.

MILES AND DIRECTIONS

0.0 Start at the Lakeshore Loop Trailhead.

1.0 Walk to the end of the Plummer Creek Marsh Interpretive Trail and return.

1.6 Cross the paved road.

2.0 Hike straight ahead, staying on the Plummer Creek Trail.

2.1 Cross the bridge over Plummer Creek.

2.2 Turn right at the junction with the Appaloosa Trail.

2.6 Turn around at the Indian Cliffs Trailhead.

3.1 Turn right at the trail junction.

3.3 Turn left on the Plummer Creek Fire Trail.

3.6 Turn right, staying on Lakeshore Loop.

4.6 Hike straight ahead at the junction with the Appaloosa Trail.

4.9 Cross the road in front of the visitor center.

5.0 Arrive back at the Lakeshore Loop Trailhead.

Options

To extend your hike, add on the Indian Cliffs Trail (Hike 38) or the CCC Nature Trail (Hike 39). For an even longer hike (15.7 miles round-trip), combine the Lakeshore Loop with the Whitetail–Shoeffler Butte Loop (Hike 37).

James E. Dewey–Iron Mountain Loop

The 5,000-acre-plus Mary Minerva McCroskey State Park, because of its remote location and no-fee policies, is a great place to spend a few days hiking and camping. Two of the three campgrounds in the park are located on mountaintops and the third is on a ridgeline. This makes for nearby, multidirectional views as you leave the tent in the morning. Wild turkeys, elk, and white-tailed deer are commonly seen throughout the vast park.

Start: Trailhead at the junction of Skyline Drive and King Valley Road

Distance: 1.9-mile shuttle or 3.5-mile loop day hike

Hiking time: About 1.5 to 2 hours

Difficulty: Easy to moderate

Best seasons: Late spring, summer, and early fall

Canine compatibility / other trail users: Dogs are allowed but must be kept under close control. The trails in McCroskey State Park are multiple-use so you may meet horses, bikes, and ORVs. Most of the time traffic is light enough that this is not a problem.

Fees and permits: None

Maps: The *Mary Minerva McCroskey State Park Map,* available as you enter the state park, covers the area and shows the trails. This map, however, is small-scale and not a topo, limiting its usefulness as a hiking map. National Geographic *Idaho* maps on CD-ROM are good topos of the area. Montana Mapping & GPS LLC's Hunting and GPS maps are good topos of the area for your GPS unit.

The map included in this book is adequate for this hike.

Trail contact: Heyburn & McCroskey State Parks, 1291 Chatcolet Rd., Plummer, ID 83851; (206) 686-1308; mcc@idpr.idaho.gov; www.parksandrecreation.idaho.gov

Special considerations: Water is available only at the junction of Skyline Drive and Mission Mountain Road (milepost 8.75 on Skyline Drive). The national forest land that borders the park is open to hunting. During the fall hunting seasons, you may want to wear orange or other bright-colored clothing while hiking.

Finding the trailhead: From exit 12 on I-90 in Coeur d'Alene, drive south on US 95 for 43 miles to Tensed. Continue south on US 95 from Tensed for 1.2 miles to the junction with Desmet Road. Turn right (west) on Desmet Road and go 0.8 mile to the junction with King Valley Road. Turn left on King Valley Road and follow it 6.2 miles to the junction with Skyline Drive. Turn right on Skyline Drive and quickly turn right again into the parking area. A small sign marks the trailhead at 3,630 feet elevation. GPS: N47 06.174'/W116 58.351'

To reach Iron Mountain Campground if this is to be a shuttle hike, continue north on Skyline Drive for 1 mile to the junction with the road to Iron Mountain Campground. Turn right and go 0.3 mile to the campground entrance. Turn left and drive into the mountaintop campground.

THE HIKE

The James E. Dewey Trail leaves from the northeast corner of the small parking area. The singletrack tread leads north-northeast through open ponderosa pine and Douglas fir (*Pseudotsuga menziesii*) forest. The open woods allow for good views to the northeast, looking down into King Valley. The route climbs gently as you traverse this east-facing slope. Walk quietly and watch the terrain around you for the flash of white that means you have spooked a white-tailed deer (*Odocoileus virginianus*). A mile and a quarter from the trailhead, the grade steepens slightly as you ascend to the ridgeline northeast of Iron Mountain's summit.

The route reaches the ridgeline 1.5 miles from the trailhead at 4,020 feet elevation. On the ridgeline is a junction with a dirt roadbed. There is a sign at this junction. Turn left on a dirt road and hike southwest along the ridgeline, passing a primitive campsite. In 0.25 mile you will reach a junction with a gravel road at the entrance to Iron Mountain Campground. Cross the road and continue southwest, taking the campground exit road (left fork). Climb slightly as you enter the campground at the very summit of 4,070-foot-high Iron Mountain. At the campground you are 1.9 miles into the hike. If this is to be a shuttle trip, this is the place to meet your ride.

To continue on the loop, which mostly follows roads from here on, walk the road on around to the southwest corner of the campground and turn left on a broad trail. You will pass an abandoned trail to the left, about 100 yards before turning off the road onto the broad trail. Descend the broad trail (which is also open to ORVs) down the ridgeline. In 0.2 mile the route crosses a gravel road. Continue descending a short distance farther to the junction with Skyline Drive. There is no sign here. Turn left on Skyline Drive and hike east along the road.

In 0.3 mile there is a road junction. Bear right (straight ahead); the road to the left goes back to the Iron Mountain Campground. Continue now generally south along Skyline Drive. In 0.3 mile King Valley Viewpoint is on your left. Stop for a minute and take in the view, then continue south on Skyline Drive for 0.7 mile to the trailhead, completing the loop.

Ponderosa Pine

The ponderosa pine (*Pinus ponderosa*) is the only three-needle pine that is native to the Northwest. Three-needle pine means that needles of up to 8 inches or more grow from the twigs in groups (or bundles) of three, not in groups of two like lodgepole pine or five like western white pine. The ponderosa, often called yellow pine, is a large tree usually 100 feet tall or slightly more at maturity and with a trunk diameter of 3 feet plus. The largest specimens reach in excess of 200 feet tall and a trunk diameter of 7 feet. The ponderosa pine is a very important timber tree in the inland Northwest.

James E. Dewey Trail

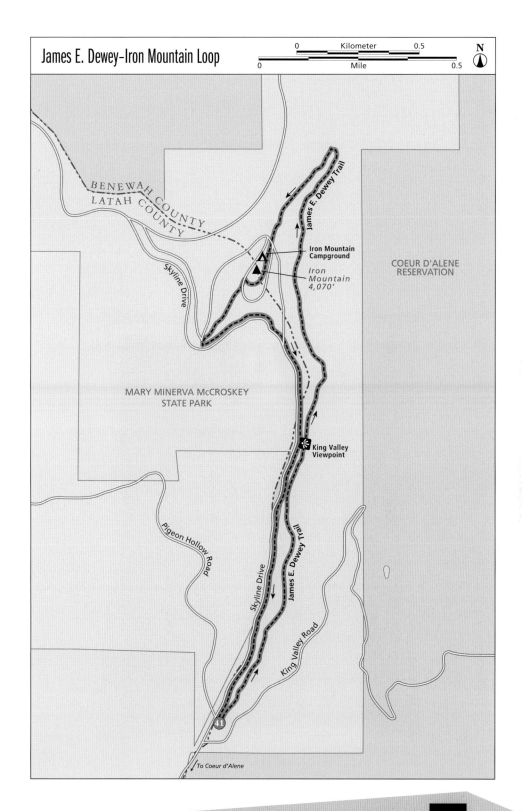

Kilometer

0   0.5

Mile

0   0.5

N

BENEWAH COUNTY
LATAH COUNTY

Skyline Drive

James E. Dewey Trail

Iron Mountain
Campground

*Iron
Mountain
4,070'*

COEUR D'ALENE
RESERVATION

MARY MINERVA McCROSKEY
STATE PARK

King Valley
Viewpoint

Pigeon Hollow Road

Skyline Drive

James E. Dewey Trail

King Valley Road

41

To Coeur d'Alene

MILES AND DIRECTIONS

0.0 Hike north-northeast from the trailhead.

1.5 Turn left at the junction with the roadbed on the ridgeline.

1.9 Pass Iron Mountain Campground (outhouse).

2.2 Turn left on Skyline Drive.

3.5 Arrive back at the trailhead.

Options

While you are in Mary McCroskey State Park, you may also want to hike Fireplace to Mission Mountain Summit (Hike 42) and or Lone Pine Viewpoint (Hike 43).

James E. Dewey Trail

Fireplace to Mission Mountain Summit

Hike the mostly gentle trail along Skyline Ridge in Idaho's second-oldest and third-largest state park. Elk or at least their tracks can be found all along this route, and white-tailed deer may be expected at any point.

Start: Fireplace Campground and Picnic Area

Distance: 1.8-mile shuttle or 3.5-mile out-and-back day hike

Hiking time: About 1-hour shuttle, 2 hours out and back

Difficulty: Easy

Best seasons: Late spring, summer, and early fall

Canine compatibility / other trail users: Dogs are allowed but must be kept under close control. The trails in McCroskey State Park are multiple-use so you may meet horses, bikes, and ORVs. Most of the time traffic is light enough that this is not a problem.

Fees and permits: None

Maps: The *Mary Minerva McCroskey State Park Map,* available as you enter the state park, covers the area and shows the trails. This map, however, is small-scale and not a topo, limiting its usefulness as a hiking map. National Geographic *Idaho* maps on CD-ROM are good topos of the area. Montana Mapping & GPS LLC's Hunting and GPS maps are good topos of the area for your GPS unit. The map included in this book is adequate for this hike.

Trail contact: Heyburn & McCroskey State Parks, 1291 Chatcolet Rd., Plummer, ID 83851; (206) 686-1308; mcc@idpr.idaho.gov; www.parksandrecreation.idaho.gov

Special considerations: Although most of this trail in within McCroskey State Park, parts of it traverse Idaho Panhandle National Forest land. The national forest is open to hunting at times during the fall. At these times it may be a good idea to wear a bright-orange vest or other bright-colored clothes.

Finding the trailhead: Take exit 12 off I-90 in Coeur d'Alene. Then drive south on US 95 for about 43 miles to Tensed. From Tensed, continue south on US 95 for 1.2 miles to the junction with Desmet Road. Turn right (west) on Desmet Road and go 0.8 mile to the junction with King Valley Road. Turn left on King Valley Road and follow it 6.2 miles to the junction with Skyline Drive. Turn left on Skyline Drive and drive south and east for 6.8 miles to Fireplace Campground and Picnic Area, at 3,800 feet elevation. There are restrooms, a picnic shelter, and campsites here but no water. Camping is free. GPS: N47 04.807' /W116 55.065'

THE HIKE

Walk west along Skyline Drive from the Fireplace Picnic Shelter. In 100 yards the broad path bears to the right, leaving Skyline Drive. The wide track is shared with ORVs as are most of the trails in McCroskey State Park. Usually traffic is light enough not to cause much interference between the diverse user groups. The course follows close to the ridgeline, heading west at first, then turning to the southwest. Ponderosa pines (*Pinus ponderosa*) and a couple of species of firs dominate the forest canopy, with Rocky Mountain maple for an understory tree in many places.

The trail climbs somewhat steeply for a short distance, gaining about 80 feet of elevation in the 300 yards to a trail junction. Bear left (nearly straight ahead) at the junction, staying on the ridgeline. Past the trail junction the track continues to climb gently. Elk tracks can usually be seen along this part of the trail, and it may be possible to catch a glimpse of some of these magnificent animals. The woods open up 0.8 mile into the hike, allowing for good views to the southeast, east, and northeast. In the fall the leaves of the Rocky Mountain maple can be spectacular here. About 1 mile from Fireplace Campground and Picnic Area, the route reaches 4,240 feet elevation, then begins to descend gently. A junction with Skyline Drive is reached in another 0.25 mile.

Fireplace Picnic Shelter

Before you make the final 0.5-mile climb to the summit of Mission Mountain, you may want to check out the informational reader board a few yards farther to the southwest along Skyline Drive. To continue to the summit, walk a few feet southwest along Skyline Drive, then bear right again. The route parallels the road for a short distance, then winds gently up the ridgeline. There is a trail junction 0.3 mile after leaving the junction with Skyline Drive. Turn left at the junction. In another 0.1 mile the track angles left across the access road for Mission Mountain Campground. Once across the road the tread climbs another 0.1 mile to the summit of Mission Mountain and the campground that's located there.

A restroom and tables are available at the campground, but there is no water. Water is available at the junction of Mission Mountain Road and Skyline Drive about 1 mile (by road) to the south. Camping is free at Mission Mountain, as it is at the other campgrounds in McCroskey State Park.

If you haven't arranged for a shuttle, return as you came to Fireplace Campground and Picnic Area.

Rocky Mountain Maple

More a shrub than a tree, the Rocky Mountain maple (*Acer glabrum*) grows up to about 20 feet tall. Its three- to five-lobed leaves are toothed on the edges and turn a bright orange-red in autumn. The fall leaves tend to be redder in open areas where the maples receive more direct sunlight. When growing beneath a conifer canopy, the fall color is more likely to be yellow. The easily bent stems of the Rocky Mountain maple were used by Native Americans for making snowshoe frames.

Rocky Mountain maple is often mistaken for vine maple (*Acer circinatum*), which generally grows in the wetter climate west of the Cascade Range. They are actually fairly easy to tell apart as the vine maple has seven to nine lobes on its leaves.

MILES AND DIRECTIONS

0.0 Hike west from Fireplace Campground and Picnic Area.

1.3 Pass the junction with Skyline Drive.

1.8 Turn around at Mission Mountain Summit or shuttle back.

3.5 Arrive back at the Fireplace Campground and Picnic Area.

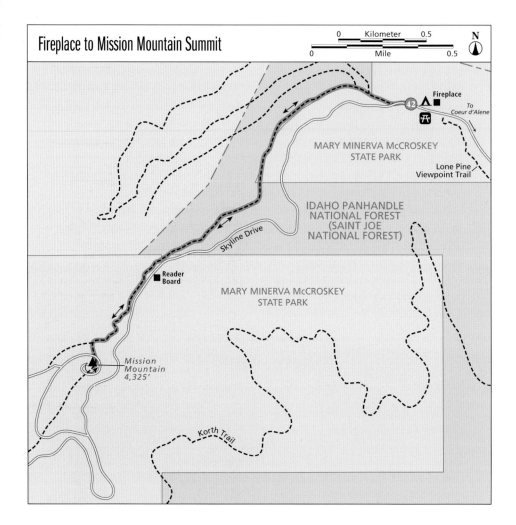

Fireplace to Mission Mountain Summit

0   Kilometer   0.5

0   Mile   0.5

N

Fireplace
To
Coeur d'Alene

42

MARY MINERVA McCROSKEY
STATE PARK

Lone Pine
Viewpoint Trail

IDAHO PANHANDLE
NATIONAL FOREST
(SAINT JOE
NATIONAL FOREST)

Skyline Drive

Reader
Board

MARY MINERVA McCROSKEY
STATE PARK

Mission
Mountain
4,325'

Korth Trail

Options

Combine this hike with the Lone Pine Viewpoint
Trail (Hike 43). They both start from Fireplace
Campground and Picnic Area. If you have the
time, camp at either Fireplace Campground and
Picnic Area or Mission Mountain Summit
Campground.

Lone Pine Viewpoint

Hike this short trail along the upper southern slope of Skyline Ridge, through diverse transitional zone forest that is being managed to mimic the way nature intended this type of woods to be. Watch for elk and white-tailed deer all along this route—they are common here.

Start: Fireplace Campground and Picnic Area
Distance: 0.8-mile shuttle or 1.6-mile out-and-back day hike
Hiking time: About 0.5-hour shuttle or 1 hour out and back
Difficulty: Easy
Best seasons: Late spring, summer, and early fall
Canine compatibility / other trail users: Dogs are allowed but must be kept under close control. The trails in McCroskey State Park are multiple-use so you may meet horses, bikes, and ORVs. Most of the time traffic is light enough that this is not a problem.
Fees and permits: None
Maps: The *Mary Minerva McCroskey State Park Map,* available as you enter the state park, covers the area and shows the trails. This map, however, is small-scale and not a topo, limiting its usefulness as a hiking map. National Geographic *Idaho* maps on CD-ROM are good topos of the area. Montana Mapping & GPS LLC's Hunting and GPS maps are good topos of the area for your GPS unit. The map included in this book is adequate for this hike.
Trail contact: Heyburn & McCroskey State Parks, 1291 Chatcolet Rd., Plummer, ID 83851; (206) 686-1308; mcc@idpr.idaho.gov; www.parksandrecreation.idaho.gov
Special considerations: If you plan to camp at Fireplace Campground, bring along all the water that you will need. The closest available potable water is along Skyline Drive, 2.7 miles to the west.

Finding the trailhead: From exit 12 on I-90 in Coeur d'Alene, drive south on US 95 for about 43 miles to Tensed. Continue south on US 95 from Tensed for 1.2 miles to the junction with Desmet Road. Turn right (west) on Desmet Road and go 0.8 mile to the junction with King Valley Road. Turn left on King Valley Road and follow it 6.2 miles to the junction with Skyline Drive. Turn left on Skyline Drive and drive south and east for 6.8 miles to Fireplace Campground and Picnic Area, at 3,800 feet elevation. There are restrooms, a picnic shelter, and campsites here but no water. Camping is free. GPS: N47 04.807' /W116 55.065'

THE HIKE

Walk a few yards east on Skyline Drive from the Fireplace Picnic Shelter, then turn right on the Lone Pine Viewpoint Trail. There is a sign where the trail leaves the road. At first the route heads south through the mixed forest consisting of Douglas fir (*Pseudotsuga menziesii*), grand fir (*Abies grandis*), western larch (*Larix occidentalis;* also called tamarack), and ponderosa pine (*Pinus ponderosa*). As it is in most of McCroskey State Park, Rocky Mountain maple (*Acer glabrum*) is an understory tree.

Shortly the track bears to the southeast and you enter a prescribed burn area. In McCroskey State Park as well as nearby Heyburn State Park, forest practices that mimic nature are practiced. These include select logging and prescribed burning to open up and clean the woods. These practices lessen the likelihood of catastrophic fire that kills nearly everything. In addition, the more-open woods allow far more animal-food-source plants to grow. This in turn feeds the white-tailed deer (*Odocoileus virginianus*), elk (*Cervus canadensis*), and wild turkeys (*Meleagris gallopavo*), as well as smaller animals and birds. Another advantage of the open forest is the views of the surrounding country.

The trail descends slightly 0.2 mile from the trailhead and joins an abandoned roadbed. Once on the roadbed the track ascends gently. The course

View from Lone Pine Viewpoint

leaves the prescribed burn area temporarily 0.4 mile from the trailhead. The abandoned roadbed, which you're still following, is nicely reverting to a trail. The tread ascends gently for a short distance. Then you bear to the right, leaving the roadbed and descending fairly steeply. Shortly the track climbs again for a short distance then flattens out. There is another prescribed burn area to the left of the trail, 0.7 mile from the trailhead. Another 0.1 mile of hiking brings you to the junction with the access road to Lone Pine Viewpoint. There is a sign at this junction that states that it is 0.8 mile to the Fireplace Picnic Area and Campground.

Across the road is an informational sign that is well worth reading. To the right on the roadbed, it's a short distance to Lone Pine Viewpoint. The viewpoint at 3,880 feet elevation provides good views to the south. If you haven't arranged for a car shuttle, turn around and hike back the way you came to Fireplace Picnic Area and Campground.

Douglas Fir

The Douglas fir (*Pseudotsuga menziesii*) is not a true fir but a separate and unique species. Its Latin name means false hemlock. In the wetter areas closer to the Pacific Ocean, the Douglas fir has been known to achieve a height of over 380 feet and a diameter of over 14 feet. You won't find any of these trees anywhere near this big in the inland Northwest, however. Mature trees here are usually 150 to 180 feet tall and 3 or 4 feet in diameter. The thick, deeply furrowed bark of the Douglas fir provides good protection from low-intensity fires, and on many old trees fire scars are in evidence. Douglas fir is a long-lived tree, sometimes reaching 1,000 years of age. Probably the most important timber tree in the Pacific Northwest, the Douglas fir (aka red fir in the inland Northwest) is used for a wide variety of wood products. It is also one of the better sources of firewood.

MILES AND DIRECTIONS

0.0 Hike east from Fireplace Picnic Area and Campground.

0.8 Turn around at Lone Pine Viewpoint.

1.6 Arrive back at the Fireplace Picnic Area and Campground.

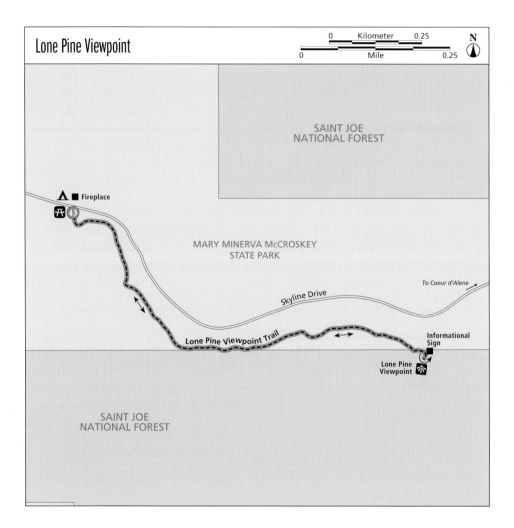

Lone Pine Viewpoint

Fireplace

SAINT JOE
NATIONAL FOREST

MARY MINERVA McCROSKEY
STATE PARK

Skyline Drive

To Coeur d'Alene

Lone Pine Viewpoint Trail

Informational
Sign

Lone Pine
Viewpoint

SAINT JOE
NATIONAL FOREST

Options

Using Fireplace Picnic Area and Campground as a base camp, hike this route as well as the trail that continues west along Skyline Ridge. See Hike 42.

Green Tip:
If you're toting food, leave the packaging at home. Repack your provisions in zip-lock bags that you can re-use and that can double as garbage bags on the way out of the woods.

D. *Honorable Mention*
Mullan Military Road

A section of the Mullan Military Road in Heyburn State Park leads from Chatcolet Campground, crosses Chatcolet Road, and soon reaches a junction with the Whitetail and Shoeffler Butte Loop Trails. This route may be used to shorten the access to the Shoeffler Butte Loop Trail. It also makes a good hike on its own.

The Art of Hiking

When standing nose to nose with a mountain lion, you're probably not too concerned with the issue of ethical behavior in the wild. No doubt you're just terrified. But let's be honest: How often are you nose to nose with a mountain lion? For most of us, a hike into the "wild" means loading up the SUV with expensive gear and driving to a toileted trailhead. Sure, you can mourn how civilized we've become—how GPS units have replaced natural instinct and Gore-Tex stands in for true grit—but the silly gadgets of civilization aside, we have plenty of reason to take pride in how we've matured. With survival now on the back burner, we've begun to understand that we have a responsibility to protect, no longer just conquer, our wild places—that they, not we, are at risk. So please, do what you can.

The following section will help you understand better what it means to "do what you can" while still making the most of your hiking experience. Anyone can take a hike, but hiking safely and well is an art requiring preparation and proper equipment.

TRAIL ETIQUETTE

Leave no trace. Always leave an area just like you found it—if not better than you found it. Avoid camping in fragile alpine meadows and along the banks of streams and lakes. Use a camp stove versus building a wood fire. Pack up all of your trash and extra food. Bury human waste at least 100 feet from water sources under 6 to 8 inches of topsoil. Don't bathe with soap in a lake or stream; use prepackaged moistened towels to wipe off sweat and dirt, or bathe in the water without soap.

Stay on the trail. It's true, a path anywhere leads nowhere new, but purists will just have to get over it. Paths serve an important purpose: They limit impact on natural areas. Straying from a designated trail may seem innocent but it can cause damage to sensitive areas—damage that may take years to recover, if it can recover at all. Even simple shortcuts can be destructive. So, please, stay on the trail.

Leave no weeds. Noxious weeds tend to overtake other plants, which in turn affects animals and birds that depend on them for food. To minimize the spread of noxious weeds, hikers should regularly clean their boots, tents, packs, and hiking poles of mud and seeds. Also, brush your dog to remove any weed seeds before heading off into a new area.

Keep your dog under control. You can buy a flexi-lead that allows your dog to go exploring along the trail while allowing you the ability to reel him in should another hiker approach or should he decide to chase a rabbit. Always obey leash laws and be sure to bury your dog's waste or pack it in resealable plastic bags.

Respect other trail users. Often you're not the only one on the trail. With the rise in popularity of multiuse trails, you'll have to learn a new kind of respect, beyond the nod-and-hello approach you may be used to. First, investigate whether you're on a multiuse trail, and assume the appropriate precautions. When you encounter motorized vehicles (ATVs, motorcycles, and 4WDs), be alert. Though they should always yield to the hiker, often they're going too fast or are too lost in the buzz of their engine to react to your presence. If you hear activity ahead, step off the trail just to be safe. Note that you're not likely to hear a mountain biker coming, so be prepared and know ahead of time whether you share the trail with them. Cyclists should always yield to hikers, but that's little comfort to the hiker. Be aware.

When you approach horses or pack animals on the trail, always step quietly off the trail, preferably on the downhill side, and let them pass. If you're wearing a large backpack, it's often a good idea to sit down. To some animals, a hiker wearing a large backpack might appear threatening. Many national forests allow domesticated grazing, usually for sheep and cattle. Make sure your dog doesn't harass these animals, and respect ranchers' rights while you're enjoying yours.

GETTING INTO SHAPE

Unless you want to be sore—and possibly have to shorten your trip or vacation—be sure to get in shape before a big hike. If you're terribly out of shape, start a walking program early, preferably eight weeks in advance. Start with a 15-minute walk during your lunch hour or after work and gradually increase your walking time to an hour. You should also increase your elevation gain. Walking briskly up hills really strengthens your leg muscles and gets your heart rate up. If you work in a storied office building, take the stairs instead of the elevator.

If you prefer going to a gym, walk the treadmill or use a stair machine. You can further increase your strength and endurance by walking with a loaded backpack. Stationary exercises you might consider are squats, leg lifts, sit-ups, and push-ups. Other good ways to get in shape include biking, running, aerobics, and, of course, short hikes. Stretching before and after a hike keeps muscles flexible and helps avoid injuries.

PREPAREDNESS

It's been said that failing to plan means planning to fail, so take the necessary time to plan your trip. Whether going on a short day hike or an extended backpack trip, always prepare for the worst. Simply remembering to pack a copy of the *US Army Survival Manual* is not preparedness. Although it's not a bad idea if you plan on entering truly wild places, it's merely the tourniquet answer to a problem. You need to do your best to prevent the problem from arising in the first place. In order to survive—and to stay reasonably comfortable—you need to concern yourself with the basics: water, food, and shelter. Don't go on a hike without having these bases covered. In addition, don't go on a hike expecting to find these items in the woods.

Water. Even in frigid conditions, you need at least two quarts of water a day to function efficiently. Add heat and taxing terrain and you can bump that figure up to one gallon. That's simply a base to work from—your metabolism and your level of conditioning can raise or lower that amount. Unless you know your level, assume that you need one gallon of water a day.

Now, where do you plan on getting the water? Preferably not from natural water sources. These sources can be loaded with intestinal disturbers, such as bacteria, viruses, and fertilizers. *Giardia lamblia,* the most common of these disturbers, is a protozoan parasite that lives part of its life cycle as a cyst in water sources. The parasite spreads when mammals defecate in water sources. Giardia can induce cramping, diarrhea, vomiting, and fatigue within two days to two weeks after ingestion. *Giardiasis* is treatable with prescription drugs. If you believe you've contracted *giardiasis,* see a doctor immediately.

The best and easiest solution to avoid polluted water is to carry your water with you. Yet, depending on the nature of your hike and the duration, this may not be an option—one gallon of water weighs 8.5 pounds. In that case, you'll need to look into treating water. Regardless of which method you choose, you should always carry some water with you in case of an emergency. Save this reserve until you absolutely need it.

There are three methods of treating water: boiling, chemical treatment, and filtering. If you boil water, it's recommended that you do so for 10 to 15 minutes. This is often impractical, however, because you're forced to exhaust a great deal of your fuel supply. You can opt for chemical treatment, which will kill giardia but will not take care of other chemical pollutants. Another drawback to chemical treatments is the unpleasant taste of the water after it's treated. You can remedy this by adding powdered drink mix to the water.

Filters are the preferred method for treating water. Many filters remove giardia and other organic and inorganic contaminants and don't leave an aftertaste. Water filters are far from perfect, as they can easily become clogged or leak if a gasket wears out. It's always a good idea to carry a backup supply of chemical treatment tablets in case your filter decides to quit on you.

Food. If we're talking about survival, you can go days without food as long as you have water. However, we're also talking about comfort. Try to avoid foods that are high in sugar and fat like candy bars and potato chips. These food types are harder to digest and are low in nutritional value. Instead, bring along foods that are easy to pack, nutritious, and high in energy (e.g., bagels, nutrition bars, dehydrated fruit, gorp, and jerky).

If you are on an overnight trip, easy-to-fix dinners include rice mixes, dehydrated potatoes, corn, pasta with cheese sauce, and soup mixes. For a tasty breakfast, you can fix hot oatmeal with brown sugar and reconstituted milk powder topped off with banana chips. If you like a hot drink in the morning, bring along herbal tea bags or hot chocolate. If you are a coffee junkie, you can purchase coffee that is packaged like tea bags. You can prepackage all of your meals in heavy-duty resealable plastic bags to keep food from spilling in your pack. These bags can be reused to pack out trash.

Shelter. The type of shelter you choose depends less on the conditions than on your tolerance for discomfort. Shelter comes in many forms—tent, tarp, lean-to, bivy sack, cabin, cave, etc. If you're camping in the desert, a bivy sack may suffice, but if you're above the tree line and a storm is approaching, a better choice is a three- or four-season tent. Tents are the logical and most popular choice for most backpackers, as they're lightweight and packable—and you can rest assured that you always have shelter from the elements. Before you leave on your trip, anticipate what the weather and terrain will be like and plan for the type of shelter that will work best for your comfort level (see the "Equipment" section).

To find a campsite, start with established campsites, when available. If not, start looking for a campsite early—around 3:30 or 4:00 p.m. Stop at the first decent site you see. Depending on the area, it could be a long time before you find another suitable location. Pitch your camp in an area that's level. Make sure the area is at least 200 feet from fragile areas like lakeshores, meadows, and stream banks. In addition, try to avoid areas thick in underbrush, as they can harbor insects and provide cover for approaching animals.

If you are camping in stormy, rainy weather, look for a rock outcrop or a shelter in the trees to keep the wind from blowing your tent all night. Be sure that you don't camp under trees with dead limbs that might break off on top of you. Also, try to find an area that has an absorbent surface, such as sandy soil or forest duff. This, in addition to camping on a surface with a slight angle, will provide better drainage. Don't dig trenches to provide drainage around your tent—remember you're practicing zero-impact camping.

If you're in bear country, steer clear of creek beds or animal paths. If you see any signs of a bear's presence (i.e., scat, footprints), relocate. You'll need to find a campsite near a tall tree where you can hang your food and other items that may attract bears such as deodorant, toothpaste, and soap. Carry a lightweight nylon rope with which to hang your food. As a rule, you should hang your food at least 20 feet from the ground and 5 feet away from the tree trunk. You can put food and other items in a waterproof stuff sack and tie one end of the rope to the stuff sack. To get the other end of the rope over the tree branch, tie a good-size rock to it and gently toss the rock over the tree branch. Pull the stuff sack up until it reaches the top of the branch and tie it off securely. Don't hang your food near your tent! If possible, hang your food at least 100 feet away from your campsite. Alternatives to hanging your food are bear-proof plastic tubes and metal bear boxes.

Lastly, think of comfort. Lie down on the ground where you intend to sleep and see if it's a good fit. For morning warmth (and a nice view to wake up to), have your tent face east.

FIRST AID

I know you're tough, but get 10 miles into the woods and develop a blister, and you'll wish you had carried that first-aid kit. Face it: It's just plain good sense. Many companies produce lightweight, compact first-aid kits. Just make sure yours contains at least the following:

- Adhesive bandages
- Moleskin or duct tape
- Various sterile gauzes and dressings
- White surgical tape
- An ACE bandage
- An antihistamine
- Aspirin
- Betadine solution
- A first-aid book
- Antacid tablets
- Tweezers
- Scissors
- Antibacterial wipes
- Triple-antibiotic ointment
- Plastic gloves
- Sterile cotton-tip applicators
- Syrup of ipecac (to induce vomiting)
- Thermometer
- Wire splint

Here are a few tips for dealing with and hopefully preventing certain ailments.

Sunburn. Take along sunscreen or sunblock, protective clothing, and a wide-brimmed hat. If you do get sunburn, treat the area with aloe vera gel and protect the area from further sun exposure. The sun's radiation can be particularly damaging to skin at higher elevations. Remember that your eyes are vulnerable to this radiation as well. Sunglasses can be a good way to prevent headaches and permanent eye damage from the sun, especially in places where light-colored rock or patches of snow reflect light up in your face.

Blisters. Be prepared to take care of these hike-spoilers by carrying moleskin (a lightly padded adhesive), gauze and tape, or adhesive bandages. An effective way to apply moleskin is to cut out a circle of moleskin and remove the center—like a doughnut—and place it over the blistered area. Cutting the center out will reduce the pressure applied to the sensitive skin. Other products can help you combat blisters. Some are applied to suspicious hot spots before a blister forms to help decrease friction to that area, while others are applied to the blister after it has popped to help prevent further irritation.

Insect bites and stings. You can treat most insect bites and stings by applying hydrocortisone 1 percent cream topically and taking a pain medication such as ibuprofen or acetaminophen to reduce swelling. If you forgot to pack these items, a cold compress or a paste of mud and ashes can sometimes assuage the itching and discomfort. Remove any stingers by using tweezers or scraping the area with your fingernail or a knife blade. Don't pinch the area, as you'll only spread the venom.

Some hikers are highly sensitive to bites and stings and may have a serious allergic reaction that can be life-threatening. Symptoms of a serious allergic reaction can include wheezing, an asthmatic attack, and shock. The treatment for this severe type of reaction is epinephrine. If you know that you are sensitive to bites and stings, carry a prepackaged kit of epinephrine, which can be obtained only by prescription from your doctor.

Ticks. Ticks can carry diseases such as Rocky Mountain spotted fever and Lyme disease. The best defense is, of course, prevention. If you know you're going to be hiking through an area littered with ticks, wear long pants and a long-sleeved shirt. You can apply a permethrin repellent to your clothing and a deet repellent to exposed skin. At the end of your hike, do a spot-check for ticks (and insects in general). If you do find a tick, grab the head of the tick firmly—with a pair of tweezers if you have them—and gently pull it away from the skin with a twisting motion. Sometimes the mouthparts linger, embedded in your skin. If this happens, try to remove them with a disinfected needle. Clean the affected area with an antibacterial cleanser and then apply triple antibiotic ointment. Monitor the area for a few days. If irritation persists or a white spot develops, see a doctor for possible infection.

Poison ivy, oak, and sumac. These skin irritants can be found most anywhere in North America and come in the form of a bush or a vine, having leaflets in groups of three, five, seven, or nine. Learn how to spot the plants. The oil they secrete can cause an allergic reaction in the form of blisters, usually about 12 hours after exposure. The itchy rash can last from ten days to several weeks. The best defense against these irritants is to wear clothing that covers the arms, legs, and torso. For summer, zip-off cargo pants come in handy. There are also nonprescription lotions you can apply to exposed skin that guard against the effects of poison ivy / oak / sumac and can be washed off with soap and water.

If you think you were in contact with the plants, after hiking (or even on the trail during longer hikes) wash with soap and water. Taking a hot shower with soap after you return home from your hike will also help remove any lingering oil from your skin. Should you contract a rash from any of these plants, use an antihistamine to reduce the itching. If the rash is localized, make a light bleach/water wash to dry up the area. If the rash has spread, either tough it out or see your doctor about getting a dose of cortisone (available both orally and by injection).

Snakebites. Snakebites are rare in North America. Unless startled or provoked, the majority of snakes will not bite. If you are wise to their habitats and keep a careful eye on the trail, you should be just fine. When stepping over logs, first step on the log, making sure you can see what's on the other side before stepping down. Though your chances of being struck are slim, it's wise to know what to do in the event you are.

If a nonpoisonous snake bites you, allow the wound to bleed a small amount and then cleanse the wounded area with a Betadine solution (10 percent povidone iodine). Rinse the wound with clean water (preferably) or fresh urine (it might sound ugly, but it's sterile). Once the area is clean, cover it with triple antibiotic ointment and a clean bandage. Remember, most residual damage from snakebites, poisonous or otherwise, comes from infection, not the snake's venom. Keep the area as clean as possible, and get medical attention immediately.

If somebody in your party is bitten by a poisonous snake, follow these steps:

1. Calm the patient.
2. Remove jewelry, watches, and restrictive clothing, and immobilize the affected limb. Do not elevate the injury. Medical opinions vary on whether the area should be lower or level with the heart, but the consensus is that it should not be above it.
3. Make a note of the circumference of the limb at the bite site and at various points above the site as well. This will help you monitor swelling.
4. Evacuate your victim. Ideally, he should be carried out to minimize movement. If the victim appears to be doing OK, he can walk. Stop and rest frequently, and if the swelling appears to be spreading or the patient's symptoms increase, change your plan and find a way to get your patient transported.
5. If you are waiting for rescue, make sure to keep your patient comfortable and hydrated (unless he begins vomiting).

Snakebite treatment is rife with old-fashioned remedies: You used to be told to cut and suck the venom out of the bite site or to use a suction cup extractor for the same purpose; applying an electric shock to the area was even in vogue for a while. Do not do any of these things. Do not apply ice, do not give your patient painkillers, and do not apply a tourniquet. All you really want to do is keep your patient calm and get help. If you're alone and have to hike out, don't run—you'll only increase the flow of blood throughout your system. Instead, walk calmly.

Dehydration. Have you ever hiked in hot weather and had a roaring headache and felt fatigued after only a few miles? More than likely, you were dehydrated. Symptoms of dehydration include fatigue, headache, and decreased coordination and judgment. When you are hiking, your body's rate of fluid loss depends on the outside temperature, humidity, altitude, and your activity level. On average a hiker walking in warm weather will lose four liters of fluid a day. That fluid loss is easily replaced by normal consumption of liquids and food. However, if a hiker is walking briskly in hot, dry weather and hauling a heavy pack, he can lose one to three liters of water an hour. It's important to always carry plenty of water and to stop often and drink fluids regularly, even if you aren't thirsty.

Heat exhaustion is the result of a loss of large amounts of electrolytes and often occurs if a hiker is dehydrated and has been under heavy exertion. Common symptoms of heat exhaustion include cramping, fatigue, lightheadedness, and nausea. You can treat heat exhaustion by getting out of the sun and drinking an electrolyte solution made up of one teaspoon of salt and one tablespoon of sugar dissolved in one liter of water. Drink this solution slowly over a period of an hour. Drinking plenty of fluids (preferably an electrolyte solution/sports drink) can prevent heat exhaustion. Avoid hiking during the hottest parts of the day, and wear breathable clothing, a wide-brimmed hat, and sunglasses.

Hypothermia is one of the biggest dangers in the backcountry, especially for day hikers in the summertime. That may sound strange, but imagine starting out on a hike in midsummer when it's sunny and 80°F out. You're clad in nylon shorts and a cotton T-shirt. About halfway through your hike, the sky begins to cloud up, and in the next hour, a light drizzle begins to fall and the wind starts to pick up. Before you know it, you are soaking wet and shivering—the perfect recipe for hypothermia. More advanced signs include decreased coordination, slurred speech, and blurred vision. When a victim's temperature falls below 92 degrees, the blood pressure and pulse plummet, possibly leading to coma and death.

To avoid hypothermia, always bring a windproof/rainproof shell, a fleece jacket, long underwear made of a breathable synthetic fiber, gloves, and a hat when you are hiking in the mountains. Learn to adjust your clothing layers based on the temperature. If you are climbing uphill at a moderate pace, you will stay warm, but when you stop for a break, you'll become cold quickly unless you add more layers of clothing.

If a hiker is showing advanced signs of hypothermia, dress her in dry clothes and make sure she is wearing a hat and gloves. Place the person in a sleeping bag in a tent or shelter that will protect her from the wind and other elements. Give the person warm fluids to drink and keep her awake.

Frostbite. When the mercury dips below 32 degrees, your extremities begin to chill. If a persistent chill attacks a localized area, say, your hands or your toes, the circulatory system reacts by cutting off blood flow to the affected area—the idea being to protect and preserve the body's overall temperature. Therefore, it's death by attrition for the affected area. Ice crystals start to form from the water in the cells of the neglected tissue. Deprived of heat, nourishment, and now water, the tissue literally starves. This is frostbite.

Prevention is your best defense against this situation. Most prone to frostbite are your face, hands, and feet, so protect these areas well. Synthetic fabrics and wool provide ample air space for insulation and draw moisture away from the skin. Do your research. A pair of light silk liners under your regular gloves is a good trick for keeping warm. They afford some additional warmth, but more important, they'll allow you to remove your mitts for intricate work without exposing the skin.

If your feet or hands start to feel cold or numb due to the elements, warm them as quickly as possible. Place cold hands under your armpits or bury them in your crotch. If your feet are cold, change your socks. If there's plenty of room in your boots, add another pair of socks. Do remember, though, that constricting your feet in tight boots can restrict blood flow and actually make your feet colder more quickly. Your socks need to have breathing room if they're going to be effective. Dead air provides insulation. If your face is cold, place your warm hands over your face, or simply wear a head stocking.

Should your skin go numb and start to appear white and waxy, chances are you've got or are developing frostbite. Don't try to thaw the area unless you can maintain the warmth. In other words, don't stop to warm up your frostbitten feet only to head back on the trail. You'll do more damage than good. Tests have shown that hikers who walked on thawed feet did more harm, and endured more pain, than hikers who left the affected areas alone. Do your best to get out of the cold entirely and seek medical attention—which usually consists of performing a rapid rewarming in water for 20 to 30 minutes.

The overall objective in preventing both hypothermia and frostbite is to keep the body's core warm. Protect key areas where heat escapes, like the top of the head, and maintain the proper nutrition level. Foods that are high in calories aid the body in producing heat. Never smoke or drink when you're in situations where the cold is threatening. By affecting blood flow, these activities ultimately cool the body's core temperature.

Hantavirus pulmonary syndrome (HPS). Deer mice spread the virus that causes HPS, and humans contract it from breathing it in, usually when they've disturbed an area with dust and mice feces from nests or surfaces with mice droppings or urine. Exposure to large numbers of rodents and their feces or urine presents the greatest risk. As hikers, we sometimes enter old buildings, and often deer mice live in these places. We may not be around long enough to be exposed, but do be aware of this disease. About half the people who develop HPS die. Symptoms are flu-like and appear about two to three weeks after exposure. After initial symptoms, a dry cough and shortness of breath follow. Breathing is difficult. If you even think you might have HPS, see a doctor immediately!

NATURAL HAZARDS

Besides tripping over a rock or tree root on the trail, there are some real hazards to be aware of while hiking. Even if where you're hiking doesn't have the plethora of poisonous snakes and plants, insects, and grizzly bears found in other parts of the United States, there are a few weather conditions and predators you may need to take into account.

Lightning. Thunderstorms build over the mountains almost every day during the summer. Lightning is generated by thunderheads and can strike without warning, even several miles away from the nearest overhead cloud. The best rule of thumb is to start leaving exposed peaks, ridges, and canyon rims by about noon. This time can vary a little depending on storm buildup. Keep an eye on cloud formation, and don't underestimate how fast a storm can build. The bigger they get, the more likely a thunderstorm will happen.

Lightning takes the path of least resistance, so if you're the high point, it might choose you. Ducking under a rock overhang is dangerous, as you form the shortest path between the rock and ground. If you dash below tree line, avoid standing under the only or the tallest tree. If you are caught above tree line, stay away from anything metal you may have brought with you. Move down off the ridge slightly to a low, treeless point and squat until the storm passes. If you have an insulating pad, squat on it. Avoid having both your hands and feet touching the ground at once and never lay flat. If you hear a buzzing sound or feel your hair standing on end, move quickly, as an electrical charge is building up.

Flash floods. The spooky thing about flash floods, especially in western canyons, is that they can appear out of nowhere from a storm many miles away. While hiking or driving in canyons, keep an eye on the weather. Always climb to safety if danger threatens. Flash floods usually subside quickly, so be patient and don't cross a swollen stream.

Bears. In the United States only Alaska and parts of the Pacific Northwest and the Northern Rockies have grizzly bear populations, although some rumors exist of sightings where there should be none. Black bears are plentiful, however. Here are some tips in case you and a bear scare each other.

Most of all, avoid surprising a bear. Talk or sing where visibility or hearing is limited, such as along a rushing creek or in thick brush. In grizzly country especially, carry bear spray in a holster on your pack belt where you can quickly grab it. While hiking, watch for bear tracks (five toes), droppings (sizable with leaves, partly digested berries, seeds, and/or animal fur), or rocks and roots along the trail that show signs of being dug up (this could be a bear looking for bugs to eat). Keep a clean camp, hang food or use bear-proof storage containers, and don't sleep in the clothes you wore while cooking. Be especially careful to avoid getting between a mother and her cubs. In late summer and fall, bears are busy eating to fatten up for winter, so be extra careful around berry bushes and oak brush.

If you do encounter a bear, move away slowly while facing the bear, talk softly, and avoid direct eye contact. Give the bear room to escape. Since bears are very curious, it might stand upright to get a better whiff of you, and it may even charge you to try to intimidate you. Try to stay calm. If a black bear attacks you, fight back with anything you have handy. If a grizzly bear attacks you, your best option is to "play dead" by lying face down on the ground and covering the back of your neck and head with your hands. Unleashed dogs have been known to come running back to their owners with a bear close behind. Keep your dog on a leash or leave it at home.

Mountain lions. Mountain lions appear to be getting more comfortable around humans, especially when deer (their favorite prey) are in an area with adequate cover. Usually elusive and quiet, lions rarely attack people. If you meet a lion, give it a chance to escape. Stay calm and talk firmly to it. Back away slowly while facing the lion. If you run, you'll only encourage the cat to chase you. Make yourself look large by opening a jacket, if you have one, or waving your hiking poles. If the lion behaves aggressively, throw stones, sticks, or whatever you can while remaining tall. If a lion does attack, fight for your life with anything you can grab.

Moose. Because moose have very few natural predators, they don't fear humans like other animals. You might find moose in sagebrush and wetter areas of willow, aspen, and pine, or in beaver habitats. Mothers with calves, as well as bulls during mating season, can be particularly aggressive. If a moose threatens you, back away slowly and talk calmly to it. Keep your pets away from moose.

Other considerations. Hunting is a popular sport in the United States, especially during rifle season in October and November. Hiking is still enjoyable in those months in many areas, so just take a few precautions. First, learn when the different hunting seasons start and end in the area in which you'll be hiking. During this time, be sure to wear at least a blaze orange hat, and possibly put an orange vest over your pack. Don't be surprised to see hunters in camo outfits carrying bows or rifles during their season. If you would feel more comfortable without hunters around, hike in national parks and monuments or state and local parks where hunting is not allowed.

Whether you are going on a short hike in a familiar area or planning a weeklong backpacking trip, you should always be equipped with the proper navigational equipment—at the very least a detailed map and a sturdy compass.

Maps. There are many different types of maps available to help you find your way on the trail. Easiest to find are Forest Service maps and BLM (Bureau of Land Management) maps. These maps tend to cover large areas, so be sure they are detailed enough for your particular trip. You can also obtain national park maps, as well as high-quality maps from private companies and trail groups, from outdoor stores or ranger stations.

US Geological Survey (USGS) topographic maps are particularly popular with hikers—especially serious backcountry hikers. These maps contain the standard map symbols such as roads, lakes, and rivers, as well as contour lines that show the details of the trail terrain, like ridges, valleys, passes, and mountain peaks. The 7.5-minute series (1 inch on the map equals approximately $\frac{2}{5}$ mile on the ground) provides the closest inspection available. USGS maps are available by mail (US Geological Survey, Map Distribution Branch, PO Box 25286, Denver, CO 80225) or at mapping.usgs.gov/esic/to_order.html.

If you want to check out the high-tech world of maps, you can purchase topographic maps on CD-ROM. These software-mapping programs let you select a route on your computer, print it out, and then take it with you on the trail. Some software-mapping programs let you insert symbols and labels, download way-points from a GPS unit, and export the maps to other software programs.

The art of map reading is a skill that you can develop by first practicing in an area you are familiar with. To begin, orient the map so the map is lined up in the correct direction (i.e., north on the map is lined up with true north). Next, familiarize yourself with the map symbols and try and match them up with terrain features around you, such as a high ridge, mountain peak, river, or lake. If you are practicing with a USGS map, notice the contour lines. On gentler terrain these contour lines are spaced farther apart, and on steeper terrain they are closer together. Pick a short loop trail, and stop frequently to check your position on the map. As you practice map reading, you'll learn how to anticipate a steep section on the trail or a good place to take a rest break, and so on.

Compasses. First off, the sun is not a substitute for a compass. So, what kind of compass should you have? Here are some characteristics you should look for: a rectangular base with detailed scales, a liquid-filled housing, protective housing, a sighting line on the mirror, luminous alignment and back-bearing arrows, a luminous north-seeking arrow, and a well-defined bezel ring.

You can learn compass basics by reading the detailed instructions included with your compass. If you want to fine-tune your compass skills, sign up for an orienteering class or purchase a book on compass reading. Once you've learned the basic skills of using a compass, remember to practice these skills before you head into the backcountry.

If you are a klutz at using a compass, you may be interested in checking out the technical wizardry of the **GPS (Global Positioning System) device.** The GPS was developed by the Pentagon and works off twenty-four NAVSTAR satellites, which were designed to guide missiles to their targets. A GPS device is a handheld unit that calculates your latitude and longitude with the easy press of a button. The Department of Defense used to scramble the satellite signals a bit to prevent civilians (and spies!) from getting extremely accurate readings, but that practice was discontinued in May 2000, and GPS units now provide nearly pinpoint accuracy (within 30 to 60 feet).

There are many different types of GPS units available, and they range in price from $100 to $400. In general, all GPS units have a display screen and keypad where you input information. In addition to acting as a compass, the unit allows you to plot your route, easily retrace your path, track your traveling speed, find the mileage between waypoints, and calculate the total mileage of your route.

Before you purchase a GPS unit, keep in mind that these devices don't pick up signals indoors, in heavily wooded areas, on mountain peaks, or in deep valleys. Also, batteries can wear out or other technical problems can develop. A GPS unit should be used in conjunction with a map and compass, not in place of those items.

Pedometers. A pedometer is a small clip-on unit with a digital display that calculates your hiking distance in miles or kilometers based on your walking stride. Some units also calculate the calories you burn and your total hiking time. Pedometers are available at most large outdoor stores and range in price from $20 to $40.

TRIP PLANNING

Planning your hiking adventure begins with letting a friend or relative know your trip itinerary so they can call for help if you don't return at your scheduled time. Your next task is to make sure you are outfitted to experience the risks and rewards of the trail. This section highlights gear and clothing you may want to take with you to get the most out of your hike.

Day Hikes
- ❏ Bear repellent spray (if hiking in grizzly country)
- ❏ Camera
- ❏ Compass/GPS unit
- ❏ Daypack
- ❏ First-aid kit
- ❏ Fleece jacket

- ❏ Food
- ❏ Guidebook
- ❏ Hat
- ❏ Headlamp/flashlight with extra batteries and bulbs
- ❏ Insect repellent
- ❏ Knife/multipurpose tool
- ❏ Map
- ❏ Matches in waterproof container and fire starter
- ❏ Pedometer
- ❏ Rain gear
- ❏ Space blanket
- ❏ Sunglasses
- ❏ Sunscreen
- ❏ Swimsuit and/or fishing gear (if hiking to a lake or river)
- ❏ Watch
- ❏ Water
- ❏ Water bottles/water hydration system

Overnight Trip

Add the following items to the list above for an overnight trip. And pack it all into a backpack instead of a day pack.

- ❏ Backpack and waterproof rain cover
- ❏ Backpacker's trowel
- ❏ Bandanna
- ❏ Bear bell
- ❏ Biodegradable soap
- ❏ Clothing—extra wool socks, shirt, and shorts
- ❏ Collapsible water container (2–3-gallon capacity)
- ❏ Cook set / utensils
- ❏ Ditty bags to store gear
- ❏ Extra plastic resealable bags
- ❏ Gaiters
- ❏ Garbage bag
- ❏ Ground cloth
- ❏ Journal/pen
- ❏ Long underwear
- ❏ Nylon rope to hang food
- ❏ Permit (if required)
- ❏ Pot scrubber
- ❏ Rain jacket and pants
- ❏ Sandals to wear around camp and to ford streams

- ❏ Sleeping bag
- ❏ Sleeping pad
- ❏ Small bath towel
- ❏ Stove and fuel
- ❏ Tent
- ❏ Toiletry items
- ❏ Water filter
- ❏ Waterproof stuff sack
- ❏ Whistle

EQUIPMENT

With the outdoor market currently flooded with products, many of which are pure gimmickry, it seems impossible to both differentiate and choose. Do I really need a tropical-fish-lined collapsible shower? (No, you don't.) The only defense against the maddening quantity of items thrust in your face is to think practically—and to do so before you go shopping. The worst buys are impulsive buys. Since most name brands will differ only slightly in quality, it's best to know what you're looking for in terms of function. Buy only what you need. You will, don't forget, be carrying what you've bought on your back. Here are some things to keep in mind before you go shopping.

Clothes. Clothing is your armor against Mother Nature's little surprises. Hikers should be prepared for any possibility, especially when hiking in mountainous areas. Adequate rain protection and extra layers of clothing are a good idea. In summer a wide-brimmed hat can help keep the sun at bay. During the winter months, the first layer you'll want to wear is a "wicking" layer of long underwear that keeps perspiration away from your skin. Wear long underwear made from synthetic fibers that wick moisture away from the skin and draw it toward the next layer of clothing, where it then evaporates. Avoid wearing long underwear made of cotton, as it is slow to dry and keeps moisture next to your skin.

The second layer you'll wear is the "insulating" layer. Aside from keeping you warm, this layer needs to "breathe" so you stay dry while hiking. A fabric that provides insulation and dries quickly is fleece. It's interesting to note that this one-of-a-kind fabric is made out of recycled plastic. Purchasing a zip-up jacket made of this material is highly recommended.

The last line of layering defense is the "shell" layer. You'll need some type of waterproof, windproof, breathable jacket that will fit over all of your other layers. It should have a large hood that fits over a hat. You'll also need a good pair of rain pants made from a similar waterproof, breathable fabric. Some Gore-Tex jackets cost as much as $500, but you should know that there are more affordable fabrics out there that work just as well.

Now that you've learned the basics of layering, you can't forget to protect your hands and face. In cold, windy, or rainy weather, you'll need a hat made of wool or fleece and insulated, waterproof gloves that will keep your hands warm and toasty. As mentioned earlier, buying an additional pair of light silk liners to wear under your regular gloves is a good idea.

Footwear. If you have any extra money to spend on your trip, put that money into boots or trail shoes. Poor shoes will bring a hike to a halt faster than anything else. To avoid this annoyance, buy shoes that provide support and are lightweight and flexible. A lightweight hiking boot is better than a heavy leather mountaineering boot for most day hikes and backpacking. Trail-running shoes provide a little extra cushion and are made in a high-top style that many people wear for hiking. These running shoes are lighter, more flexible, and more breathable than hiking boots. If you know you'll be hiking in wet weather often, purchase boots or shoes with a Gore-Tex liner, which will help keep your feet dry.

When buying your boots, be sure to wear the same type of socks you'll be wearing on the trail. If the boots you're buying are for cold-weather hiking, try the boots on while wearing two pairs of socks. Speaking of socks, a good cold-weather sock combination is to wear a thinner sock made of wool or polypropylene covered by a heavier outer sock made of wool or a synthetic/wool mix. The inner sock protects the foot from the rubbing effects of the outer sock and prevents blisters.

Many outdoor stores have some type of ramp to simulate hiking uphill and downhill. Be sure to take advantage of this test, as toe-jamming boot fronts can be very painful and debilitating on the downhill trek.

Once you've purchased your footwear, be sure to break them in before you hit the trail. New footwear is often stiff and needs to be stretched and molded to your foot.

Hiking poles. Hiking poles help with balance and, more importantly, take pressure off your knees. The ones with shock absorbers are easier on your elbows and knees. Some poles even come with a camera attachment to be used as a monopod. Moreover, heaven forbid you meet a mountain lion, bear, or unfriendly dog, the poles can make you look a lot bigger.

Backpacks. No matter what type of hiking you do, you'll need a pack of some sort to carry the basic trail essentials. There are a variety of backpacks on the market, but let's first discuss what you intend to use it for: day hikes or overnight trips?

If you plan on doing a day hike, a daypack should have some of the following characteristics: a padded hip belt that's at least 2 inches in diameter (avoid packs with only a small nylon piece of webbing for a hip belt); a chest strap (the chest strap helps stabilize the pack against your body); external pockets to carry water and other items that you want easy access to; an internal pocket to hold keys, a knife, a wallet, and other miscellaneous items; an external lashing system to hold a jacket; and, if you so desire, a hydration pocket for carrying a hydration system (which consists of a water bladder with an attachable drinking hose).

For short hikes, some hikers like to use a fanny pack to store just a camera, food, a compass, a map, and other trail essentials. Most fanny packs have pockets for two water bottles and a padded hip belt.

If you intend to do an extended overnight trip, there are multiple considerations. First off, you need to decide what kind of framed pack you want. There are two pack types for backpacking: the internal frame and the external frame. An internal frame pack rests closer to your body, making it more stable and easier to balance when hiking over rough terrain. An external frame pack is just that, an aluminum frame attached to the exterior of the pack. Some hikers consider an external frame pack to be better for long backpack trips because it distributes the pack weight better and allows you to carry heavier loads. It's often easier to pack, and your gear is more accessible. It also offers better back ventilation in hot weather.

The most critical measurement for fitting a pack is torso length. The pack needs to rest evenly on your hips without sagging. A good pack will come in two or three sizes and have straps and hip belts that are adjustable according to your body size and characteristics.

When purchasing a backpack, go to an outdoor store with salespeople who are knowledgeable in how to properly fit a pack. Once the pack is fitted for you, load the pack with the amount of weight you plan on taking on the trail. The weight of the pack should be distributed evenly, and you should be able to swing your arms and walk briskly without feeling out of balance. Another good technique for evaluating a pack is to walk up and down stairs and make quick turns to the right and to the left to be sure the pack doesn't feel out of balance. Other features that are nice to have on a backpack include a removable daypack or fanny pack, external pockets for extra water, and extra lash points to attach a jacket or other items.

Sleeping bags and pads. Sleeping bags are rated by temperature. You can purchase a bag made with synthetic insulation, or you can buy a goose down bag. Goose down bags are more expensive, but they have a higher insulating capacity by weight and will keep their loft longer. You'll want to purchase a bag with a temperature rating that fits the time of year and conditions you are most likely to camp in. One caveat: The techno-standard for temperature ratings is far from perfect. Ratings vary from manufacturer to manufacturer, so to protect yourself, you should purchase a bag rated 10° to 15° below the temperature you expect to be camping in.

Synthetic bags are more resistant to water than down bags, but many down bags are now made with a Gore-Tex shell that helps to repel water. Down bags are also more compressible than synthetic bags and take up less room in your pack, which is an important consideration if you are planning a multiday backpack trip. Features to look for in a sleeping bag include a mummy-style design, a hood you can cinch down around your head in cold weather, and draft tubes along the zippers that help keep heat in and drafts out.

You'll also want a sleeping pad to provide insulation and padding from the cold ground. There are different types of sleeping pads available, from the more expensive self-inflating air mattresses to the less expensive closed-cell foam pads. Self-inflating air mattresses are usually heavier than closed-cell foam mattresses and are prone to punctures.

Tents. The tent is your home away from home while on the trail. It provides protection from wind, rain, snow, and insects. A three-season tent is a good choice for backpacking and can range in price from $100 to $500. These lightweight and versatile tents provide protection in all types of weather, except heavy snowstorms or high winds, and range in weight from 4 to 8 pounds. Look for a tent that's easy to set up and will easily fit two people with gear. Dome-style tents usually offer more headroom and places to store gear. Other handy tent features include a vestibule where you can store wet boots and backpacks. Some nice-to-have items in a tent include interior pockets to store small items and lashing points to hang a clothesline. Most three-season tents also come with stakes so you can secure the tent in high winds.

Before you purchase a tent, set it up and take it down a few times to be sure it is easy to handle. Also, sit inside the tent and make sure it has enough room for you and your gear.

Cell phones. Many hikers are carrying their cell phones into the backcountry these days in case of emergency. That's fine and good, but please know that cell phone coverage is often poor to nonexistent in valleys, canyons, and thick forest. More importantly, people have started to call for help because they're tired or lost. Let's go back to being prepared. You are responsible for yourself in the backcountry. Use your brain to avoid problems, and if you do encounter one, first use your brain to try to correct the situation. Only use your cell phone, if it works, in true emergencies. If it doesn't work down low in a valley, try hiking to a high point where you might get reception.

HIKING WITH CHILDREN

Hiking with children isn't a matter of how many miles you can cover or how much elevation gain you make in a day—it's about seeing and experiencing nature through their eyes. Kids like to explore and have fun. They like to stop and point out bugs and plants, look under rocks, jump in puddles, and throw sticks. If you're taking a toddler or young child on a hike, start with a trail that you're familiar with. Trails that have interesting things for kids, like piles of leaves to play in or a small stream to wade through during the summer, will make the hike much more enjoyable for them and will keep them from getting bored.

You can **keep your child's attention** if you have a strategy before starting on the trail. Using games is not only an effective way to keep a child's attention, it's also a great way to teach him or her about nature. Quiz children on the names of plants and animals. Pick up a family-friendly outdoor hobby like geocaching (geocaching.com) or letterboxing (atlasquest.com), both of which combine the outdoors, clue solving, and treasure hunting. If your children are old enough, let them carry their own daypack filled with snacks and water. So that you are sure to go at their pace and not yours, let them lead the way. Playing follow-the-leader works particularly well when you have a group of children. Have each child take a turn at being the leader.

With children, a lot of clothing is key. The only thing predictable about weather is that it will change. Especially in mountainous areas, weather can change dramatically in a very short time. Always bring extra clothing for children, regardless of the season. In the winter have your children wear wool socks and warm layers such as long underwear, a fleece jacket and hat, wool mittens, and good rain gear. It's not a bad idea to have these along in late fall and early spring as well.

Good footwear is also important. A sturdy pair of high-top tennis shoes or lightweight hiking boots are the best bet for little ones. If you're hiking in the summer near a lake or stream, bring along a pair of old sneakers that your child can put on when he or she wants to go exploring in the water. Remember: When you're near any type of water, watch your child at all times. Also, keep a close eye on teething toddlers who may decide a rock or leaf of poison oak is an interesting item to put in their mouths.

From spring through fall, you'll want your kids to wear wide-brimmed hats to **keep their faces, heads, and ears protected from the hot sun.** Also, make sure your children wear sunscreen at all times. Choose a brand without PABA—children have sensitive skin and may have an allergic reaction to sunscreen that contains PABA. If you are hiking with a child younger than six months, don't use sunscreen or insect repellent. Instead, be sure that the head, face, neck, and ears are protected from the sun with a wide-brimmed hat, and that all other skin exposed to the sun is protected with the appropriate clothing.

Remember that food is fun. Kids like snacks, so it's important to bring a lot of munchies for the trail. Stopping often for snack breaks is a fun way to keep the trail interesting. Raisins, apples, granola bars, crackers and cheese, cereal, and trail mix all make great snacks. Also, a few of their favorite candy treats can go a long way toward heading off a fit of fussing. If your children are old enough to carry their own backpack, let them fill it with some lightweight "comfort" items such as a doll, a small stuffed animal, or a little toy (you'll have to draw the line at bringing the ten-pound Tonka truck). If your kids don't like drinking water, you can bring some powdered drink mix or a juice box.

Avoid poorly designed child-carrying packs—you don't want to break your back carrying your child. Most child-carrying backpacks designed to hold a forty-pound child will contain a large carrying pocket to hold diapers and other items. Some have an optional rain/sun hood.

HIKING WITH YOUR DOG

Bringing your furry friend with you is always more fun than leaving him behind. Our canine pals make great trail buddies because they never complain and always make good company. Hiking with your dog can be a rewarding experience, especially if you plan ahead.

First, note that national parks and many wilderness areas do not allow dogs on trails. Your best bet is to hike in national forests, BLM lands, and state parks. Always call ahead to see what the restrictions are.

Getting your dog in shape. Before you plan outdoor adventures with your dog, make sure he's in shape for the trail. Getting your dog in shape takes the same discipline as getting yourself in shape, but luckily your dog can get in shape with you. Take your dog with you on your daily runs or walks. If you have a large yard or there is a park near your home, hit a tennis ball or play Frisbee with your dog. Swimming is also an excellent way to get your dog in shape. If there is a nearby lake or river and your dog likes the water, have him retrieve a tennis ball or stick.

Gradually build your dog's stamina up over a two- to three-month period. A good rule of thumb is to assume that your dog will travel twice as far as you will on the trail. If you plan on doing a 5-mile hike, be sure your dog is in shape for a 10-mile hike.

Training your dog for the trail. Before you go on your first hiking adventure with your dog, be sure he has a firm grasp of the basics of canine etiquette and behavior. Make sure he can sit, lie down, stay, and come. One of the most important commands you can teach your canine pal is to "come" under any situation. It's easy for your friend's nose to lead him astray or possibly get lost.

Another helpful command is the "get behind" command. When you're on a hiking trail that's narrow, you can have your dog follow behind you when other trail users approach. Nothing is more bothersome than an enthusiastic dog that runs back and forth on the trail and disrupts the peace of the trail for others—or worse, jumps up on other hikers and gets them muddy. When you see other trail users approaching you on the trail, give them the right-of-way by quietly stepping off the trail and making your dog lie down and stay until they pass.

Equipment. The most critical pieces of equipment you can invest in for your dog are proper identification and a sturdy leash. Flexi-leads work well for hiking because they give your dog more freedom to explore but still leave you in control.

Make sure your dog has identification that includes your name and address and a number for your veterinarian. Other forms of identification for your dog include a tattoo or a microchip. You should consult your veterinarian for more information on these last two options.

The next piece of equipment you'll want to consider is a pack for your dog. By no means should you hold all of your dog's essentials in your pack—let him carry his own gear! Dogs that are in good shape can carry 30 to 40 percent of their own weight.

Most packs are fitted by a dog's weight and girth measurement. Companies that make dog packs generally include guidelines to help you pick out the size that's right for your dog. Some characteristics to look for when purchasing a pack for your dog include a harness that contains two padded girth straps, a padded chest strap, leash attachments, removable saddlebags, internal water bladders, and external gear cords.

You can introduce your dog to the pack by first placing the empty pack on his back and letting him wear it around the yard. Keep an eye on him during this first introduction. He may decide to chew through the straps if you aren't watching him closely. Once he learns to treat the pack as an object of fun and not a foreign enemy, fill the pack evenly on both sides with a few ounces of dog food in resealable plastic bags. Have your dog wear his pack on your daily walks for a period of two to three weeks. Each week add a little more weight to the pack until your dog will accept carrying the maximum amount of weight he can carry.

You can also purchase collapsible water and dog food bowls for your dog. These bowls are lightweight and can easily be stashed in your or your dog's pack. If you are hiking on rocky terrain or in the snow, you can purchase footwear for your dog that will protect his feet from cuts and bruises.

Always carry plastic bags to remove feces from the trail. It is a courtesy to other trail users and helps protect local wildlife.

The following is a list of items to bring when you take your dog hiking: collapsible water bowls, a comb, a collar and a leash, dog food, plastic bags for feces, a dog pack, flea/tick deterrent, paw protection, water, and a first-aid kit that contains eye ointment, tweezers, scissors, stretchy foot wrap, gauze, antibacterial wash, sterile cotton-tip applicators, antibiotic ointment, and cotton wrap.

First aid for your dog. Your dog is just as prone—if not more prone—to getting in trouble on the trail as you are, so be prepared. Here's a rundown of the more likely misfortunes that might befall your little friend.

Bees and wasps. If a bee or wasp stings your dog, remove the stinger with a pair of tweezers and place a mudpack or a cloth dipped in cold water over the affected area.

Porcupines. One good reason to keep your dog on a leash is to prevent him from getting a nose full of porcupine quills. You may be able to remove the quills with pliers, but a veterinarian is the best person to do this nasty job because most dogs need to be sedated.

Heatstroke. Avoid hiking with your dog in really hot weather. Dogs with heatstroke will pant excessively, lie down and refuse to get up, and become lethargic and disoriented. If your dog shows any of these signs on the trail, have him lie down in the shade. If you are near a stream, pour cool water over your dog's entire body to help bring his body temperature back to normal.

Heartworm. Dogs get heartworms from mosquitoes that carry the disease in the prime mosquito months of July and August. After testing for heartworm, your veterinarian may suggest a monthly pill for your dog that easily prevents this condition.

Plant pitfalls. One of the biggest plant hazards for dogs on the trail are fox-tails. Foxtails are pointed grass-seed heads that bury themselves in your friend's fur, between his toes, and even get in his ear canal. If left unattended, these nasty seeds can work their way under the skin and cause abscesses and other problems. If you have a long-haired dog, consider trimming the hair between his toes and giving him a summer haircut to help prevent foxtails from attaching to his fur. After every hike always look over your dog for these seeds—especially between his toes and in his ears.

Other plant hazards include burrs, thorns, thistles, and poison ivy, oak, and sumac. If you find any burrs or thistles on your dog, remove them as soon as pos-sible before they become an unmanageable mat. Thorns can pierce a dog's foot and cause a great deal of pain. If you see that your dog is lame, stop and check his feet for thorns. Dogs are immune to poison ivy, but they can pick up the sticky, oily substance from the plant and transfer it to you.

Protect those paws. Be sure to keep your dog's nails trimmed so he avoids getting soft tissue or joint injuries. If your dog slows and refuses to go on, check to see that his paws aren't torn or worn. You can protect your dog's paws from trail hazards such as sharp gravel, foxtails, lava scree, and thorns by purchasing dog boots.

Sunburn. If your dog has light skin, he is an easy target for sunburn on his nose and other exposed skin areas. You can apply a nontoxic sunscreen to exposed skin areas that will help protect him from overexposure to the sun.

Ticks and fleas. Ticks can easily give your dog Lyme disease, as well as other diseases. Before you hit the trail, treat your dog with a flea and tick deterrent. The most popular nowadays is the once-a-month pour-on treatment that repels both insects.

Mosquitoes and deerflies. These little flying machines can do a job on your dog's snout and ears. Best bet is to spray your dog with fly repellent for horses to discourage both pests.

Giardia. Dogs can get *giardiasis,* which results in diarrhea. It is usually not debilitating, but it's definitely messy. Ask your veterinarian about prevention and treatment options.

Mushrooms. Make sure your dog doesn't sample mushrooms along the trail. They could be poisonous to him, but he doesn't know that.

Hike Index

REGION SOUTH OF COEUR D'ALENE

About the Author

A native of the Northwest, Fred Barstad has spent a large part of the last forty-five years hiking, climbing, skiing, and snowshoeing in the region's canyons, deserts, and mountains. He has climbed most of the Cascades Volcanoes, including more than sixty summit climbs of Mount Hood, as well as Mount McKinley in Alaska and the Mexican Volcanoes. Fred has written eleven other FalconGuides including *Best Hikes Near Portland, Hiking Hells Canyon and Idaho's Seven Devils Mountains,* and *Hiking Washington's Mount Adams Country.* Fred makes his home in Enterprise, Oregon, at the base of the Wallowa Mountains.

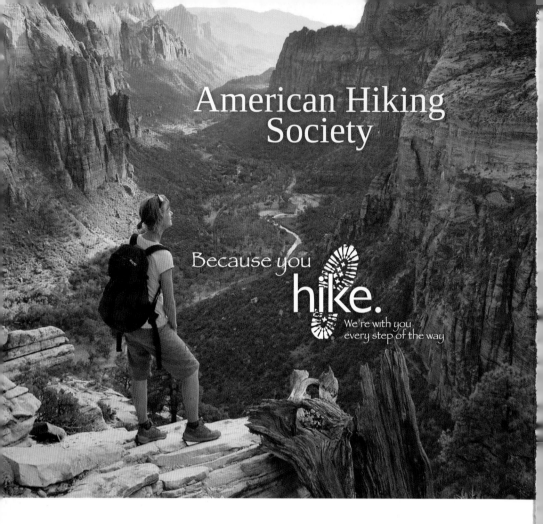

As a national voice for hikers, **American Hiking Society** works every day:

- Building and maintaining hiking trails
- Educating and supporting hikers by providing information and resources
- Supporting hiking and trail organizations nationwide
- Speaking for hikers in the halls of Congress and with federal land managers

Whether you're a casual hiker or a seasoned backpacker, become a member of American Hiking Society and join the national hiking community! You'll enjoy great member benefits and help preserve the nation's hiking trails, so tomorrow's hike is even better than today's. We invite you to join us now!